"Eat and love,
to be sure, but you'd better
eat first."

JIM HARRISON, *"Midrange Road Kill"*

CHIC
SIMPLE ®

COOKING

ALFRED A. KNOPF   NEW YORK 1995

KIM JOHNSON GROSS   JEFF STONE

RECIPES WITH SALLY SAMPSON
WRITTEN BY TODD LYON
PHOTOGRAPHS BY GENTL AND HYERS
FOOD STYLING BY GEORGIA DOWNARD
PROP STYLING BY EDWARD KEMPER DESIGN

ICON ILLUSTRATION BY WAYNE WOLF
ILLUSTRATIONS BY GREGORY NEMEC
CHAPTER ILLUSTRATIONS BY ALEXANDRA WEEMS
ART DIRECTION BY WAYNE WOLF
PHOTOGRAPHY CONSULTANT ROBERT VALENTINE

LC 94-15627
ISBN 0-679-43225-6

Manufactured in the United States of America
First Edition

GRATEFUL ACKNOWLEDGMENT IS MADE TO
THE FOLLOWING FOR PERMISSION TO REPRINT
PREVIOUSLY PUBLISHED MATERIAL:

BANTAM BOOKS: Two recipes "Couscous Salad with Apricots, Pine Nuts, and Ginger" and "Corn and Bulgur Salad with Cilantro and Lime" and excerpts of text from *Fields of Greens* by Annie Somerville, copyright © 1993 by Annie Somerville. Reprinted by permission of Bantam Books, a division of Bantam Doubleday Dell Publishing Group, Inc.

CROWN PUBLISHERS, INC.: Two recipes "Pasta with Tomatoes, Mozzarella, and Basil" and "Baked Peaches Stuffed with Walnuts and Chocolate" and excerpts of text from *A Tuscan in the Kitchen* by Pino Luongo, Barbara Raives, and Angela Hederson, copyright © 1988 by Pino Luongo, Barbara Raives, and Angela Hederson. Reprinted by permission of Crown Publishers, Inc.

HARPERCOLLINS PUBLISHERS, INC. and LESCHER & LESCHER, LTD.: One recipe "Stewed Potatoes with Tomatoes and Feta" and excerpts of text from *The Cooking of the Eastern Mediterranean* by Paula Wolfert, copyright © 1994 by Paula Wolfert; one recipe "Shrimp in Tomato Sauce with Almonds and Pine Nuts" from *Mediterranean Cooking Revised with 75 New Recipes* by Paula Wolfert, copyright © 1994 by Paula Wolfert. Reprinted by permission of HarperCollins Publishers, Inc. and Lescher & Lescher, Ltd.

ALFRED A. KNOPF, INC.: One recipe "Chicken Simmered in White Wine" and excerpts of text from *The Way to Cook* by Julia Child, copyright © 1989 by Julia Child; excerpts of text from *The Fannie Farmer Cookbook* by Marion Cunningham, copyright © 1979, 1990 by The Fannie Farmer Cookbook Corporation. Reprinted by permission of Alfred A. Knopf, Inc.

ALFRED A. KNOPF, INC. and LESCHER & LESCHER, LTD.: One recipe "Theater Steak" and excerpts of text from *The Supper Book* by Marion Cunningham, copyright © 1992 by Marion Cunningham. Reprinted by permission of Alfred A. Knopf, Inc. and Lescher & Lescher, Ltd.

WILLIAM MORROW & COMPANY, INC.: One recipe "Grilled West Indies Spice-Rubbed Chicken Breast with Grilled Banana" and excerpts of text from *The Thrill of the Grill* by Chris Schlesinger and John Willoughby, copyright © 1990 by Chris Schlesinger and John Willoughby. Reprinted by permission of William Morrow & Company, Inc.

RANDOM HOUSE, INC.: One recipe "Spicy Chicken Pizza" from *Adventures in the Kitchen* by Wolfgang Puck, copyright © 1991 by Wolfgang Puck. Reprinted by permission of Random House, Inc.

RANDOM HOUSE, INC. and LESCHER & LESCHER, LTD.: One recipe "Warm Green Bean Salad with Rocket and Garden Lettuces" and excerpts of text from *Chez Panisse Menu Cookbook* by Alice Waters, copyright © 1982 by Alice L. Waters. Reprinted by permission of Random House, Inc. and Lescher & Lescher, Ltd.

THE TAB NEWSPAPERS: Excerpts from "Grilling with the Schlesingers" by Sally Nirenberg Sampson (*The TAB*, June 16, 1992). Reprinted by permission of The TAB Newspapers, Boston, Massachusetts.

TIMES BOOKS: Two recipes "Broiled Flounder à la Moutarde" and "Zucchini Bordelaise" and excerpts of text from *Pierre Franey's Low-Calorie Gourmet* by Pierre Franey and Richard Flaste, copyright © 1984 by Billi-Bi Enterprises. Reprinted by permission of Times Books, a division of Random House, Inc.

To my grandmother Gerda Andersen, my friend Molly's mom, Priscilla Friedrich,
and to Pierre Franey's *Sixty-Minute Gourmet* for inspiring me and empowering me with the joy
of cooking and for the privilege of eating many memorable meals.

K.J.G.

For Jane, whose unimaginable culinary skills inspired me to cook, and Pino Luongo, whose sense of Zen
simplicity in cooking has led to many happy kitchen encounters—some even with food (though usually with Jane).

J.S.

And special thanks to Knopf editor Judith Jones for her invaluable guidance and friendship.

K.J.G. & J.S.

For MS, LS, and BOS—all more sustenance than any food could ever be. And for CS, with absolution.

S.S.

To the Flyin' Lyons, authentic and honorary, in celebration of
the audacious, rambunctious, hilarious, and—yes, Mom—delicious
holiday dinners we continue to share.

T.L.

"The more you know, the less you need."

AUSTRALIAN ABORIGINAL SAYING

CONTENTS

USE US—PLEASE. We've opened each section of the book with a quintessential basic recipe. These recipes provide the foundation to good cooking and are the building blocks of a cooking repertoire. Throughout the book you'll find OPTIONAL INGREDIENTS: are suggestions for enhancing a recipe according to your liking; OTHER CHOICES: are another way to personalize a recipe, with substitutions; TIPS and also a series of icons that identify: [🧰 *first aid*], which includes information from removing stains to learning where to store your eggs to choosing the freshest food in the market; a FIRE ENGINE indicates the ingredients that control the spiciness; an ALARM CLOCK means additional time is involved—i.e., a marinade or cake-baking time; and WARNINGS indicate food dangers you should know about. Throughout there are [VOICES] of wise chefs and cookbook gurus, and [LEXICONS], or visual glossaries, introducing the wide spectrum of vital foods.

A SIMPLE TALE

THREE SOLDIERS ENTER A TOWN SEEKING LODGING AND NOURISHMENT. THE TOWNSPEOPLE, FOREWARNED AND HOSTILE TO STRANGERS, EACH USE A DIFFERENT AND CREATIVE EXCUSE to deny the soldiers, claiming to have neither spare beds nor spare food. The soldiers, however, are even more creative than the townspeople and announce that, since no one will feed them, they will make stone soup, fit for a king, for all to enjoy. The soldiers are crafty fellows but they're not magicians. They borrow a large pot, fill it with water, and add three stones. As each cooking step draws near, they assert their need for an ingredient that will perfect their glorious soup of water and stones. Salt. Pepper. Carrots. Barley. Cabbages. Beef. And so on. By the time soup's on, the townspeople have contributed all they had wanted to retain. In fact, the originally selfish townspeople end up rounding out the meal with bread and cider, and reward the soldiers with the best beds in town. The soldiers are proclaimed to be wise and splendid, never mind good, resourceful cooks.

Go and wake up your cook.

ARABIAN PROVERB

CHIC SIMPLE COOKING IS A BOOK ABOUT THE ESSENTIAL TANGIBLES— INGREDIENTS, MEASUREMENTS, METHODS—AND SUCH SUBLIME INTANGIBLES AS DESIGN, PROPORTION, FLEXIBILITY. IT'S about blending the familiar and the unfamiliar, about knowing the rules and when to break them. Mostly, it's about having fun and feeding yourself at the same time. ☞ We've opened each section of the book with a Simple recipe, a panic-proof basic. For beginners, they're the building blocks of a cooking repertoire; for more experienced cooks, they serve as reminders that the simplest dishes are still, sometimes, the best dishes. ☞ Throughout the book you'll find practical tips, advice, and hopefully, inspiration. One of the key benefits of preparing your own food is getting it exactly as you like it: salt and pepper to taste, *your* taste; garlic pungent and pressed or mild and sliced; if you love lemon, you can add extra zing by grating the zest before squeezing it for fresh juice; if you crave a more complicated interplay of flavors, throw in all the optional ingredients offered—the possibilities are in your capable hands. ☞ Cooking is deeply personal;

seasoning alone can be the makings of a character study. What's important to you, how you taste and smell and see things is reflected in the food you prepare. With all the varied constraints of time, it's easy to forget how nurturing and literally creative preparing a meal can be. It is time to stop and reflect, to measure time in savored tastes instead of choked down mouthfuls. ☞ Let's face it, this cookbook doesn't reinvent the wheel—we just tapped into the collective wealth of cooking know-how and adapted the recipes we loved the most. Wise as any professional chef may be, the most successful cook of all is the one who loves his or her own cooking, who can't wait to dig into the heavenly smelling output of his or her own kitchen. What more needs to be said? Experiment, laugh, smell, sample, enjoy—and most of all, cook.

SOUP

"Beautiful Soup!

Who cares for fish, game

or any other dish?

Who would not give all

else for two pennyworth

only of beautiful Soup?"

CHICKEN STOCK

Homemade stock is a happy habit to acquire. Leftover roasted chicken? Simply throw those bones in a pot, add cold water, and let 'er simmer. Or do as Sally, our recipe developer, does, and add all the trimmings. Either way is guaranteed to be soul-satisfying.

MAKES 5–7 CUPS

1 carcass and neck of a 6–7-pound chicken

OPTIONAL INGREDIENTS

1 Spanish onion, quartered
2 carrots, sliced
2 stalks celery, with greens, sliced
8 sprigs fresh parsley
1 teaspoon tarragon
1 bay leaf

1. Place ingredients in a large soup pot and generously cover with cold water. (If you have vegetables left over from roasting the chicken, add them too.)

2. Cook over medium heat until the mixture comes to a slow boil. Reduce heat to low and gently simmer, partially covered, for 3 hours.

3. Strain and cool the stock, uncovered. Discard the carcass and vegetables. Refrigerate.

4. When the stock has completely cooled several hours later, skim off and discard the hardened fat. Refrigerate or freeze the stock.

OTHER CHOICES: To create a beef stock, see page 260.

WHEN FRANKENSTEIN

WANDERED, LOST IN THE WOODS, HE WAS KINDLY TAKEN

IN BY A BLIND MAN WHO OFFERED HIM SOUP. THE INHUMAN SAVAGE

BEAST WAS DULY SOOTHED AND NOURISHED. EVEN OUT OF STORYBOOKS,

soup is an all-season, all-occasion answer: warming in the winter, refreshing in the summer. And it can be

made from almost anything. The secret to the most savory soups is a well-flavored

stock, a broth that can even stand on its own in economical splendor. Stock

isn't just for the soup bowl, either: you can use it to baste a roasting

turkey, moisten stuffing, flavor rice, or become the base for simple

pan gravy. And just when you think you can't afford to eat well,

remember: when you've got stock, you've got food. And when

you've got food, you've got life.

FISH STOCK

MAKES ABOUT 10 CUPS

1 Spanish onion, quartered
2 carrots, sliced into chunks
2 stalks celery, including greens, sliced
8 sprigs fresh parsley
1 teaspoon dried thyme
1 bay leaf
2 cups dry white wine
8 cups cold water
   Bones and heads of 5–6 white-fleshed fish (such as flounder or sole)
   Salt and pepper to taste

1. Combine all the ingredients except salt and pepper in a large stockpot and bring to a boil over high heat. Reduce heat to low and cook, partially covered, for 30 minutes, stirring occasionally.

2. Strain the soup and discard solids. Add salt and pepper to taste.

3. Cover and refrigerate until ready to use.

STOCKPILE

Many people don't make soups because they are intimidated by the prospect of making stock from scratch. Although it is very easy to make your own, alternatives abound. Many gourmet shops sell their own stocks, which are usually excellent. Supermarkets and health-food stores carry large supplies of good canned stocks and bouillon cubes. If available, buy products that are low in sodium and without MSG. If those products are not available, little salt, if any, will be needed. Always skim the fat off canned stocks before using them.

VEGETABLE STOCK

MAKES ABOUT 8 CUPS

2 Spanish onions, quartered
3 carrots, sliced into chunks
2 stalks celery, including greens, sliced
3 potatoes, quartered
8 sprigs fresh parsley
4 cloves garlic
4 sun-dried tomatoes
2 bay leaves
12 black peppercorns
8 cups cold water
   Salt

1. Combine all the ingredients except salt in a large stockpot and bring to a boil over high heat. Reduce heat to low and cook, partially covered, for 1 hour, stirring occasionally.

2. Strain the soup and discard the vegetables, bay leaf, and peppercorns. Add salt to taste.

3. Cover and refrigerate until ready to use.

[SOUP *first aid—page 262*]

CHICKEN SOUP WITH LEMON ZEST, THYME, AND POTATOES

This may look and cook like chicken soup, but it is utterly and inexplicably transformed by lemon, taking on an entirely new character.

MAKES ABOUT 14 CUPS

1   teaspoon unsalted butter or olive oil
1   small Spanish onion, coarsely chopped
3   carrots, halved lengthwise and thinly sliced
2   stalks celery, halved lengthwise and sliced
10 cups chicken stock (see page 19)
1   bay leaf
1   strip lemon zest
1   teaspoon dried thyme
2   medium potatoes, finely diced (about 2 cups)
2–3 cups cooked chicken, shredded or diced

1. Heat a large stockpot over medium-low heat and add the butter or oil. When the butter is melted or the oil is hot, add the onion, carrots, and celery, and cook until the vegetables begin to soften, about 10 minutes. Add the stock, bay leaf, lemon zest, and thyme, and cook over low heat for about 1 hour.

2. Place the potatoes in a separate pot and cover with cold water. Bring to a boil and cook for about 10 minutes or until the potatoes are tender. Drain the potatoes.

3. Add the potatoes and the chicken to the soup and cook 5 minutes, or until the chicken and the potatoes are just heated. Remove the bay leaf and the lemon zest just prior to serving.

OTHER CHOICES: You can substitute 1 cup cooked pasta or rice for the potatoes.

POTATO LEEK SOUP

MAKES ABOUT 8 CUPS

2   tablespoons unsalted butter
1   large bunch leeks, julienned (see page 262)
6   red new potatoes, cubed, and peeled, if desired
6   cups chicken or vegetable stock (see pages 19, 21)
3/4 cup milk, light cream, or heavy cream
1/2 teaspoon ground nutmeg
1/4 teaspoon black pepper
    Salt
    Fresh chives, for garnish

1. Melt the butter in a large stockpot over medium-low heat and add the leeks. Cook, covered, for about 15 minutes, or until they have softened.

2. Raise the heat to high, add the potatoes and stock, and bring to a boil. Reduce heat to low and cook, partially covered, about 25 minutes, or until the potatoes are tender.

3. Transfer the solids to a blender or food processor fitted with a steel blade and gradually add broth, pulsing until just puréed. Do not overbeat or the potatoes will become elastic. Add milk or cream, nutmeg, black pepper, and salt to taste. Serve garnished with chives.

NOTE: When served cold, this soup goes by its French name, vichyssoise. Before adding milk or cream, chill the soup for at least 2 hours.

"Soup is sensitive. You don't catch steak hanging around when you're poor and sick, do you?"

JUDITH MARTIN (MISS MANNERS)

CHICKEN SOUP WITH LEMON ZEST, THYME, AND POTATOES

CORN SOUP WITH BELL PEPPERS AND CILANTRO

MAKES ABOUT 10 CUPS

2 teaspoons olive oil
1 Spanish onion, coarsely chopped
2–3 cloves garlic, finely chopped or pressed
2 bell peppers, 1 red and 1 green, diced (see Note)
6 large ears corn (approximately 4 cups of kernels)
7–8 cups chicken or vegetable stock (see pages 19, 21)
1/4 cup chopped fresh cilantro, for garnish

OPTIONAL INGREDIENT

1/4–1/2 teaspoon cayenne pepper

1. Heat a large stockpot over medium-low heat and add the oil. When the oil is hot, add the onion, garlic, bell peppers, and, if desired, the cayenne pepper. Cook for about 15 minutes, or until the vegetables are softened.

2. Raise the heat to high, add the corn and the stock, and bring to a boil. Reduce the heat to low and cook, partially covered, for 25 minutes.

3. Transfer half of the solids to a blender or food processor fitted with a steel blade and purée. Return the purée to the soup and stir.

4. Garnish each serving with fresh cilantro.

NOTE: You can add the bell peppers at the end if you prefer them crisp.

WHY PUT OFF THE BOIL?

It is recommended that cold water be used when starting a soup so that the flavors are drawn out of the ingredients as they are brought to the first boil.

PUTTING A LID ON IT

By partially covering the pot, liquid will escape throughout the simmering process, resulting in more concentrated flavors.

THE THIN & THE THICK OF IT

Many soups are excellent served cold or hot. Like any cold food, cold soup needs more spices. It will also have a thicker consistency, which you may choose to thin with more broth, cream, milk, buttermilk, or yogurt. To prevent curdling, always add some flour —it will help bind the soup—and heat very gently.

FOR AN EXTRA NIP

Many soups are enhanced by dark beers and wines, such as sherry and Madeira.

BUTTERNUT SQUASH SOUP WITH PEAR, ORANGE, AND ROSEMARY

MAKES ABOUT 12 CUPS

2 teaspoons olive oil
1 Spanish onion, chopped
1 butternut squash, peeled, seeded, and sliced (see page 41)
1 large pear, peeled, cored, and sliced
1 sprig fresh rosemary or 1 teaspoon dried
6–7 cups chicken or vegetable stock (see pages 19, 21)
1/2 cup orange juice
2–3 teaspoons grated fresh orange zest
  Salt and pepper
  Fresh orange slices, for garnish

OPTIONAL INGREDIENT

Croutons (see page 31)

1. Heat a large stockpot over medium-low heat and add the oil. When the oil is hot, add the onion and sauté for about 5–10 minutes, or until the onion is golden.

2. Add the remaining ingredients, raise heat to high, and bring to a boil. Reduce heat to low and cook, partially covered, for 25 minutes, or until the squash is tender.

3. Transfer the mixture in batches to a blender or food processor fitted with a steel blade and purée until smooth.

4. Garnish each serving with orange slices.

CORN SOUP WITH BELL PEPPERS AND CILANTRO

WINTER BORSCHT

Family recipes are wealthy legacies indeed. This soup comes down through the generations by way of Toby Gross, Kim's mother-in-law. Traditional garnishes include chopped hard-boiled egg and crumbled matzo. A more modern accompaniment is a baked potato on the side. This is definitely a soup you will always "eat! eat!" with pleasure.

MAKES ABOUT 12 CUPS

3   pounds turkey legs
2   medium-sized Spanish onions, chopped
3   large cloves garlic, minced
3   bunches beets, peeled and sliced
1/2 cup sugar
1/2 teaspoon citric acid or 2 tablespoons lemon juice
    Salt

1. Place the turkey, onions, and garlic in a large stockpot. Add water to cover plus 1 inch. Bring to a boil, reduce heat to low, partially cover, and cook for about 45 minutes.

2. Add the beets, sugar, and citric acid or lemon juice. Raise heat to high and bring the soup to a boil. Reduce heat to low and cook for about 15 minutes. Skim fat off the top. Add salt to taste.

OTHER CHOICES: Substitute flanken or short ribs for the turkey legs, and cook for 15 minutes longer (1 hour total) in step 1.

BORSCHT BELT

The word "borscht" is derived from Yiddish. In the 1930s, the term "Borscht Belt" referred to the kosher hotels and cabarets of the Catskill Mountains.

BEET GREENS

When buying beets, don't throw out the tops. Beet greens are high in beta carotene, calcium, and iron. When picking beets with the intention of eating the greens, use the same criteria as for any greens: seek out small, crisp, dark green leaves. Even if you don't intend to eat the greens, they can indicate the quality of the beets. If the tops are yellowed, limp, or otherwise appear unfresh, check the roots extra carefully.

SUMMER BORSCHT

MAKES ABOUT 12 CUPS

2   large bunches beets, peeled and thinly sliced
6   cups water or chicken stock (see page 19)
1/3 cup sugar
2   tablespoons fresh lemon juice
3   cups buttermilk or yogurt, more if yogurt is desired for garnish
    Salt and pepper
1–2 tablespoons chopped fresh dill
1   salad cucumber, peeled and thinly sliced

1. Place the beets, the water or stock, and the sugar in a large stockpot and bring to a boil. Reduce heat to low and cook, partially covered, for about 35 minutes, or until the beets are tender. Allow to cool to room temperature.

2. Place half the beets in a blender or food processor fitted with a steel blade and process, gradually adding half the broth, lemon juice, and yogurt or buttermilk until smooth. Repeat this step with the remaining beets and broth until all are processed.

3. Combine all the ingredients in a large bowl. Refrigerate for at least 2 hours.

4. Add salt and pepper to taste and garnish with dill, cucumber, and additional yogurt, if desired.

"To a man with an empty stomach, food is god."

MAHATMA GANDHI

ROOT VEGETABLES

ARE WAITING IN YOUR CELLAR RIGHT NOW, SUSPENDED IN A KIND OF INCOGNITO SUBTERRANEAN HALF-LIFE, READY TO REVIVE YOUR VEGGIE-DEPRIVED BODY. ROOTS ARE OFTEN DESCRIBED as "lowly" and can go entirely ignored at the table, playing only a supporting role in the composition of thick soups. Unless, of course, it's Thanksgiving, the one day of the year when root vegetables show off their true colors and flavors. And think of those colors—though they grow underground in the dark, carrots come up bright orange; beets are magenta; parsnips are pale ivory; and turnips are blushed with violet. Lately our increasingly multicultural greengrocers have brought us more exotic roots: taro, yucca, and other longtime staples of South American and African cuisines. Root vegetables are poised on the edge of culinary stardom. They're waiting to be discovered, waiting to come out of the cellar and into the spotlight.

CARROTS. The best carrots are young and slender. Like beets, the greens rob the roots of moisture and vitamins, so remove them immediately. Carrots are wonderful both raw and cooked. They are an ideal ingredient for soups, stir-fries, salads, juice, and a cake. Orange carrots were developed relatively recently by Dutch farmers. Until the seventeenth century, carrots were black, white, or purple.

BEETS. Choose firm beets with smooth, unblemished skins. Beet greens should be removed as soon as possible, as they leach moisture from the beet. Don't peel the skin off beets until after cooking. Beets are sweet and are widely eaten cooked in salads, but they can also be boiled, baked, or cooked in a microwave. Beet greens are flavorful and can be cooked like spinach.

PARSNIPS. Naturally sweet, they can be used like carrots. The most popular way of preparing parsnips is to boil and mash them. But they are also tasty when roasted, or sautéed with chopped tart apples. Add chopped parsnips to stews and soups, but be sure to add them toward the end of the cooking time, as they quickly become mushy.

RADISHES. Choose radishes that feel firm when gently squeezed. While wonderful raw and in salads, radishes are also delicious when sautéed in olive oil and seasoned with salt, pepper, and a touch of sugar.

TURNIPS. Members of the cabbage family, turnips come in several varieties. The smaller ones are good when glazed like carrots, added to rich stews, or mashed. The larger ones, like the yellow rutabagas, have a stronger flavor and are good mashed and well seasoned with butter, pepper, and nutmeg.

CARROT

BEET

RADISH

TURNIP

PARSNIP

CROUTONS

SPICY GAZPACHO

We forget how good gazpacho is until tomatoes reach their deep summertime blush. Although chopping can be a chore, we can always opt for the blender, and drink our gazpacho by the glass.

SERVES 6–8

 2 cucumbers, peeled, seeded, if desired, and diced
 3 beefsteak tomatoes, diced
 4 cloves garlic, finely chopped or pressed
 1 red onion, coarsely chopped
 1 red bell pepper, diced
 1 yellow bell pepper, diced
 2 tablespoons olive oil
 1/4 cup red wine vinegar
 1/4 cup balsamic vinegar
 2–3 cups tomato juice
 1 teaspoon black pepper
 1 teaspoon salt
 1/4 cup chopped fresh parsley, basil, dill, or cilantro
 1/2 teaspoon cayenne pepper

1. Mix the cucumbers, tomatoes, garlic, onion, and peppers in a large glass or ceramic bowl.

2. Add remaining ingredients, except for the fresh herbs and cayenne pepper. Toss to combine.

3. Place half the mixture in the bowl of a blender or food processor fitted with a steel blade and pulse until it is the desired consistency.

4. Return the mixture to the original bowl with the chunky remaining ingredients and stir by hand.

5. Cover and refrigerate for at least 4 hours.

6. Add fresh herbs and cayenne pepper just before serving.

CURRIED VEGETABLE SOUP WITH FRESH GINGERROOT

SERVES 4

 1 teaspoon olive oil
 1 small Spanish onion, chopped
 2–3 cloves garlic, sliced
 1–2 thin slices fresh gingerroot (about the size of a quarter)
 1 tablespoon curry powder
 5 1/2–6 cups chicken or vegetable stock (see pages 19, 21)
 1 large potato, diced
 1 bunch broccoli: stems, peeled and chopped; florets, chopped (or substitute 4 medium-sized zucchini, 1 head cauliflower, or 1 pound carrots)
 Salt and pepper

1. Heat a medium-sized saucepan over medium-low heat and add the oil. When the oil is hot, add the onion, garlic, gingerroot, and curry powder. Cook, partially covered, for about 7 minutes, or until the vegetables begin to soften.

2. Add 1 cup of the stock, the potato, and the broccoli stems (not the florets), and bring to a boil.

3. Reduce the heat to low, cover, and cook for about 15 minutes, or until broccoli stems and potato are tender.

4. Add the broccoli florets, 1/2 cup of the stock, cover, and cook for about 10 minutes, or until the florets are tender.

5. Place the remaining 4 to 4 1/2 cups of chicken or vegetable stock in a separate pot and bring to a boil over high heat.

6. Put all the vegetable ingredients in a food processor fitted with a steel blade and gradually add the boiling chicken stock. If necessary, this can be done in 2 batches. Add salt and pepper to taste.

CROUTONS

By just adding croutons to a soup or salad, a side dish can become the main meal.

SERVES 4

 1–2 tablespoons olive oil
 2 cloves garlic, finely chopped or pressed
 1/2 teaspoon kosher salt
 1/2 loaf day-old bread or half a French baguette, cut in cubes or on diagonal, as desired

1. Preheat oven to 325° F.

2. Combine the olive oil, garlic, and salt in a large bowl and add the croutons. Toss lightly to coat. Place croutons on a cookie sheet in the oven and bake for about 10 minutes, or until lightly golden.

3. The croutons should be cooled and used immediately.

NOTE: Planning ahead option: as soon as croutons are finished cooling, place in plastic bags and freeze.

TURMERIC. An Indian spice made from a ground root that gives a yellow color and an exotic flavor to foods.

CRACKED BLACK PEPPERCORN. For the liveliest, most vivid taste, buy whole black peppercorns and use them freshly ground—it really does make a difference.

GINGER. Ground ginger is used primarily in baking. Fresh gingerroot is used especially in Chinese cooking and can be found in many markets.

WHITE PEPPERCORN. Less flavorful than black pepper, it is used in light-colored sauces when black specks in food are undesirable.

WHOLE BLACK PEPPERCORN. When whole black peppercorns are called for, be sure to crush them slightly first or they won't release any flavor.

CUMIN. This pungent, caraway-like spice comes from the seed of the cumin plant, a native of the Mediterranean region. Used in soups and in Indian and Mediterranean cuisine.

POULTRY

"It was Napoleon

who had such a passion for chicken that he kept his chefs working around the clock.

What a kitchen that was, with birds in every state of undress; some still cold and slung over hooks, some turning slowly on the spit, but most in wasted piles because the Emperor was busy. Odd to be so governed by appetite. It was my first commission. I started as a neck wringer and before long I was the one who carried the platter through inches of mud to his tent. He liked me because I am short. I flatter myself. He did not dislike me. He liked no one except Joséphine and he liked her the way he liked chicken."

JEANETTE WINTERSON, *The Passion*

ROASTED CHICKEN

A perfect roasted chicken is the epitome of the art of simplicity. It is an experience of juxtaposed textures, heady juices, and seductive aromas—yet there is something beautifully elementary about a roasted chicken. Master this simple chicken recipe, its nuances of time and temperature, and all cooking wisdom is yours.

SERVES 4

1 whole roaster chicken (about 6–7 pounds)
2 cloves garlic, finely chopped or pressed
¼ teaspoon black pepper

OPTIONAL INGREDIENT

1–1½ teaspoons kosher salt

1. Preheat oven to 450° F.

2. Remove the giblets and neck from the chicken cavity; set them aside and refrigerate them if you are going to make stock, or add them to the roasting pan if you are going to make gravy; if neither, discard.

3. Rinse the chicken in several changes of cold water and pat dry.

4. Rub the skin and flesh with the garlic, black pepper, and, if desired, kosher salt (to make skin very crispy). Place on a roasting rack in a pan.

5. ☼ Cook for approximately 70 minutes (10 minutes per pound) or until internal temperature reaches 160° F.

"Poultry is for the
cook what canvas is
for the painter."

JEAN-ANTHELME
BRILLAT-SAVARIN

P O U L T R Y

IS THE WHITE SHIRT OF THE CULINARY WORLD:

IT'S EQUALLY AT HOME IN A PICNIC BASKET AT A LITTLE LEAGUE

BASEBALL GAME, IN A BUFFET AT A CHAMPAGNE RECEPTION FOR A VISITING

dignitary, or on an everyday plate at a simple supper in your own kitchen. No wonder it's a favorite item in

our culinary wardrobe—poultry goes with everything. How do we count the fine qualities of domestic fowl? Here's

a start: It's economical for both the wallet and the waistline. It can be as obvious as a 20-pound roasted turkey or as

subtle as slivers of white meat in a pasta sauce. As soup, it's good medicine. It bakes, it roasts, it fries, it grills, it stews, it

boils, it stuffs...then it chills. As the centerpiece of a sit-down dinner, it pleases the palates of almost everyone you love.

BROILER AND FRYER. They are specifically bred to produce tender meat, and are usually 3–5 pounds and about 6–8 weeks old when slaughtered. Best used in parts and broiled or fried, but can also be roasted.

CAPON. Usually 8–10 pounds and 10 weeks old when slaughtered, these are castrated cocks. They're more delicate and fatter than other chicken, and usually have a greater proportion of white meat. Good for roasting and stuffing. Usually more expensive.

CORNISH GAME HEN. Usually 5–6 weeks old when slaughtered, weighing 1–2 pounds each. These miniature chickens are best roasted or split and broiled. Usually more expensive.

FREE-RANGE. These birds are not cooped up but instead are allowed to run free. They are fed grain, are leaner than other fowl, and their skin is whitish. Usually more expensive.

KOSHER. According to Jewish dietary law, meat most be "kosher" (or "kasher"), or free from blood. Meat is considered kosher once it has been properly slaughtered and salted under rabbinical supervision. Depending on how thoroughly the meat is rinsed after salting, kosher meat can be higher in sodium.

ROASTER. Roasters are usually 4–8 pounds each, and about 10 weeks old when slaughtered. Best roasted whole, but can be cut up and roasted, sautéed, or broiled in parts.

[POULTRY *first aid—page 258*]

ROASTING

IF YOUR OVEN IS RELIABLE AND YOUR TIMING IS TRUE,

YOU KNOW YOUR ROASTED CHICKEN IS GOING TO BE PERFECT. SO WHY NOT GO

AHEAD AND PUSH IT A LITTLE. TRY NEW FLAVOR COMBINATIONS, LIKE LEMON AND

tarragon or red pepper flakes and tomatoes. When you surround your chicken with fruits or vegetables, or rub its body

with spices, that slow-roasting causes almost any combination of flavors to mingle in the most alluring and savory way.

ROASTED CHICKEN WITH GARLIC, ROSEMARY, POTATOES, AND ONIONS

SERVES 4

 1 whole roaster chicken, about 6–7 pounds
 6 cloves garlic
 3 branches fresh rosemary or 2 tablespoons dried
 1/4 teaspoon black pepper
12–16 small new potatoes, halved or quartered
 2 red or Spanish onions, cut in eighths, through the root

OPTIONAL INGREDIENT

 2 1/2 teaspoons kosher salt

1. Preheat oven to 450° F.

2. Clean per Simple Roasted Chicken recipe (see page 37), steps 2 and 3.

3. Place the garlic cloves in between the skin and flesh of the chicken. Sprinkle the inside cavity with half the rosemary and 1 teaspoon of the kosher salt, if desired. Sprinkle the skin with pepper and 1 teaspoon of the kosher salt, if desired.

4. Place on a flat roasting rack in a broiler pan.

5. In a bowl, combine the potatoes and onions, and sprinkle them with 1/2 teaspoon of kosher salt, if desired, and the remaining rosemary. Place the combined ingredients on the rack in the pan, surrounding the chicken.

6. Cook for approximately 70 minutes (10 minutes per pound), or until internal temperature reaches 160° F. Do not baste.

SIMPLE POULTRY GRAVY

This is a misnomer: Gravy makes one think of wonderful, thick, artery-clogging rapture, and this is actually more of a slender sauce, though still wanton.

SERVES 4

 Pan drippings, including garlic and herbs
 Giblets and neck from poultry
 1/2 cup water or chicken broth

1. When the fowl has finished cooking, remove the pan drippings, garlic, and

herbs from the roasted poultry's cavity to a saucepan with the refrigerated giblets and neck.

2. Add ½ cup water or chicken broth and bring to a boil, then immediately remove from heat. Strain gravy and remove fat by skimming clear liquid off top.

3. Serve on the side with the main poultry dish.

ROASTED CHICKEN WITH BUTTERNUT SQUASH AND PEARS

SERVES 4

1 whole roaster chicken or capon (about 6–7 pounds)
1½ teaspoons dried sage
12 shallots, or 3 Spanish onions, quartered
2 ripe pears (any kind will do), peeled, if desired, cored, and diced

1 butternut squash, peeled, seeded, and cut into 1-inch cubes; reserve seeds for roasting (recipe follows)

OPTIONAL INGREDIENT

1 tablespoon kosher salt

1. Preheat oven to 450° F.

2. Clean per Simple Roasted Chicken recipe (page 37), steps 2 and 3.

3. Combine sage and salt, if desired, and set aside. Place the chicken on a roasting rack in a pan and surround it with the vegetables and pears. Rub the sage mixture into the flesh, skin, and cavity.

4. ⏰ Cook approximately 70 minutes (10 minutes per pound) or until internal temperature reaches 160° F.

ROASTED SQUASH SEEDS

Don't throw out those seeds! Recycle them into an elegant garnish that adds welcome crunch to an evening meal or into a protein-rich trail-side snack.

SERVES 4

Seeds from 1 butternut squash
2 teaspoons olive oil or butter
Salt

1. To clean the seeds, discard the membranes and rinse. Air-dry the seeds on a towel for a couple of hours or on a cookie sheet in an oven at 200° F. for 20 minutes.

2. Heat 2 teaspoons olive oil or butter in a large nonstick skillet. Add seeds and cook over medium heat until they start to turn golden.

3. Season with salt and serve on the side with the chicken.

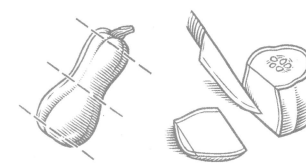

PEELING AND DESEEDING A BUTTERNUT SQUASH

The easiest way to peel a butternut squash is to cut it horizontally into halves or thirds, then place the individual pieces flat side down and cut off the peel. To deseed, cut across the peeled chunks and scoop out seeds with a spoon.

ROASTED TURKEY WITH CORN BREAD STUFFING

Everyone has figured out that turkey doesn't need a holiday to justify it. This moist, slow-cooked turkey acquires a surprising kick with the addition of dry vermouth.

SERVES 8

1   turkey (about 10–12 pounds)
¼   cup olive oil or unsalted butter, melted
1   teaspoon kosher salt
    Freshly ground pepper
1   tablespoon chopped fresh rosemary or 1 teaspoon dried
¼   cup dry vermouth or fresh lemon juice (about 1 lemon)

1. Preheat oven to 450° F.

2. Clean per Simple Roasted Chicken recipe (page 37), steps 2 and 3.

3. Combine the oil or butter, salt, pepper, rosemary, and vermouth or lemon juice, if desired, and rub or brush into flesh and skin.

4. Loosely fill the cavity with stuffing (recipe follows) and place the bird on a rack in a roasting pan in the oven. Roast, uncovered, for 30 minutes.

5. ⏲ Cover with aluminum foil. Reduce heat to 350° F. and cook for 3–4 hours (or about 15–20 minutes per pound). If desired, baste with drippings every 30 minutes.

6. If you are using a thermometer, place it deep in the inner thigh. The turkey is done when the internal temperature reaches 160° F. If you do not have a thermometer, you can tell that the turkey is done when the juices run clear from the breast and the leg moves easily.

CORN BREAD STUFFING

Though homemade corn bread is best in this stuffing, store-bought is okay, too, as long as it's not too sweet and canned corn is added.

MAKES 8–10 CUPS

2   tablespoons olive oil
2   leeks, diced
4   stalks celery, diced
3   Granny Smith apples, peeled, if desired, and diced
7–8 cups crumbled day-old homemade corn bread (see page 166 and omit the optional scallions, jalapeño, and black pepper)
1   cup chopped walnuts, pecans, or hazelnuts
3   tablespoons chopped fresh parsley
3   tablespoons chopped fresh sage or 1 tablespoon dried
3   tablespoons chopped fresh rosemary or 1 tablespoon dried
3   tablespoons chopped fresh thyme or 1 tablespoon dried
1   teaspoon salt
¼   cup vermouth
2   large eggs, beaten
½–1 cup apple juice

1. Heat a large skillet over low heat and add the oil. When the oil is hot, add the leeks, celery, and apples and cook for about 15–20 minutes or until soft. Remove from heat.

2. Add the remaining ingredients and mix. Place the stuffing in the turkey cavity or in an ovenproof dish and bake for about 35 minutes at 350° F.

OTHER CHOICES: Our homemade corn bread may be substituted with store-bought corn bread stuffing with one 16-ounce can of corn kernels, drained.

> ## "The discovery of a new dish does more for the happiness of man than the discovery of a star."
>
> ### JEAN-ANTHELME BRILLAT-SAVARIN

ROASTED TURKEY WITH CORN BREAD STUFFING

SPICE-RUBBED ROASTED TURKEY WITH FRUIT AND NUT STUFFING

Turkey goes downtown. Infused with the sophisticated flavors of garlic, cumin, pepper, and cinnamon, it leaves the farm in the dust.

SERVES 8

SPICE RUB

2–4 tablespoons chili powder
½ cup olive oil
4 cloves garlic, chopped or pressed
2 teaspoons ground cumin
½ teaspoon black pepper
1 teaspoon ground cinnamon
1 turkey, about 10–12 pounds

1. Combine the chili powder, oil, garlic, cumin, pepper, and cinnamon in a small saucepan over medium-low heat and bring to a low boil. Simmer for 5 minutes and set aside to cool.

2. Clean per Simple Roasted Chicken recipe (page 37), steps 2 and 3.

3. Rub or brush the spice rub all over the flesh, the skin, and inside the cavities. Cover and refrigerate overnight. Reserve remaining spice rub for basting.

4. Preheat oven to 450° F.

5. Loosely fill the cavity with stuffing (recipe follows) and place the bird on a rack in a roasting pan in the oven. Bake, uncovered, for 30 minutes.

6. Reduce heat to 350° F. and cook, covered with aluminum foil, for 3–4 hours (or about 15–20 minutes per pound). Baste with spice rub and drippings every 30 minutes.

7. The turkey is done when the internal temperature reaches 160° F.

FRUIT AND NUT STUFFING

This cornucopia of fruits (dried and fresh) and nuts (domestic and imported) finds harmony with bourbon and ginger.

MAKES 9 CUPS

18 prunes, pitted and chopped
½ cup raisins or currants
12 dried apricot halves, chopped
¼ cup bourbon
1 tablespoon corn, canola, or olive oil
3 large Spanish onions, coarsely chopped
2 stalks celery, with greens, coarsely chopped
3 Granny Smith or other tart apples, peeled, if desired, and diced
2 cups (1 bag) fresh or frozen cranberries
1 cup toasted pine nuts (see page 181)
1 cup finely chopped almonds, hazelnuts, pecans, or walnuts
1 teaspoon chopped fresh gingerroot
1 teaspoon ground cinnamon
1 teaspoon salt
1 teaspoon black pepper
2 large eggs, beaten

1. Combine the prunes, raisins or currants, apricots, and bourbon in a small bowl. Cover and let sit overnight at room temperature.

2. Heat a medium-sized pan over medium heat and add oil. When the oil is hot, add the onions and celery and cook until golden, about 10 minutes.

3. Place the onion mixture in a large mixing bowl, add the dried fruit mixture and the remaining ingredients.

4. Place the stuffing in turkey cavities or in an ovenproof dish and bake for about 35 minutes at 350° F.

TIP: Any leftover stuffing should always be taken out of the turkey, placed in a separate container, and refrigerated.

TIP: Drizzle gravy on stuffing cooked outside of the turkey for additional moistness and flavor.

CRANBERRIES AND BOSC PEAR

CHICKEN PAILLARDS WITH BALSAMIC VINAIGRETTE AND WILTED GREENS

4 whole chicken breasts,
  boneless and skinless, halved and
  trimmed of fat and membranes
2–3 cloves garlic
1 teaspoon Dijon mustard
4 tablespoons balsamic vinegar
6 tablespoons olive oil
8 cups assorted salad greens
  Salt and pepper

1. Flatten each breast by pounding it between 2 pieces of waxed paper with a mallet or rolling pin. You can make it paper-thin or as thick as ¼ inch.

2. Place the garlic, mustard, balsamic vinegar, and olive oil in a blender or a food processor fitted with a steel blade. Blend until the mixture starts to thicken. Add salt and pepper to taste.

3. Place the paillards in a large shallow ceramic or glass container and pour about ¼ cup of the marinade over them. Cover them and let them sit at room temperature no longer than 1 hour, or refrigerate for 4 hours or overnight. Refrigerate the remaining vinaigrette.

4. Heat a large nonstick or cast-iron skillet over high heat. Remove as much of the marinade as possible from the paillards and discard. When the skillet is hot, add the paillards, reduce the heat to medium, and cook for about 1–2 minutes per side, depending on the thickness of the chicken. This will probably take 2 batches, depending on size of pan.

5. Serve the hot paillards, whole or shredded, over the greens, which will wilt. Drizzle remaining vinaigrette over the paillards. Salt and pepper to taste.

"Turkey? Already?" Danny asked his aunt. "I'm trying this new method," she said. "It's supposed to save energy. You set your oven extremely low and cook your meat all night." "Weird." But in the middle of the night, Macon woke with a start and gave serious thought to that turkey. She was cooking it till tomorrow? At an extremely low temperature? What temperature was that, exactly?... He made his way downstairs in the dark, and he crossed the icy kitchen linoleum and turned on the little light above the stove. One hundred and forty degrees, the oven dial read. "Certain death," he told Edward, who had tagged along behind him. Then Charles walked in, wearing large, floppy pajamas. He peered at the dial and sighed. "Not only that," he said, "but this is a *stuffed* turkey." "Wonderful." "Two quarts of stuffing. I heard her say so."

"Two quarts of teeming, swarming bacteria."

ANNE TYLER, *The Accidental Tourist*

CHICKEN PAILLARDS WITH BALSAMIC VINAIGRETTE AND WILTED GREENS

GARLIC HEAD

VAMPIRES ARE PERHAPS THE ONLY KNOWN BIPEDS WHO DON'T LOVE GARLIC. MOST OF US MORTALS ARE SO MAD FOR THE STUFF THAT WE'VE BEEN KNOWN TO HOST PARADES AND FESTIVALS IN ITS honor. It even has a fan club: the Order of the Stinking Rose. Garlic is a member of the lily family, as are onions, shallots, leeks, and scallions. (Now, don't get any ideas about eating flowering lily bulbs.) Besides being an essential ingredient in many dishes, garlic is believed to have powerful health benefits. In ancient times it was used to cure broken bones, tuberculosis, and bronchitis; today it is still favored as a folk remedy for putting the common cold on the run. Culinary uses of garlic are divided along geographical lines. In ancient Mediterranean and Asian cuisines it has been as indispensable as water and heat. In the U.S. it was once thought of as a strictly Italian ingredient (shame on us). Now we love garlic with meats, vegetables, salads, breads, or eaten all alone, roasted and sweet.

CHILENO. This Mexican member of the garlic family has a sharp taste and a reddish skin.

ELEPHANT GARLIC. Don't let looks deceive you. Elephant garlic may look like regular garlic on steroids, but in fact it is a type of leek. Its mild flavor has its own merits, but elephant garlic cannot be substituted for white garlic.

WHITE GARLIC. Nearly 300 varieties of garlic are grown worldwide, but in the U.S. one type rules: It is the white-sheathed garlic with plump, tightly packed cloves. Ninety percent of it is grown in California and is classified as "early" or "late" with respect to the growing season. The early type has a white or off-white color. "Late" garlic has a longer shelf life. It looks the same from the outside, but its inner cloves are covered by a pinkish skin.

ELEPHANT

WHITE

CHILENO

JULIA

Julia Child was a late bloomer—at least as far as cooking is concerned. At 34 years old, the grande dame of Euro-American cuisine could barely put a meal together. As a child, she was rarely allowed in the kitchen; at various times in her life she aspired to be a novelist, a basketball star (she's 6 feet 2 inches tall), and, during World War II, a spy. Instead, she became a clerk for the Office of Strategic Services. It was there she met her husband, Paul, "a hungry man interested in food." He eventually persuaded her to enroll at the Cordon Bleu. From these inauspicious beginnings, Julia Child went on to revolutionize American cooking. She brought European and, notably, French cuisine into the home and subsequently inspired an entire generation of homemakers with her first book, *Mastering the Art of French Cooking*. She made cooking both accessible and fun. As *Time* magazine reported in 1966, "Even her failures and faux pas are classic. When a potato pancake falls on the worktable, she scoops it back into the pan, bats her big blue eyes at the camera and advises: 'Remember, you're all alone in the kitchen and no one can see you.'" She's become so much a part of American culture that even *Sesame Street* has made a Muppet in her honor: Julia Grown-Up.

> "I would much rather swoon over a few thin slices of prime beefsteak, or one small serving of chocolate, or a sliver of foie gras than indulge to the full on such nonentities as fat-free gelatin puddings."

C H I L D

ON STOCK. "Chicken stock is always useful to have on hand for use in a quick sauce or for soups. Why buy it when you can make your own for free, and know exactly what's in it? You may wish to freeze raw bones and scraps, then boil them up when you have collected a worthwhile group."

ON FISH. "Your nose is the best judge. The fish should have a fresh, natural, appetizing aroma. If it smells "fishy" or chemical, ...get your money back."

ON PASTA SALAD. "Just because pasta is easy to cook doesn't mean you don't have to go about it carefully. It is hopeless, for instance, to try mixing a salad when the cooked pasta has glued itself together into an unyielding mass, and it is horrid to be served a salad of dried-out, badly cooked pasta. I therefore suggest that it be tossed in oil and seasonings as soon as it is cooked, and a little garlic is often a happy addition, too."

CHICKEN SIMMERED IN WHITE WINE

Claiming it as her all-time favorite chicken recipe, Julia Child designates the following as a Master Recipe in The Way to Cook, *because it's quick and uncomplicated to prepare. She also marvels that something that tastes so good can actually be considered diet food.*

SERVES 4–6

2   medium carrots, trimmed and peeled
2   medium leeks, the tender part only, cleaned and washed
4–6   tender celery stalks, trimmed and washed
      Seasoning salt
      Fresh ground pepper
1/4   teaspoon dried tarragon
1   imported bay leaf
3 1/2   pounds cut-up frying chicken
1 1/2   cups dry white French vermouth or dry white wine
1 1/2   cups (approximately) clear chicken broth

1. Cut the vegetables into 1 1/2-inch julienne strips.

2. Toss the vegetables with salt, pepper, tarragon, and bay leaf; strew a third of them in the bottom of the casserole.

3. Season the chicken pieces with salt and pepper, and bury them in layers with the rest of the vegetables. Pour in the wine and enough chicken broth barely to cover the chicken.

4. Bring to a simmer, cover, and simmer slowly for 25 to 30 minutes, or until the chicken is done (the legs and thighs are tender when pierced, and their juices run clear with no trace of rosy color). Let the chicken steep in its cooking liquid for 10 to 15 minutes before proceeding—it will pick up flavor.

5. Degrease the liquid and remove the bay leaf. You may wish to peel the skin off the chicken pieces.

NOTE: May be cooked even a day in advance, and reheated.

EQUIPMENT: A covered flameproof casserole, chicken fryer, or electric frying pan that will hold the chicken and vegetables comfortably.

[🍲 OTHER FACTS—*page 279*]

LEMON ZEST WITH BASIL

CHICKEN WITH FRESH BASIL AND LEMON

Homey fried chicken gets a sophisticated marinade; the result is a family dinner that will enrapture just about any palate.

SERVES 4

Zest of 2 lemons, grated or finely julienned

$\frac{1}{2}-\frac{3}{4}$ cup fresh basil, about 1 small bunch (do not substitute dried)

3 cloves garlic

$2\frac{1}{2}$ teaspoons kosher salt

$2\frac{3}{4}$ teaspoons black pepper

4–8 tablespoons olive oil

$\frac{1}{2}$ cup unbleached all-purpose flour

1 4-pound fryer chicken, cut into 8 pieces, or 6–8 chicken breasts, boneless, halved and trimmed of excess fat and membrane

1. Place the lemon zest, basil, garlic, $\frac{1}{2}$ teaspoon of the salt, $\frac{3}{4}$ teaspoon of the pepper, and 2 tablespoons of the olive oil in the bowl of a food processor fitted with a steel blade and pulse until it forms a chunky paste.

2. ⏲ Place the chicken pieces in a large shallow glass or ceramic bowl and add the lemon and basil mixture. Cover and let sit at room temperature for no more than 1 hour, or refrigerate for at least 4 hours or overnight.

3. Combine the flour, the remaining kosher salt, and the rest of the pepper in a shallow bowl or plate and set it aside for dredging the chicken.

4. Heat a large skillet over medium-high heat and add 2 tablespoons of the olive oil. Remove the chicken from the marinade and dredge it in the flour mixture. Place the chicken directly in the hot oil.

5. Because cooking the chicken will take 2–3 batches, you may need to clean out the pan between batches with a paper towel and add more oil. If you are using a whole, cut-up chicken, cook it for about 10 minutes on the first side and about 7 on the second. If you are using boneless breasts, cook for about 5 minutes on the first side and 3 on the second.

6. Remove the chicken from the pan and place on paper towels.

NOTE: As this chicken recipe has the potential to smoke up the kitchen, be sure to remove all excess fat before cooking. Good ventilation is a must.

ZEST

The zest is the outermost, brightly colored part of the rind of citrus fruits. It adds visual excitement to presentation and also enhances both bouquet and taste. The zest can be freshly grated, dried into a loose powder, or simply left as a peel. (Its uninhibited brother, the twist, can often be found making trouble in a martini.)

"A cook's best friend is her nose."

EDEN PHILLPOTTS

CHICKEN FAJITA

FAJITAS

Fillings are served buffet-style, so you can create them as you like it — and you'll like it even more with bright, chunky salsa and fresh guacamole. A personal fiesta!

SERVES 4

1¼ pounds chicken or turkey breast, boneless and skinless, trimmed of fat and membrane and cut into thin strips, or 1¼ pounds flank steak, London broil, or sirloin steak, trimmed of fat and cut into thin strips
¼ large red onion, coarsely chopped
½ cup salsa, store-bought or homemade (recipe follows)
¼ cup chopped fresh cilantro
⅓ cup fresh lime juice (2–3 limes)
¼–½ teaspoon crushed red pepper flakes
1 teaspoon vegetable oil
1–2 red onions, thinly sliced
1–2 red or yellow bell peppers, thinly sliced
8–12 flour tortillas

TOPPINGS

Chopped fresh cilantro
Sour cream or yogurt
Avocado or guacamole (recipe follows)

1. Place the chicken or meat strips in a medium-sized shallow glass or ceramic bowl and add onion, salsa, cilantro, lime juice, and red pepper flakes. Cover and let stand at room temperature for no more than 1 hour, or refrigerate for 4 hours.

2. Preheat oven to 250° F.

3. Heat a large nonstick or cast-iron skillet over a medium flame and add oil. When the oil is hot, add the onions and peppers. Cook for 10–15 minutes, or until the vegetables begin to soften and brown. Remove to an ovenproof dish and set in the oven to keep warm.

4. Wrap the tortillas in aluminum foil and place in the oven to warm.

5. Reheat the skillet over a high flame and add the chicken or meat strips. Cook about 2–3 minutes, or until browned, turning once. (If using poultry, be sure strips are cooked through—the flesh should just turn white but still be juicy.)

6. Serve buffet-style, with toppings in separate bowls, allowing each person to assemble his own fajitas.

SALSA

MAKES 4 CUPS

2½–3 pounds fresh ripe tomatoes, seeded, if desired, and diced
1 red onion, coarsely chopped
2–4 cloves garlic, chopped
2 green or yellow bell peppers, coarsely chopped
⅓–½ cup finely chopped fresh cilantro
½–1 teaspoon cayenne pepper
½ teaspoon salt
2 tablespoons fresh lime juice

OPTIONAL INGREDIENT

1 jalapeño pepper or chipotle chile, seeded and finely chopped

Combine all the ingredients, cover, and refrigerate for 3–4 hours.

GUACAMOLE

MAKES 4 CUPS

4 very ripe avocados, chopped
1 small tomato, coarsely chopped
2 scallions, root and 1 inch of green part trimmed and discarded, remainder chopped
½ cup chopped fresh cilantro
1 pinch of cayenne pepper
¼–⅓ teaspoon salt
⅛ teaspoon crushed red pepper flakes
1½ tablespoons fresh lime juice
½ jalapeño pepper, finely minced

Combine all the ingredients in a bowl. Do not overmix; it should be somewhat chunky. To store the guacamole, cover and refrigerate, keeping a few avocado pits in the finished dip to prevent discoloration.

O N I O N S

OUR WORD "ONION" COMES FROM THE LATIN *UNIO*, A TERM THAT ORIGINALLY REFERRED TO A SINGLE, EXTRAORDINARILY LARGE PEARL, BUT WHICH FARMERS APPROPRIATED TO IDENTIFY the pick of their onion crops. Today we sauté our edible pearls while sweeping their fine, papery skins from our pantry floors. We dream of leeks in the winter and scallions in the spring, knowing our salads will swing and our soups will smell like heaven. Is the onion, in fact, the proverbial pearl of wisdom?

CHIVES. Chives grow in bunches of long, slender green leaves that grow back like grass when snipped. An herb (like the onion), chives are used to season vegetables and delicately flavor egg and seafood dishes. Chives do not do well with heat, so only use them raw, sprinkled on foods. Fresh, frozen, or dried chives can be used interchangeably in most recipes. If necessary, you can substitute the dark green stem of a scallion for chives. Chives are best when dark green and free of brown or yellowed spots.

LEEKS. Leeks look like large, fat scallions and are both sweeter and milder than onions. In France, leeks are known as the poor man's asparagus, although they are actually quite expensive.

PEARL ONIONS. Cooking onions that are often used whole, either roasted, grilled, or stewed; they have a mildly sweet flavor.

RAMPS. Ramps are wild leeks that are available only in the spring and are celebrated at a festival in West Virginia called the Ramp Romp. They are stronger and earthier in taste than leeks, but can be substituted for cultivated leeks in smaller quantities. They should be cleaned the same way as leeks.

RED ONIONS. Red onions are mild and sweet, which makes them particularly good eaten raw on salads and burgers and as garnishes for chili and cold soups. They are also good grilled but are generally not recommended for sautéing.

SCALLIONS. Scallions are milder than yellow onions and are best when cooked slightly or left raw. The entire scallion is edible, although the root end and the last inch of the green stem should be discarded. The white bulb is the strongest-tasting. Scallions are ripe when the green stems are bright and the white bulbs firm.

SHALLOTS. Shallots are the mildest-tasting member in the onion family and are reminiscent of both garlic and onions, although milder than either.

SPANISH ONIONS. In this book, when an onion is called for, we mean a Spanish onion. They are strong but somewhat sweeter and larger than the better-known yellow onion. They are great all-purpose onions and are particularly good for sautéing.

SWEET ONIONS. Vidalia onions and Walla Walla onions are the sweetest onions of all. They can be baked, fried, or sautéed, are extremely perishable, and should be eaten the day they are purchased.

VIDALIAS. Large and exceptionally sweet onions native to Vidalia, Georgia.

WHITE ONIONS. Cooking onions with a mild, flat taste, white onions are often included in cream sauces.

YELLOW ONIONS. Yellow onions are the strongest, most popular and widely used onion and are best when cooked.

SCALLION

YELLOW

WHITE

PEARL

RED

RAMP

SHALLOT

VIDALIA

SPANISH

LEEK

ROOT (DISCARDED)

BULB (EDIBLE)

GREENS (USUALLY DISCARDED)

HUNTER'S CHICKEN

Hunter's Chicken is a classic Italian dish made several different ways, depending upon the region and the cook's whim. It's always simmered with onions, garlic, tomatoes, and herbs; the rest is your creative license. We like it best with everything.

SERVES 4

1   4–4½-pound fryer chicken, cut into 8 pieces
1   small Spanish or yellow onion, sliced
3   cloves garlic, chopped, pressed, or thinly sliced
1   28-ounce can whole tomatoes, chopped, with juice
1   tablespoon chopped fresh thyme or 1–2 teaspoons dried
1   tablespoon chopped fresh rosemary or 1–2 teaspoons dried
    Salt and pepper

OPTIONAL INGREDIENTS

2   carrots, chopped
2   stalks celery, chopped
1   red or orange bell pepper, chopped
½–1   ounce dried porcini mushrooms, chopped

1. Heat a large nonstick or cast-iron skillet over medium-high heat. Add the chicken pieces and cook for about 3–5 minutes per side, or until the skin has browned. Remove the chicken pieces and set aside. Discard all but 1 tablespoon of fat from the pan.

2. Add the onion and garlic, carrots, celery, and pepper, if you are using them, and cook over medium-low heat for 10–15 minutes, or until the vegetables are golden. Add the tomatoes and the optional mushrooms and cook for 5 minutes. If you are using dried herbs, put them in now.

3. Add the chicken and cook over low heat for about 20 minutes.

4. If you are using fresh herbs, put them in now. Add salt and pepper to taste, and serve.

CURRIED CHICKEN WITH RAISINS AND CASHEWS

The combination of worldly-wise curry and ginger with sweet, innocent raisins has always been a winner; the addition of mellow buttermilk and rich cashews lends surprising depth.

SERVES 4

4   whole chicken breasts, boneless and skinless, halved and trimmed of fat and membrane
2   teaspoons olive oil
2   garlic cloves, chopped or pressed

MARINADE

3   cups buttermilk
2–3   tablespoons curry powder
1½   tablespoons ground ginger
2   teaspoons ground cinnamon
¼   teaspoon cayenne pepper
1   teaspoon salt

TOPPINGS

½   cup chopped fresh cilantro
¾   cup chopped cashews
½   cup raisins
¼   cup shredded coconut
½   bunch scallions, cut diagonally into 1-inch pieces
½–1   cup chutney

1. ⏰ Combine the buttermilk, curry, ginger, cinnamon, cayenne, and salt in a small shallow bowl and add the chicken pieces. Cover and refrigerate for 4 hours.

2. Take the chicken out of the buttermilk marinade. Refrigerate the remaining marinade.

3. Heat a large skillet over a high flame and add the oil. When the oil is hot, add the chicken breasts, a few at a time, and brown them on both sides. Reduce heat to medium, add the garlic cloves and cook 2 minutes, or until golden. Add the reserved marinade to make a curry sauce. Cook the chicken about 7–10 minutes on each side, depending on the thickness of the breasts.

4. Serve the curry sauce over the chicken and offer any or all of the following toppings in little bowls: cilantro, cashews, raisins, coconut, scallions, and chutney.

DRIED SHIITAKE MUSHROOMS

SALTIMBOCCA

IS A CLASSIC ROMAN DISH, ALTHOUGH ITS EASE OF PREPARATION

MAKES IT THOROUGHLY MODERN. IT'S USUALLY MADE WITH VEAL,

BUT WE'VE DEVELOPED A VERSION THAT USES CHICKEN AND FULLY DESERVES

the name Saltimbocca—"to jump into the mouth." Serve with roasted squash and a green salad.

CHICKEN SALTIMBOCCA

SERVES 4

3	whole chicken breasts, boneless and skinless, halved and trimmed of fat and membrane (about 1½ pounds)
2	tablespoons olive oil
6	cloves garlic, thinly sliced
16–20	fresh sage leaves (do not substitute dried)
¼–⅓	cup shaved Parmesan cheese
1	tablespoon unbleached all-purpose flour
½	teaspoon kosher salt
1½	cups white wine

OPTIONAL INGREDIENT

3	slices prosciutto

1. Flatten each breast by pounding it between 2 pieces of waxed paper with a mallet, rolling pin, or bottle. Pound it as thinly as possible, being careful not to tear the chicken. Set it aside.

2. Heat a large nonstick or cast-iron skillet over medium heat and add 1 tablespoon of the oil. When the oil is hot, add the garlic and sage and cook until both are toasted, about 2 minutes. Remove them with a slotted spoon and place on a paper towel. Do not wash the pan.

3. On each chicken breast, place half a slice of prosciutto, if desired, 1 tablespoon of Parmesan cheese, and equal amounts of half the reserved garlic and sage. Fold each chicken breast and seal the edges by pinching with your fingers. Reheat the skillet.

4. If necessary, add the remaining tablespoon of oil. Dust each chicken breast with flour. Sprinkle salt in pan and add the chicken. Cook, over medium heat, about 4 minutes on the first side and 3 on the second.

5. Remove the chicken and set aside. Raise the heat in the pan to high and add the wine; bring it to a boil, and pour it over the chicken. Top each breast with reserved garlic and sage.

OTHER CHOICES: Substitute 12 small veal medallions (about 1½ pounds) for the chicken breasts.

CHICKEN SALTIMBOCCA

CHRIS SCHLESINGER

"It didn't matter what was going on," says Chris Schlesinger. "Dad was going to the beach on weekends. And it was the men's job to go out to the wilds of the back porch and do this incredibly dangerous and skillful thing of cooking hamburgers and hot dogs." Who knew that Schlesinger would go on to become a master? Maybe his dad did. "I took over the grilling as the baton was passed down from father to son," he says, and remembers being attracted not only to the process of grilling but to the ambiance of flame-cooked meals: "They had a different tone. More relaxed, more jovial, not so formal." Schlesinger's 1990 book, *The Thrill of the Grill,* written with John Willoughby, introduced backyard cowboys to the nuances of coal and spice rubs. Two books later he's managed to create a culinary culture that weds spicy sauces to open-fire meats, fish, and vegetables. But even though Schlesinger's cookouts have reached far beyond the back porch, he hasn't lost touch with the primal act of grilling, "a throwback to prehistoric times."

GRILLED WEST INDIES SPICE-RUBBED CHICKEN BREAST WITH GRILLED BANANA

The culinary arts of the West Indies reveal a special genius for combining sweet, fresh fruits with age-old, mysterious spices. Chris Schlesinger adds his grilling finesse to achieve a perfect balance with this exotic offering.

SERVES 4

4   boneless chicken breasts, skin on
3   tablespoons curry powder
3   tablespoons ground cumin
2   tablespoons allspice
3   tablespoons paprika
2   tablespoons powdered ginger
1   tablespoon cayenne pepper
2   tablespoons salt
2   tablespoons freshly cracked black pepper
4   firm bananas, skin on and halved lengthwise
2   tablespoons vegetable oil
1   tablespoon soft butter
2   tablespoons molasses
    Lime halves for garnish

1. Mix all the spices together well and rub this mixture over both sides of each chicken breast. Cover and refrigerate for 2 hours.

2. Over a medium fire, grill the chicken breasts skin-side down for 7–8 minutes, until well browned and heavily crusted. Turn them and grill an additional 10 minutes. Check for doneness by nicking the largest breast at the fattest point: The meat should be fully opaque with no traces of red. Remove the chicken from the grill.

3. Rub the banana halves with vegetable oil and place them on the grill, flat-side down. Grill them for about 2 minutes, or until the flat sides are slightly golden in color. Flip them and grill for an additional 2 minutes.

4. Remove the banana halves from the grill. Mix the butter and molasses together and paint this over the bananas. Serve the chicken breasts and banana halves together, sprinkled with a little lime juice.

CHRIS SCHLESINGER

ON EQUIPMENT. "Use long-handled, spring-loaded, heavy-duty tongs."

ON FIRE. "The best way to start a fire is with a metal flue. It is a cylinder made of sheet metal with a grid about 2 inches from the bottom and open at both ends."

ON SALT. "This coarse-grained sea salt containing natural iodine is the only type I use. It dissolves more quickly and has a better flavor than the free-flowing variety. Besides, it just feels better when you are sprinkling it on with your fingers."

ON BALSAMIC VINEGAR. "My personal favorite, a sprinkle of balsamic vinegar, will bring a simple piece of grilled meat or poultry to life, drawing out its innate flavor."

"Part of the fun of grilling is...not just [the danger of] having a bad meal but of ruining a meal beyond recognition. I think that's a great appeal for guys."

[OTHER FACTS—*page 279*]

B A R - B - Q

CLUBBING YOUR DINNER IS ONLY THE FIRST PART OF THE BATTLE. COOKING RAW MEAT OVER AN OPEN FLAME IS THE SECOND. SAUCING IT IS THE THIRD. THE HOTTEST MIXED with the sweetest mixed with the spiciest—that's the sauce that kept cowpokes from slittin' ol' cook's throat in the dead of night. Even the most common foods get wild with a good sauce and a hot, hot flame.

BAR-B-Q CLEAR

The Carolinas as well as the Caribbean islands favor clear sauces that look innocent but can tickle or destroy your palate.

MAKES ABOUT 2 CUPS

- 1½ cups cider vinegar
- ½ cup olive or canola oil
- 1 tablespoon fresh lemon or lime juice
- 2–3 cloves garlic, minced
- ¼ teaspoon crushed red pepper flakes or ½ tablespoon Inner Beauty Real Hot Sauce (see page 274)
- 2–4 tablespoons chopped fresh cilantro
  Salt and pepper

Combine all the ingredients in a bowl and stand back.

NOTE: This doubles as a salad dressing.

BAR-B-Q RED

This is the sloppy big red from the smoky roadside pit house we shared with family and friends when we were kids— you still don't have to apologize for wanting to lick your fingers.

MAKES ABOUT 2-3 CUPS

- 1 tablespoon olive or canola oil
- 1 medium Spanish onion, coarsely chopped
- 2 cloves garlic, minced
- ½ cup cider vinegar
- 1½ cups ketchup
- 1 tablespoon Dijon mustard
- 2 tablespoons light brown sugar
- ¼ cup fresh lemon juice
- 2 teaspoons chili powder

1. Heat a medium-sized saucepan over medium heat and add the oil. When the oil is hot, add the onion and garlic and stir occasionally until they are soft, about 5 minutes.

2. Add the remaining ingredients and simmer 5–10 minutes.

TIP: Barbecue sauces should be made far enough in advance to divide into three batches: one for marinating, one for basting, and one for the table.

"Burn me a good thick one, Pete. Meat and potatoes."

JOHN WAYNE, *The Man Who Shot Liberty Valance*

BAR-B-Q RED

M E A T

Thou mayest eat flesh,

DEUTERONOMY XII:20

whatsoever thy soul lusteth after

GRILLED OR BROILED STEAK

What put the "grill" in "bar & grill"?
Steaks and chops, of course. Whether
served all sauced and spiced or touched by
nothing but a flame, a good-quality steak or
chop is likely to elicit a primal scream or
two. This basic recipe adds only salt, pepper,
and oregano to your favorite cut
and is easily supplemented.

SERVES 4

4 filet mignons, pork chops,
   veal chops, lamb chops, or
   1 sirloin, T-bone, porterhouse,
   or rib steak (all about
   1½–2 inches thick and
   totaling about 2 pounds)

   Kosher salt and freshly
   ground black pepper

   OPTIONAL INGREDIENT

   Dried oregano or herb of
   choice

1. Preheat broiler, prepare grill (see page 261), or gather round the campfire.

2. Sprinkle the meat with salt and pepper to taste.

3. Place the meat about 3–4 inches from the heat source and cook for about 3–4 minutes on each side.

TIP: Use tongs, not a fork, when turning meat to prevent punctures that would allow juices to flow out.

VANISHING BEEF

ONCE IN A WHILE, STEAK CALLS. IT'S NOT A CONSTANT

CRAVING—WE'VE WEANED OURSELVES OF THE RED-MEAT HABIT.

KNOWING THAT WE WON'T WEAKEN AND WASTE AWAY FOR WANT OF BURGERS

and roasts, we've retired beef from our diet and replaced it with chicken, fish, vegetables, salads, and pasta. Still,

every now and then, we are inexplicably overwhelmed by an urgent desire for a great hunk of steak, broiled over

the hottest flame, served sizzling and sauced on a kingly platter. When steak-lust consumes us, we consider

Mark Twain's prescription for a happy, stress-free life: "Eat what you like and let the food fight it out inside."

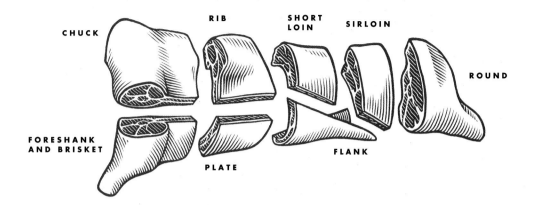

BRISKET. Usually sold as corned beef, but excellent for stew or pot roast.

CHUCK. Of all the cuts from the beef carcass, the one that offers the greatest money-saving potential is the chuck. The chuck is the entire front shoulder section of the beef, including the neck. Some familiar names and uses for chuck are pot roast, market steak, patio steak, blade-cut chuck roast, rib-eye steak, and ground chuck.

FLANK. One of the tastiest and most versatile cuts in the butcher's case. As the classic London broil, the flank steak is delicious marinated, broiled, or grilled, and (important!) sliced diagonally across the grain in thin slices. A stuffed, rolled flank steak also makes an attractive presentation.

FORESHANK. The front leg of the beef. Usually deboned and used for ground beef. It is likely to be about as tender as the sole of an old boot.

PLATE. The plate comes off the beef just below the rib and is usually boned out and sold as stew or ground beef. Occasionally it is sold boneless and rolled for a Yankee pot roast. Needs moist heat and long, slow cooking.

ROUND. Not a naturally tender cut, but versatile and usually a very good buy. The rump is the most tender section and can be cooked with dry heat, but the other cuts (farther away from the loin) are best treated with moist heat. Round is merchandised as round steak, top round (often sold as London broil and good for marinating/grilling treatment), bottom round (rump roast, Swiss steak), eye of the round, and ground round. Other cuts of meat from the round include the knuckle, the round tip, and the crescent. These cuts are best for kebabs, stroganoff, and London broil.

RIB. The rib is the carcass just in front of the short loin, between the small end of the short loin and the blade end of the chuck. The rib qualifies as naturally tender, comparable to the loin cuts, which can be cooked with dry heat. The rib is merchandised for standing rib roast (the king of beef roasts in this country), rib steak, and rib eye.

SHORT LOIN. The most naturally tender portion of the animal. The short loin is the sources of the best steaks. The porterhouse, the T-bone, the New York, filet mignon, tournedos, club steaks, Kansas City Strips, chateaubriand, to name a few, all come from the short loin.

SIRLOIN. Almost as tender as short loin is sirloin, though the steaks will be a little tougher. Cuts from the sirloin are top sirloin, tenderloin, bottom sirloin, cube steak, and culotte steak.

> "I won't eat anything that has intelligent life, but I'd gladly
> eat a network executive or a politician."
>
> **M A R T Y   F E L D M A N**

[🥩 MEAT *first aid—page 259*]

MARINADES

While a marinade can tantalize and tenderize tough cuts of meat, marinades aren't just for steak anymore. Gather the spices and flavors of the world and let them work their multicultural magic on poultry, vegetables, even fruit. The following marinades are in amounts suitable for a 2-pound steak. Double or triple the recipe if needed.

SOY, SHERRY, AND DIJON MUSTARD MARINADE

2 tablespoons soy sauce
2 tablespoons sherry
2 tablespoons Dijon mustard
3 tablespoons light brown sugar
2 teaspoons curry powder

LIME, SOY, AND GARLIC MARINADE

4 tablespoons fresh lime juice (about 1–2 limes)
3 tablespoons soy sauce
3–4 cloves garlic, finely chopped or pressed
1 tablespoon fresh gingerroot, finely chopped
6 tablespoons orange juice
1/2 teaspoon crushed red pepper flakes
Zest of 1 lime, finely chopped

MARINADE TIPS

TIME. Meats should be marinated for at least 1 hour at room temperature or overnight, refrigerated—or even longer if a stronger flavor is desired. If you plan to marinate a dish for more than an hour, wrap it well and refrigerate.

CONTENTS. Typically a wet marinade contains oil, seasoning, and an acid such as lemon juice, wine vinegar, or some kind of fermented liquid. Try wine, sake, dry sherry, bourbon, or flavored brandy.

TENDERIZE. The acid breaks down muscle fibers for a more tender final product, while the oil adds moisture.

PLANNING AHEAD. When you purchase a steak for marinating, buy two and freeze one, with the marinade, in a plastic freezer bag. When you are ready to cook it, simply place the bag in the refrigerator to defrost. It will have marinated as it froze and will marinate still more as it defrosts.

BOURBON, BALSAMIC VINEGAR, AND FRESH GINGER MARINADE

3 tablespoons bourbon
2 tablespoons light brown sugar
3 tablespoons balsamic vinegar
2 tablespoons fresh gingerroot, finely chopped
1/2 teaspoon black pepper

MARINATED STEAK

SERVES 4–6

Marinade of choice (see this page)

1 1/2–2 pounds flank steak or London broil

1. Mix marinade ingredients together.

2. Score the steak (see below). Combine the steak and the marinade in a large, shallow glass bowl and let sit at room temperature 1–2 hours, or cover and refrigerate for 4 hours or overnight.

3. Preheat the broiler or prepare a grill.

4. Remove the steak from marinade. Reserve the remaining marinade.

5. Broil or grill the steak for about 5 minutes per side, basting with reserved marinade.

6. Before serving, thinly slice the steak, cutting diagonally against the grain.

A SCORE FOR MEAT **1.** Top cuts of steaks (e.g., T-bones) usually have a line of gristle between the fat and the meat that can shrink and deform the steak during broiling. Using a very sharp knife, make cuts through the toughest areas of the gristle before cooking. **2.** If you'd like your marinade to infuse the meat more deeply, first make diagonal cuts on each side of the steak or chop. **3.** With extra tender cuts (e.g., veal fillets), gently score the meat with the back of a heavy knife. **4.** When preparing a sauced steak (e.g., *steak moutarde*), broil or grill one side, then make diagonal slashes on the uncooked side. Spread sauce deep in the crevices, then return the steak to the flame.

LIME, SOY, AND GARLIC

BOURBON, BALSAMIC VINEGAR,
AND FRESH GINGER

SOY, SHERRY, AND DIJON
MUSTARD

SIMPLE BURGER

Have you forgotten how delicious burgers really can be? They come to mind whenever we see an outdoor grill, but they're equally tasty as winter fare and always open to interpretation.

SERVES 1

6   ounces ground beef, formed
    into a patty
    Kosher salt and pepper

BROILING. Preheat the broiler. Sprinkle the beef patty with salt and pepper. Place the patty on a broiler pan about 2½–3 inches from the broiler. Broil for about 3–5 minutes per side, or longer for well done.

GRILLING. Prepare a grill. Sprinkle the beef patty with salt and pepper. Place the burger on the grill and cook for about 3–5 minutes on each side, or longer for well done.

OTHER CHOICES: If you would like to substitute ground chicken, turkey, or veal for ground beef in any of the burger recipes, cook them according to the same directions, but for a shorter time. All three have a lower fat content than beef, and shorter cooking times will keep the juices in.

WARNING: To guard against salmonella, be sure the poultry is thoroughly cooked.

MOROCCAN BURGERS

SERVES 4

1½–2   pounds lean ground beef
    4   tablespoons pine nuts, raw or
        toasted (see page 181)
    ½   teaspoon ground cinnamon
    8   dried apricots, chopped
    ½   teaspoon garlic powder
    ½   teaspoon ground cumin
        Zest of ½ lemon, finely grated
        or julienned
    ½–1 teaspoon cayenne pepper

1. Prepare a grill or broiler.

2. Combine all the ingredients by hand and divide into 4 patties of equal size.

3. Cook the patties for about 7–10 minutes on each side or until desired doneness is reached.

CARAMELIZED ONIONS

What happens to onions when they're sautéed and made transparent? Call it magic. A burger could hardly hope for a better companion.

SERVES 4

2   tablespoons olive oil
2   large red or Spanish onions, peeled
    and sliced into thin rounds
½   teaspoon regular or kosher salt, or
    more, to taste
2   teaspoons light brown sugar, honey,
    or ⅛ cup bourbon
4   tablespoons chicken stock
    (see page 19)

1. Heat a large nonstick skillet over medium heat and add the oil. When the oil is hot, add the onions and salt and cook, stirring occasionally, until soft, about 15 minutes.

2. Reduce heat to low and incrementally stir in the sugar and stock. Cook until liquid is completely absorbed, about 5–10 minutes.

BURGERS

PREPARATION. If possible, remove the meat from refrigerator 1 hour before cooking.

MOISTNESS. For additional moisture, mix in, with your hands, 1 tablespoon of nonfat ricotta cheese, applesauce, or barbecue sauce per burger.

HOW TO MAKE A HAMBURGER PATTY

Using your fingers, gently toss ground beef with seasonings. Try herbs, capers, minced onions, dill, black pepper—whatever the bun or your budget desires. Divide meat into balls. Flatten, but don't squash. A rare burger can be as thick as 2 inches; even for burgers that are to be well cooked, the thickness should be no less than 1 inch, so the outside doesn't dry out before the middle is done.

TOPPINGS

1. Ketchup 2. Mustard 3. Chili
4. Pesto 5. Mayonnaise 6. Relish
7. Raw red onions 8. Guacamole
9. Salsa 10. Caramelized onions
11. Roasted peppers 12. Roasted
garlic 13. Barbecue sauce
14. Cheese: Cheddar, goat,
Swiss, smoked Gouda
15. Sautéed mushrooms

BURGER WITH CARAMELIZED ONIONS

MEAT LOAF SANDWICH

SPICY BLUE CHEESEBURGERS

A burger for grown-ups. This one matches the intensity of creamy blue cheese with the snap, crackle, and pop of a spicy Cajun crust.

SERVES 4–6

2 teaspoons dried oregano
1 teaspoon cayenne pepper
1 teaspoon black pepper
2 teaspoons garlic powder
2 teaspoons dried thyme
1 teaspoon paprika
1 teaspoon salt
1½–2 pounds lean ground beef
½ pound blue cheese, crumbled or cut into 6 equal pieces

1. Preheat the broiler.

2. In a medium-sized bowl mix the herbs and spices.

3. Divide the meat into 4 balls of equal size and shape into patties.

4. To stuff the burgers, divide each patty in half and flatten. Place 1 piece of blue cheese on each half and top with the other half. Seal the edges by pinching and re-form into patties.

5. Evenly coat each patty with the herb mixture.

6. Place burgers on a broiler pan about 2½–3 inches from the heat and broil for about 3–5 minutes per side, or longer for well done.

OTHER CHOICES: For the blue cheese, substitute smoked Cheddar, Montrachet, or another goat cheese. You can also use ground veal, pork, turkey, or chicken.

MEAT LOAF

Meat loaf has come into its own. We're glad for that, because this one can be prepared in minutes and then left in the oven for an hour or so. Feel free to add corn, peas, or chopped fresh tomatoes. Just be sure to reserve a quarter-loaf for tomorrow's sandwiches.

SERVES 6–8

1 teaspoon olive oil
1 small Spanish onion, chopped
1 red, yellow, or green bell pepper, diced
2–3 cloves garlic, finely chopped or pressed
1 teaspoon dried oregano
2 slices of white bread
1½ cups milk, water, or beef stock
2 large eggs, lightly beaten
2 pounds lean ground beef
3 tablespoons Dijon mustard
1 teaspoon black pepper
¼–½ teaspoon salt
¾ cup ketchup or barbecue sauce
½ cup chopped fresh parsley or cilantro

1. Preheat oven to 350° F. Lightly grease an 8 x 4-inch loaf pan.

2. Heat a medium-sized skillet over medium heat and add the oil. When the oil is hot, add the onion and bell pepper and cook about 3–5 minutes, or until golden. Reduce heat to low, add the garlic and oregano, and cook 3 minutes. Place in a large mixing bowl and set aside to cool.

3. In the meantime, soak the bread in the liquid until moist. Squeeze excess liquid out of the bread. Add the bread to the cooled onion mixture.

4. Add the eggs and remaining ingredients to the ground beef and mix, by hand, until everything is thoroughly incorporated. Place the mixture in a loaf pan.

5. Bake for about 1 hour and 15 minutes.

OTHER CHOICES: For the beef, you can substitute ground turkey or chicken, but add an extra egg to the mixture for moistness.

SHISH KEBAB

SHISH KEBAB

SERVES 4

1½ pounds beef cubes, from sirloin tips, London broil, or sirloin end steaks
¾ cup white wine
6–8 cloves garlic, chopped or pressed
1 small red onion, chopped
2 teaspoons dried oregano
12–16 cherry tomatoes
12–16 button mushrooms, wiped clean
1 large red bell pepper, cubed into 12–16 pieces
1 zucchini, cubed into 12–16 pieces
12–16 pearl onions, blanched and peeled

1. Place the meat, wine, garlic, onion, and oregano in a shallow glass or ceramic bowl. Cover and refrigerate overnight or let sit at room temperature for no more than 2 hours.

2. Preheat the broiler. Set aside 12 skewers.

3. Remove the meat from the marinade and discard marinade.

4. Cooking time of meat and vegetables will vary, so it's best not to combine them on the same skewer. Fill some skewers with meat pieces and fill other skewers with individual vegetables.

5. Place skewers under a broiler and cook for about 5 minutes; turn them over about halfway through.

6. When finished cooking, remove vegetables and meat from skewers and place in a serving bowl. Serve with a dipping sauce.

OTHER CHOICES: Substitute lamb, chicken, or pork for the beef. Substitute 3 small red onions, quartered, for the pearl onions.

YOGURT AND MINT DIPPING SAUCE

Here's a sauce that's cool, creamy, and refreshing—the perfect complement to warm nights and hot kebabs.

SERVES 4

2 cloves garlic, finely chopped or pressed
1 tablespoon red wine vinegar
1 cup plain yogurt
½ teaspoon salt
½ teaspoon black pepper
Chopped fresh mint

Combine all the ingredients in a small serving bowl. Garnish with more mint, if desired. Serve with hot or cold kebabs.

DIPPING SAUCE

Dipping sauce is a nice extra addition to the supper table, as it allows guests to custom-dress grilled meats, veggies, and bread. While some dipping sauces are made from the same stuff (though never the same batch) as marinades, others are a flavorsome foil.

SKEWERS

It doesn't matter, in terms of taste, efficiency, or appearance, whether you use metal or wooden skewers. Metal is good if you skewer often—but avoid skewers that are round, as the meat will turn and twist. Wooden skewers are good because they're disposable and inexpensive.

TIP. Before using wooden skewers, soak them in water for 10 minutes so they don't burn when grilling or broiling.

CONSUMPTION

Since 1976 beef consumption has decreased by 28 percent.

"Beef is pleasure food, and we deserve pleasure."

JIM HARRISON, *"Piggies Come to Market"*

FAIRY UMBRELLAS

MAY BE WHAT YOUR GRANDMOTHER CALLED THEM. THEY SPROUT IN THE NIGHT, PALE AND SMOOTH, LIKE SMALL BEINGS ENCASED IN A THIN SKIN. THEY ARE THE FRIENDS OF WITCHES, the source of potions and spells. They cook like vegetables, but don't be fooled. Unencumbered by roots, seeds, flowers, or photosynthesis, mushrooms have their own nocturnal category: fungus. Tens of thousands of varieties sprout on the earth. There are poisonous toadstools and dotted monstrosities that cling to tree bark. Then there are the benign varieties, gathered in baskets to enrich our meals with the deep flavors of earth and evening.

CHANTERELLES. Shaped like trumpets, chanterelles are used predominantly in French cooking and range in flavor from mild and meaty to sweet and spicy.

CREMINI. These brown cultivated mushrooms are, like button mushrooms, mild and readily available.

ENOKI (also called Enokitake, or Enoki-Daki). Long-legged, bright yellowish-white, and slightly crunchy, they are mild and sweet and are best eaten raw or added to cooked dishes at the very end, like fresh herbs.

MOREL. These mushrooms are small and dark with conical tops. They are intense, earthy, and especially good in sauces.

OYSTER. Often a purplish-beige color with a fluted shape, they are creamy, delicate, and should be cooked as briefly and as simply as possible.

PORCINI (also called Cèpes, or Boletes). Porcini mushrooms have brown tops and pale stems and are creamy-textured. When fresh, they are best cooked very simply: In Italian dishes, they are often grilled, broiled, or sautéed with a small amount of olive oil and garlic, while in French cuisine, they're often braised with shallots and olive oil.

PORTOBELLO. These very large and flat-topped mushrooms are usually beige-colored and flecked with black dirt. Used extensively in Italian cooking, they are meaty and taste great grilled with a balsamic vinaigrette.

SHIITAKE. These brown, umbrella-shaped mushrooms are the most popular of all the wild mushrooms. Rich and fleshy, they are best simply prepared or in combination with other wild mushrooms.

WHITE BUTTON. These mild, small white mushrooms are the most widely available mushrooms in stores.

DRIED. Since the flavor of dried mushrooms is highly concentrated, they should be used more like an herb than a vegetable. To reconstitute them, rinse in cold water—several times if necessary—then place them in a bowl and cover with hot water. Let them sit for 20–30 minutes and strain. Save the soaking liquid for soups.

PORTOBELLO

WHITE BUTTON

ENOKI

SHIITAKE

PORCINI

CREMINI

VEAL SCALOPPINE

Veal's subtle flavor and neutral texture make it the perfect meat for the creative cook—it absorbs any sauce and takes to the most subtle herb.

SERVES 4–6

- ½ cup unbleached all-purpose flour
- 2 large eggs, lightly beaten
- 1¼ cups plain bread crumbs
- 1½ teaspoons dried basil or rosemary
- 1½ teaspoons salt
- 1 teaspoon black pepper
- 12 veal scaloppine, or 12 veal medallions (about 1½ pounds) pounded ¼ inch thick
- 2 tablespoons olive oil
- 2 lemons, cut into 8 wedges

1. Place the flour on a plate, the eggs in a shallow bowl, and the bread crumbs, herbs, salt and pepper on another plate. Pat dry each scaloppine with a paper towel. Dredge each in the flour, then the egg, then the bread crumb mixture. Let sit for about 20 minutes so the crumbs adhere.

2. Heat a large nonstick skillet over medium heat and add 1 tablespoon of the oil. When the oil is hot, add the veal. Cook until the veal is golden, or about 2–3 minutes per side. If necessary, clean the skillet with paper towel and add the remaining oil. Serve with lemon wedges.

BREAD CRUMBS

Lightly toast, cool, and quarter bread slices. Place no more than 3 at a time in a food processor fitted with a steel blade, and pulse until the crumbs are the desired consistency. If you want seasoned bread crumbs, add a small amount of dried herbs, such as oregano, basil, rosemary, sage, or tarragon.

VEAL REVEALED

Veal comes from young calves and has, ounce for ounce, about one third less fat than beef does. It should be light pink and finely grained, with little marbling, and should be cooked more like poultry than beef. Milk-fed veal is considered premium. Veal raised on grain or grass has a stronger flavor and less delicate texture. As a general rule, the darker the meat, the older the calf. Usually the veal comes from calves 1–3 months old; sometimes calves of up to 9 months are used.

VEAL CHOP WITH LEMON AND ROSEMARY

Freshly squeezed lemon, garlic, and fresh rosemary on a veal chop evoke memories of simple country dining in Tuscany.

SERVES 4

- 4 veal chops, about ¾ inch thick, trimmed of fat
- 4 cloves garlic, finely chopped or pressed
  Juice of ½ lemon
- 1 tablespoon chopped fresh rosemary, or 1 teaspoon dried

OPTIONAL INGREDIENTS

- ½ teaspoon kosher salt
- 1 lemon, quartered, for garnish

1. Preheat the broiler.

2. Sprinkle the veal chops with garlic, a squeeze of lemon juice, the dried rosemary (if using fresh rosemary or any fresh herb, do not add it at this time; in order to retain the full flavor of the herb, add it just prior to serving), and salt, if desired. Place the chops on a rack in a roasting pan about 6 inches from the broiler and broil for about 4 minutes per side.

3. Remove the veal from the broiler. Serve with the lemon wedges.

"Veal, what is veal?"

JAMES LEEDS, *Children of a Lesser God*

VEAL CHOP WITH LEMON AND ROSEMARY

M A R I O N   C U

When Marion Cunningham turned fifty, she had neither arrived on the culinary map nor had she left her home state of California. (Never one to stray far, she married a man she met in kindergarten.) But she was an avid cook, a casual cooking teacher, and a great admirer of James Beard; when she learned he was giving a two-week cooking class in his hometown of Seaside, Oregon, she took a risk and jumped on a plane. She describes it as a "magical experience." The feeling must have been mutual because Beard asked her back for years, to be his cooking assistant. Beard later recommended to his editor that Cunningham revise *The Fannie Farmer Cookbook.* Having barely graduated from high school, Cunningham wasn't confident in her ability to do the job. But she once again accepted the challenge. It took five years, but in the process of writing the book, she emerged as a practical, down-to-earth voice of culinary reason. A sample: "We'd all be better off today if we admitted that there is really no such thing as gourmet cooking—there is simply good cooking." Cunningham has been writing cookbooks ever since.

> "Supper is more a state of mind than a meal bound by rules. Above all, it shouldn't be prepared watching the clock and racing through all the cooking.... The kitchen should be a soothing place, especially after a hectic day in the work world."

N N I N G H A M

THEATER STEAK

Marion calls this the theater steak because one can cook and eat it and still make first curtain.

SERVES 4

- ½ cup butter or vegetable oil
- 2 large onions, in thin rings
- ½ pound fresh mushrooms, sliced
- 2 beef fillets, each about ½ pound, cut in half lengthwise
- 1 cup water
- 4 slices good fresh white bread
- 2 bunches fresh watercress, stemmed, washed, and dried
   Salt and freshly ground pepper

1. Melt the butter in a large skillet, and when butter is hot, stir in the onions and mushrooms. Add salt and pepper and sauté over medium-high heat, stirring constantly, until the vegetables are just soft. Remove the vegetables from the skillet and keep warm on a plate.

2. Salt and pepper the steak amply. Turn the heat to high, and fry the steak quickly, turning it over as soon as the steak is well browned. Remove to a plate and keep warm. Over high heat, stir in the water and deglaze the skillet (scraping and stirring the remaining bits from the bottom of the pan) for a minute. Quickly dip one side of each of the slices of bread into the drippings in the skillet and place each on the serving plate.

3. Assemble by placing some of the watercress on each slice of bread. (Reserve a little of the watercress and onion for garnish.) Add the onions and mushrooms, then add any remaining juices from the skillet, and place the steak on top. Press the steak gently down so some of its juices flow into the watercress and bread. Garnish with the watercress and onion and serve.

ON PRESENTATION. "Butter should be in a butter dish with its own knife; milk in a pitcher; bottled sauces and condiments, unless the jar is particularly pretty, should be removed from their commercial containers and placed in small bowls with spoons. If your table looks like a hash-house counter, you encourage people to eat accordingly."

ON ENHANCING FLAVORS. "I use garlic, citrus, and ginger quite often to flavor food. If you chop these ingredients with salt or sugar, the flavors are magically diffused throughout the dish. The salt and sugar crystals act like little missionaries, spreading the flavors."

[OTHER FACTS—*page 279*]

F I S H

In the back room Brett and Bill were sitting on barrels surrounded by the dancers. Everybody had his arms on everybody else's shoulders, and they were all singing. Mike was sitting at a table with several men in their shirt-sleeves, eating from a bowl of tuna fish, chopped onions and vinegar. They were all drinking wine and mopping up the oil and vinegar with pieces of bread. "Hello, Jake. Hello!" Mike called.

ERNEST HEMINGWAY, *The Sun Also Rises*

"Come here. I want you to meet my friends. We're all having hors-d'oeuvres." I was introduced to the people at the table. They supplied their names to Mike and sent for a fork for me. "Stop eating their dinner, Michael," Brett shouted from the wine-barrels. "I don't want to eat up your meal," I said when someone handed me a fork. "Eat," he said. "What do you think it's there for?"

GRILLED OR BROILED FISH STEAKS

If you know this recipe, then you know fish. It works wonderfully with just about anything caught in an ocean or a brook, and tastes best of all if you're cooking your own catch. Two things to keep in mind: 1. the fresher the fish, the better the dish; 2. never overcook fish.

SERVES 4

4	swordfish steaks, 1½ inches thick (2 pounds)
1	tablespoon olive oil
½	teaspoon salt
½	teaspoon black pepper
1–2	lemons, quartered

1. Preheat the broiler or prepare a grill.

2. Rub the swordfish steaks with oil and sprinkle them with salt and pepper.

3. Place the steaks about 3–4 inches from the heat source and cook for about 3–4 minutes per side. Serve immediately with lemon wedges.

OTHER CHOICES: Salmon and tuna steaks work equally well. As an alternative to lemon juice try Pesto or Roasted Bell Pepper Sauce (see page 180).

FISH COOKING TECHNIQUES. Generally, fish should be cooked until it is opaque—when the translucent quality of the flesh disappears. Tastes have changed in the last decade, and now there is a trend to leave some fish rare in the center. However, no matter your preference, overcooked fish is tough and flavorless. **PAN-FRYING.** Heat butter or oil over medium-high heat. Add fish and sauté until lightly browned on one side. Turn when edges become opaque (3–5 minutes). Fish is done when it flakes at the touch of a fork in the thickest section. **ROASTING.** Preheat oven to 400° F., rub a little olive oil into the fish, and bake until the fish is opaque. **BROILING.** Always preheat broiler. Place broiler pan about 4 inches from the heat

IF IT WEREN'T FOR FISH,

NUTRITIONISTS WOULD HAVE LITTLE TO TALK ABOUT.

WHATEVER THE CATCH OF THE DAY, WE CAN BE PRETTY

SURE THAT IT'S FULL OF VITAMINS AND PROTEIN,

and relatively low in calories. It's incredibly delicious and easy

to prepare—dinners can be broiled, poached, or

blackened in a matter of minutes. Fish isn't called brain

food for nothing, you know. Supping often on fish is rumored to make

you slim and witty.

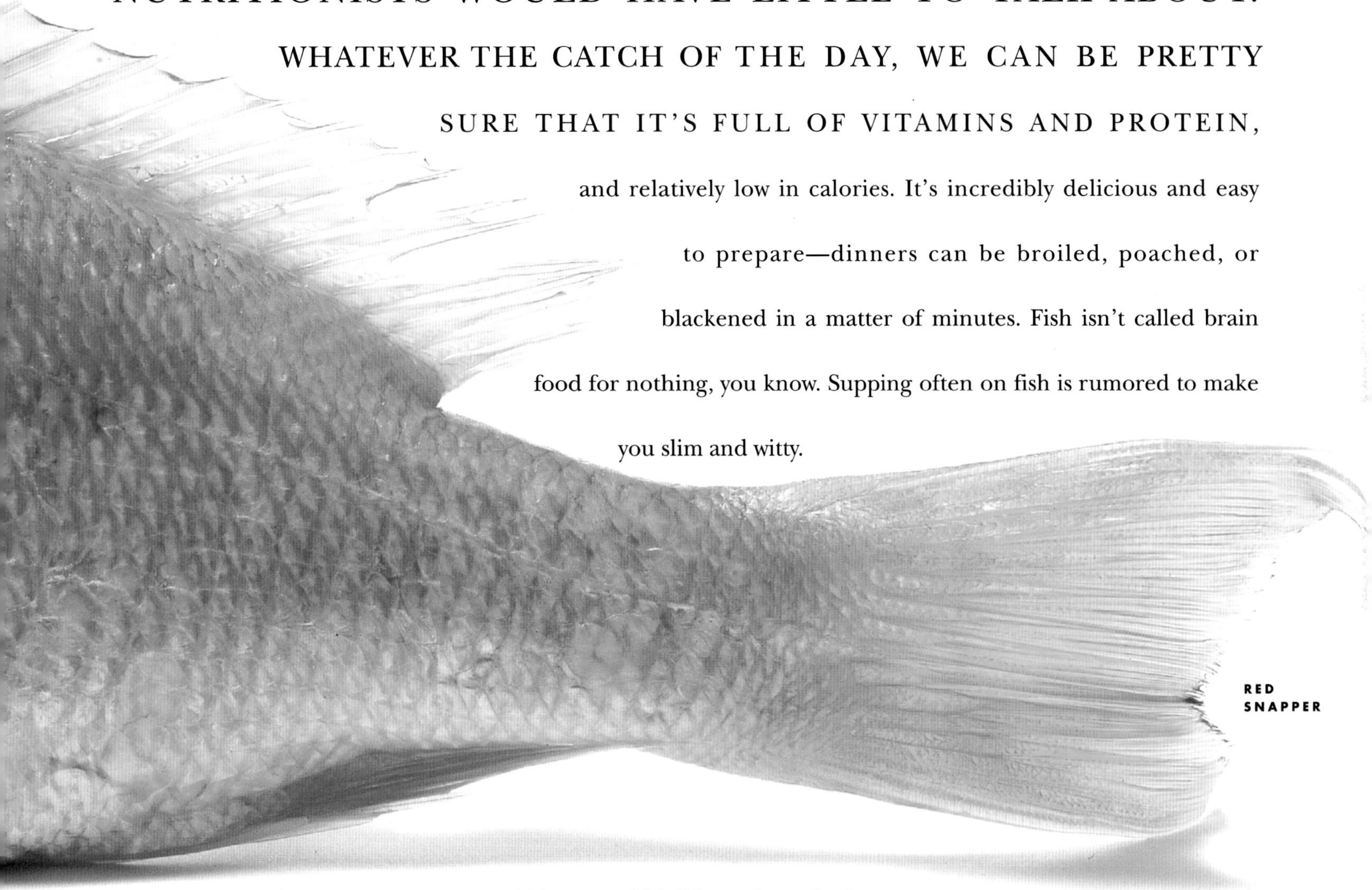

RED SNAPPER

source—a little less if the fish is thin or small, more if thick or large. Fish being broiled may or may not be turned—a general guide to length of cooking time for any and all methods is 10 minutes total per inch of thickness and/or when the thickest part of fish flakes at the touch of a fork. **POACHING.** Poaching requires a gentle simmer in wine or fish stock. Start the fish in warm liquid, and simmer it in enough wine or fish stock to cover it. Cover and cook until opaque. **BLACKENED OR CAJUN FISH.** A firm-fleshed fillet is dipped in melted butter, then in a special herb seasoning mixture and "dry-fried" in an extremely hot cast-iron skillet without any oil. Fish is cooked on each side until it looks charred—about 2 minutes.

[FISH *first aid—page 262*]

SALMON ON A BED OF LEEKS AND CARROTS

COD AND POTATOES

Robert Hughes is a senior writer at Time *and is the author of* The Fatal Shore, Barcelona, *and* The Culture of Complaint. *He came across this recipe, which has nursery-comfort-food appeal, while he was researching* Barcelona.

SERVES 4

4 potatoes (Idaho or russet)
    Small amount of whole milk or skim milk and butter or margarine
    Salt and pepper
1½ pounds fresh codfish, cut into 4 steaks, 2 inches by 4 inches
½ cup olive oil
2–3 cloves garlic, chopped
½ tablespoon paprika
    Chopped fresh parsley, for garnish

1. Peel and cut up the potatoes. Boil them in salted water until they're soft. Drain and then mash. Add milk and butter or margarine to taste. Don't make the potatoes too soft. Season with salt and pepper. Keep mashed potatoes warm in the oven or in a pot. These should be made just before you need them.

2. Put the cod steaks in a heated vegetable or fish steamer with water. Cover and steam until they're firm but not flaking. It should take 7–10 minutes depending on the thickness of the steaks. Drain the water, but leave the fish in the steamer.

3. In a small pan heat the olive oil and add garlic; cook the garlic until nut brown. Add paprika and set aside. (The oil will turn a bright orange.)

4. Put scoops of mashed potatoes on individual plates and flatten them slightly. Place the pieces of drained cod on the potatoes. Then spoon the oil and garlic mixture over the cod, enough to drizzle down the sides. Serve it garnished with chopped parsley.

SALMON ON A BED OF LEEKS AND CARROTS

SERVES 4

2 teaspoons olive oil
2 large leeks, julienned (see page 264)
3 carrots, julienned
¼ teaspoon salt
¼ teaspoon black pepper
3 tablespoons vermouth or white wine
4 6-ounce salmon fillets

1. Heat a large nonstick skillet over medium heat and add the oil. When the oil is hot, add the leeks and carrots and cook for about 15 minutes, or until the carrots are al dente. Stir occasionally.

2. Add salt, pepper, vermouth or wine, and salmon fillets. Cover and cook for about 10–12 minutes. Serve at once.

NOTE: Be sure you have a cover for your large nonstick skillet.

TUNA AU POIVRE

The rare tuna, the crunchy pepper crust—an explosive combination that is so much more than the sum of its parts.

SERVES 4

1 tuna steak (about 1¼ pounds), 1–1¼ inches thick
3 tablespoons soy sauce
2–3 cloves garlic, finely chopped or pressed
    Juice of 1 lime
½ teaspoon sugar
1 tablespoon olive oil
3–4 teaspoons coarsely ground black pepper

1. Place tuna steak in a shallow glass or ceramic bowl and cover with soy sauce, garlic, lime juice, and sugar.

2. Cover, then refrigerate for no more than 2 hours or let sit at room temperature for one hour, turning occasionally.

3. Heat a large nonstick skillet over high heat and add oil.

4. Lightly coat both sides of the tuna with pepper. When oil is hot, place tuna in skillet and cook for about 3 minutes on each side, or until tuna is of desired doneness.

OTHER CHOICES: Can also be made with swordfish.

PROVENÇAL

BOY, DO WE FEEL STUPID. ALL THIS TIME, WHILE WE AMERICANS WERE DISCOVERING THE JOYS of TV dinners, home cooks in the South of France were eating beans, garlic, and fresh fish. We felt a little sorry for them because their meals seemed so inconvenient. Of course, now we know that the Mediterranean region has one of the healthiest and most delicious cuisines of the world, and that traditional Provençal dishes are almost as easy to prepare as—well, as TV dinners.

PROVENÇAL SALAD WITH TUNA AND WHITE BEANS

SERVES 4

Fresh tuna and white beans come together in this winning dish. Because it is served at room temperature, perfect timing is not a problem.

2 teaspoons olive oil
1 leek, julienned (see page 264) or ¼ Spanish onion, coarsely chopped
2 stalks celery, julienned
2 carrots, julienned
1 bay leaf
1 teaspoon dried thyme
1 19-ounce can white kidney beans, drained and rinsed
½ cup water, vegetable stock, or fish stock (see page 21)
1 fresh tuna steak (about 1 pound), 1–1½ inches thick
2–4 tablespoons balsamic vinegar
1–2 tomatoes, diced
¼ cup chopped fresh parsley or basil

1. Heat a large nonstick skillet over medium-low heat and add 1 teaspoon of olive oil. Add the leek or onion, celery, carrots, bay leaf, and thyme, and cook until the vegetables are soft, about 10 minutes. Add the beans and water or stock and cook about 5 minutes, or until the beans are soft and heated through.

2. Remove the bay leaf. Scoop the vegetables and beans into a large serving dish.

3. In the same pan, heat the remaining teaspoon of olive oil over medium-high heat and add the tuna. Cook for about 5 minutes per side or until desired doneness.

4. Cut the tuna into large chunks and arrange them on top of the bean mixture. Sprinkle with balsamic vinegar, tomatoes, and parsley or basil.

"There was no doubt about the most important ingredient in a Provençal Christmas....[The] clothes and toys and stereo equipment and baubles were of incidental importance; the main event of Christmas was food."

PETER MAYLE, *A Year in Provence*

PROVENÇAL SALAD WITH TUNA AND WHITE BEANS

"The carp was dead, killed, assassinated, murdered in the first, second, and third degree. Limp, I fell into a chair, with my hands still unwashed, reached for a cigarette, lighted it, and waited for the police to come and take me into custody."

ALICE B. TOKLAS

PROVENÇAL FISH STEW WITH ROUILLE

Rouille is a traditional sauce of Provence, served as a colorful accompaniment to fish dishes, especially hearty stews. Made with red peppers and potatoes, it is named "rust" in French for its brownish-red color.

SERVES 4

2	teaspoons olive oil
1	Spanish onion, chopped
2	stalks celery, diced
½	fennel bulb, diced
4	cloves garlic, finely chopped or pressed
¼	teaspoon crushed red pepper flakes
2	teaspoons dried thyme
1	bay leaf
¼	teaspoon cayenne pepper
½	teaspoon turmeric
1	28-ounce can whole tomatoes, chopped, including liquid
4	cups fish stock (see page 21)
1	cup white wine
¾	cup orzo
½	pound cod, cut into 1-inch or bite-size cubes
½	pound halibut, cut into 1-inch or bite-size cubes

1. Heat a medium-sized skillet or pot over a medium flame and add olive oil. When the oil is hot, add the onion, celery, and fennel. Stir occasionally until the onion is golden, about 10 minutes.

2. Mix in the garlic, herbs, and spices, and cook for 5 minutes. Add the tomatoes, fish stock, and wine. Stir, then cook over medium-low heat for 20–25 minutes.

3. Increase heat to high and bring the mixture to a boil. Add the orzo and stir. Reduce the heat to medium and cook for about 5 minutes.

4. Reduce heat to low, add cod and halibut, and cook until the fish is done, about 7–10 minutes.

OTHER CHOICES: Clam juice and water may be substituted for the fish stock. If you like this slightly thicker, add forkfuls of cooked potato until the desired consistency is reached.

ROUILLE

SERVES 4

1	small new red potato, quartered
2–3	cloves garlic
1	small red bell pepper, cleaned, cored, and quartered
½	teaspoon cayenne pepper
2	tablespoons warm water
5	tablespoons olive oil

1. To make the rouille, place the potato in a small pot and cover with cold water. Bring to a boil over high heat and cook for 10 minutes, or until the potato is tender. Drain and place in bowl of a food processor fitted with a steel blade and blend.

2. Add the garlic, bell pepper, cayenne, and water to the food processor and process until smooth. While the machine is running, gradually add the olive oil.

3. Serve a dollop of rouille on each bowl of stew.

P I E R R E

Perhaps best known to most Americans as the "Sixty-Minute Gourmet," Pierre Franey had a different nickname as a child: "Pierre Le Gourmand." At a very young age Franey was a disciplined cook who contributed to the family meals. First he learned to clean fish; by the time he was eight, he was dredging fish in salt and pepper, sautéing it in butter, and drizzling it with fresh lemon juice. His future as a chef was sealed. "There was little else," says Franey, "that I ever imagined I would be, and Burgundy was one of the best places on earth to start." In his long career Pierre Franey has authored fourteen books, is a regular columnist for *The New York Times*, and has gained special fame as a master of fish cookery. But for all the thousands of dishes he's prepared, privately and publicly, Franey has such a true feeling for food that he still vividly remembers tastes from his childhood. He says, "It is literally possible for a single taste of some beloved dish to evoke a lifetime of relationships and experiences."

"Some of the simplest dishes can be food for the gods."

FRANEY

PIERRE FRANEY

ON INGREDIENTS. "The key to simple, fast cooking is magnificent, fresh ingredients whose flavors can virtually stand on their own without a cook's intervention."

ON EQUIPMENT. "I use nonstick skillets and pans. The nonsticking quality of the pans allowed me to add just as much oil or butter as the flavor of the dish required and not a drop more, since I was confident the food could be removed from the pot in the end without damage.... Some pans are much better than others and, as with every other piece of equipment you buy, high quality will pay for itself over and over again."

ON SAUCES. "In the absence of cream or starch, I find that simply chopping some tomatoes or other vegetables into a sauce will give it body.... Mushrooms, especially, puréed into a sauce with an electric blender will yield exquisite smoothness, much the same body, in fact, that one obtains through the use of cream."

BROILED FLOUNDER À LA MOUTARDE

This dish is typical of Franey's oeuvre in that it is designed not to dominate but to liberate the true flavors of the fillets. So be sure your fish is ultra-fresh and cooked with the lightest hand.

SERVES 4

4 skinless and boneless flounder fillets (about 1½ pounds)
Freshly ground black pepper (7 turns of the pepper mill)
1 tablespoon olive oil
2 tablespoons Dijon mustard
2 tablespoons chopped chives
4 lime wedges

1. Preheat the broiler.

2. Arrange the fillets on a baking sheet or in a baking dish, and sprinkle them with pepper. Then pastry-brush them with the oil.

3. Using a pastry brush, spread the mustard evenly over the fish.

4. Put the fillets into the broiler, about 3 inches from the heat source. Broil for about 2 minutes, or until golden brown. Do not overcook. Place on individual dishes, sprinkled with chives and accompanied by a wedge of lime.

ZUCCHINI BORDELAISE

SERVES 6

1½ pounds small zucchini
2 tablespoons olive oil
½ teaspoon salt
Freshly ground black pepper (6 turns of the pepper mill)
2 tablespoons fresh bread crumbs
1 tablespoon butter
2 tablespoons chopped shallots
4 tablespoons chopped fresh parsley

1. Rinse the zucchini and pat them dry. Trim off the ends, but do not peel them.

2. Heat the oil in a nonstick frying pan and, when it is hot, add the zucchini. Sauté the zucchini over high heat, shaking the pan and tossing the vegetable gently. Add the salt and pepper. Cook a total of 5 minutes.

3. Add the bread crumbs and butter to the pan. When the crumbs start to brown, add the shallots and toss the mixture for another minute. Serve the zucchini hot, sprinkled with the parsley.

[EDITOR'S NOTE: This recipe requires tiny zucchini, which are difficult to find. For best results with regular-sized zucchini, cut zucchini into rounds ¼ inch thick.]

[🐚 OTHER FACTS—*page 279*]

VEGETABLES

One AUGUST,

years ago, I was wandering around the spacious property of a château up in Normandy, trying to work up a proper appetite for lunch. The land doubled as a horse farm, and a vicious brood mare had tried to bite me, an act rewarded with a stone sharply thrown against her ass. Two old men I hadn't seen laughed beneath a tree. I walked over and sat with them around a small fire. They were gardeners and it was their lunch hour, and on the flat stone they had made a circle of hot coals. They had cored a half-dozen big red tomatoes, stuffed them with softening cloves of garlic, and added a sprig of thyme, a basil leaf, and a couple of tablespoons of soft cheese. They roasted the tomatoes until they were soft and the cheese melted. I ate one with a chunk of bread and healthy-sized swigs from a jug of red wine. When we finished eating, and since this was Normandy, we had a sip or two of calvados from the flask. A simple snack but indescribably delicious.

JIM HARRISON, *"Hunger, Real and Unreal"*

STEAMED BROCCOLI

*Steamed and spritzed with lemon,
broccoli is a marvelous side dish—as much
for its flavor as for its lively green presence.
But think of what else you can do with
broccoli: You can fold it in a pasta dish
just before serving, integrate it with sauces
and soups, or use it as a garnish for
platters of meat or fish.*

SERVES 4

1 head broccoli (about
1½–2 pounds): cut off bottom
third of stalk; peel and slice
cut-off stalk and discard; peel
remaining stalks of leaves and
cut into 3 lengthwise pieces
1 lemon, quartered

ON THE STOVE

Place broccoli with 1 inch of water in a
large stockpot and bring water to a
boil over high heat. Cover and reduce
heat to medium. Steam for about 5–6
minutes, or until al dente. Serve immediately with lemon wedges.

IN THE MICROWAVE

Place the broccoli stems in a 2-quart
microwave-proof casserole with ½ cup
water. Cover and cook on high for 3½
minutes.

TIP: Never add lemon juice before
serving, as it will bleach the vegetable.

GREEN AND BEYOND

ANIMAL, VEGETABLE, MINERAL? OF THESE, PERHAPS THE VEGETABLE IS THE GREATEST BLESSING TO HUMANKIND: DELICIOUS, NUTRITIOUS, AND LOW-CALORIE TO BOOT. VEGETABLES ALSO COULDN'T BE MORE accommodating, whether puréed into soups, adding variety to salad greens, or elevating pasta and pizza to new nutritional heights beyond just starch. As with so many vegetables, there is a certain genius to the bean. In its immature state, a bean is a single unit, consisting of a squeaky-sweet pod and the edible seeds within. As it matures, the pod contributes its moisture and nutrients to the seeds, which can then be harvested and served fresh, or dried to sustain us through our long winters.

FAVA BEANS. Fresh fava beans, also known as broad beans, are large beans with a smooth, buttery texture and a nutty, sweet, and slightly bitter taste. Their thick, bright green pod holds the intense, pale green bean, which may be served with or without the skin. They come about 4–6 beans in a pod and need to be shelled. They are used extensively in Mediterranean cooking. They can be eaten raw, as well as cooked. Some recipes call for peeling each bean individually, but this is not necessary; cooking unpeeled beans results in a slightly stronger flavor.

GREEN BEANS. These are the young, green, edible pods of haricot beans. While they are often called string beans, today they have been bred so as to be stringless. They are available in different varieties, including pole beans and yellow wax beans, but there is little difference in taste.

HARICOTS VERTS. A French variety of immature, small, tender green beans. Particularly wonderful in salads.

SNAP PEAS. Bred from the snow pea to be fatter and sweeter. They are about $2\frac{1}{2}$–3 inches long, bright green, plump with mature peas, and are eaten whole, pod and peas together.

SNOW PEAS. These peas are crisp and are often eaten barely cooked in their flat pods.

> "I ate his liver with fava beans and a nice Chianti."
>
> DR. HANNIBAL LECTER, *The Silence of the Lambs*

FRESH PEAS

DRIED SPLIT PEAS

FLAT BEANS

YELLOW WAX BEANS

STRING OR GREEN BEANS

HARICOTS VERTS

FAVA BEANS

SPINACH WITH GARLIC AND PINE NUTS

This tasty no-brainer is accented by the flavorful crunch of pine nuts. Health note: By heating spinach without oil in a nonstick skillet, you can cut down on fat absorption.

SERVES 4

1½–2 pounds fresh spinach, ends
     trimmed and discarded
1 teaspoon olive oil
2 tablespoons pine nuts
2–4 cloves garlic, chopped
     Salt and pepper

1. Wash the spinach well and shake out the water. Heat a large saucepan over high heat and add the spinach. Cook for about 5–7 minutes or until tender, tossing frequently. Transfer the spinach to a colander and set aside.

2. Heat the saucepan over a medium flame and add the olive oil. When the oil is hot, add the pine nuts and chopped garlic and cook until both are golden, about 2 minutes. Return the spinach to the saucepan, toss to combine, and cook until heated through, about 2 minutes. Add salt and pepper to taste.

OTHER CHOICES: Substitute broccoli rabe for the spinach.

SPINACH

CAUTION. Spinach reacts with aluminum, carbon, and silver, causing discoloration in both the metal and the spinach, so it is best to use stainless steel when cooking spinach.

NUTRITION. While spinach is a rich source of vitamins A and C, calcium, and potassium, it also contains oxalic acid. This actually inhibits the body's absorption of calcium and iron from the spinach (luckily, it doesn't affect other foods). So eat as much spinach as you like, but don't rely on it as a calcium or iron source.

SUPPLEMENTARY SPINACH

Cooked chopped spinach can enhance many dishes with added texture, color, flavor, and nutrition. Here are some suggestions: 1. Topping for mashed potatoes 2. Vegetable dips 3. Add to stuffing for poultry, mushrooms, bell peppers 4. Eggs: scrambled, omelettes, quiches, deviled 5. Garlic bread 6. With pesto over pasta 7. Rice 8. As a "bed" for an already cooked serving of beef, chicken, or fish.

CHERRY TOMATOES WITH A CHOICE OF HERBS

Goes with everything, yet can work as the main event when spooned over pasta. Just add a drizzle of olive oil and a shaving of Parmesan.

SERVES 4

2 teaspoons olive oil
1–2 cloves garlic, pressed or finely
     chopped
1 pint cherry tomatoes, halved
1 pint pear tomatoes, halved
2 tablespoons chopped fresh
     tarragon, rosemary, or sage
     Salt and pepper

1. Heat a large nonstick skillet over medium-low heat and add the olive oil. When the oil is hot, add the garlic and cook for about 3 minutes, or until it just begins to turn golden. Remove garlic from oil.

2. Raise heat to medium, add the tomatoes, and cook, with an occasional stir, until the tomatoes are tender, or about 3 minutes. Do not overcook or the tomatoes will get mushy.

3. Add the herb and cook for 1 minute. Add salt and pepper to taste.

OTHER CHOICES: Use half red cherry tomatoes and half yellow.

"Kissing don't last: cookery do."

GEORGE MEREDITH

CHERRY TOMATOES WITH CHOICE OF HERBS

ACORN SQUASH WITH GARLIC, THYME, AND HONEY

SERVES 4

1 large acorn squash, seeded and cut into 8 pieces, skin left on
1 cup chicken stock or water
1 tablespoon unsalted butter
1 clove garlic, pressed or finely chopped
1½ teaspoons chopped fresh thyme or ½ teaspoon dried
½ teaspoon salt or more, to taste
1–2 teaspoons honey

1. Place the squash and stock or water in a large saucepan or skillet and bring to a boil.

2. Reduce the heat to low, cover, and simmer until the squash is tender, or about 20 minutes. Push the squash to one side to make room for the butter.

3. Add the butter and garlic and cook for about 3 minutes.

4. Sprinkle the squash with the remaining ingredients and cook, stirring occasionally, for about 5 minutes.

SPAGHETTI SQUASH WITH TOMATO SAUCE

SERVES 4

1 spaghetti squash
1 recipe Tomato Sauce (see page 178)
   Parmesan or Fontina cheese, freshly grated

ON THE STOVE

1. Place the squash in a large pot and cover with water. Cover and boil until squash is cooked (outer skin of squash should be soft enough to easily pierce with a fork), about 45 minutes. Drain and set squash aside.

2. Once squash is cool, about 10-15 minutes, cut squash lengthwise and comb out seeds and discard.

3. Place the squash in a serving dish, comb out the spaghettilike strands of squash, top with tomato sauce, and sprinkle with cheese.

GRILLED YELLOW SQUASH AND ZUCCHINI WITH BALSAMIC VINEGAR

SERVES 4

1 cup balsamic vinegar
4 squash: 2 yellow, 2 zucchini (about 1½ pounds; the smaller the better)
   Enough olive oil for lightly brushing the vegetables

1. Put a rack high in the oven and preheat the broiler.

2. To thicken the vinegar, bring it to a boil in a saucepan and then reduce heat and continue at a low boil until reduced by half.

3. Cut off and discard the ends of the squash and then cut the squash into lengthwise strips ⅓ inch thick.

4. Lightly brush the squash strips with olive oil and put them on a broiling pan. Grill each side under the broiler until lightly browned (2–4 minutes).

5. As soon as the vegetables come out of the oven, drizzle the reduced vinegar over them and serve.

"To get the best results, you must talk to your vegetables."

CHARLES, PRINCE OF WALES

S Q U A S H

THE DIFFERENCE BETWEEN SUMMER AND WINTER SQUASH

IS THAT SUMMER SQUASH IS PICKED WHEN IT IS YOUNG AND

ITS SKIN IS TENDER AND EDIBLE. WINTER SQUASH IS PICKED WHEN IT IS

mature, resulting in a tough, generally inedible shell. Most winter squash can be kept in a cool, dry place for several

months. The seeds of winter squash, which are high in fat and protein, can be baked or pan-fried with a

small amount of oil and salt. Summer squash is an especially low-calorie food, and no wonder—it's 95 percent water.

ACORN SQUASH (winter). Shaped like acorns, they are dark green and deeply ridged. They are best baked, served with honey and butter, or stuffed. **GOLDEN ACORN** varieties are also available.

BABY SQUASH (summer). The French call them *courgettes* and Italians *zuchette*, meaning "small" squash. Baby squash can be any variety of squash, usually harvested with the flower still on, or when they are less than 3 inches long.

BUTTERNUT SQUASH (winter). These large (3–5 pounds each), creamy orange, bell-shaped squash are slightly sweet, with a dense consistency. They are best peeled and are great in soups, or baked.

GOLDEN NUGGETS (winter). Orange-skinned, and sweet, like butternut squash, golden nuggets are somewhat reminiscent of pumpkin, a big-brother squash. They are good baked, or boiled and mashed with butter.

SPAGHETTI SQUASH (winter). So named because its flesh resembles spaghetti strands, this squash is yellow, large, oval-shaped, and mild in flavor. Spaghetti squash are available mainly in the winter and make a great substitute for pasta.

YELLOW SQUASH (summer). Mild and long with slightly pebbled skin, they range in color from pale to brilliant yellow. They are best prepared with zucchini and can be substituted for them.

ZUCCHINI (summer). They are the most popular, prolific, and widely available of all the squashes, summer or winter. Zucchinis resemble cucumbers but are thinner, smoother, and often a darker green. They are quite mild and can be eaten raw, steamed, deep-fried, grilled, baked, or pan-fried. They do not need to be peeled.

YELLOW SQUASH

SPAGHETTI SQUASH

BABY SQUASH (PATTYPAN)

ZUCCHINI

BUTTERNUT SQUASH

ACORN SQUASH

GOLDEN ACORN SQUASH

PAULA WOLFERT

What comes to mind when someone mentions Mediterranean culture? If you're like most people, you envision the coasts of Italy or Greece. But not Paula Wolfert. Wolfert's Mediterranean includes all the countries on that seashore, including Slavic Macedonia, Turkey, and the Levant. She even counts in the Republic of Georgia, "a country that is Mediterranean in spirit and agriculture." Wolfert's career was born of a restless spirit. She dropped out of Columbia University and became a cook, but only because she didn't know what else to do. "I later went to Tangiers to be a writer, but I didn't lift a pencil," she remembers. "I was a house-wife/drifter/bohemian." Wolfert eventually met Bill Bayer, a writer, with whom she traveled and whom she later married. With his encouragement she began to write about her travels with food, and has since produced a groundbreaking cookbook every five years. Wolfert may be a drifter at heart, but her books have staying power: Her first, *Couscous and Other Good Food*, was published in 1973 and is still in print.

"For me, one of the best desserts imaginable is
figs, and a glass of chilled

SHRIMP IN TOMATO SAUCE WITH ALMONDS AND PINE NUTS

This delicious Spanish dish combines the richness of nuts with the subtlety of shrimp and a little nip of cayenne.

SERVES 4

- ⅓ cup olive oil
- 1 cup chopped onion
- 3 cups fresh or canned tomatoes, peeled, seeded, and chopped
- ½ cup ground blanched almonds
- ⅓ cup pine nuts
- 4 cloves garlic, peeled and chopped
- 2 tablespoons chopped parsley
- ¼ teaspoon cayenne
  Salt
- 2 cups shelled cooked small shrimp

1. Heat the oil in the skillet and cook the onion until soft and golden. Add the tomatoes. Cook uncovered for 15–20 minutes, stirring often.

2. In a blender, grind the almonds, pine nuts, garlic, parsley, and 3 tablespoons water to a paste. Stir into the tomato sauce. Cook while stirring for 5 minutes. If sauce is very thick, thin with ¾–1 cup water. Season with cayenne and salt.

3. Fold in the shrimp. Allow to heat through. Serve on a bed of boiled rice.

STEWED POTATOES WITH TOMATOES AND FETA

These ingredients couldn't be more elementary; it's the slow cooking and the resulting thickening of the sauce that make Wolfert's creation a Mediterranean marvel.

SERVES 4

- 1½ tablespoons olive oil
- 1 cup chopped Spanish onion
- 2 cloves garlic, peeled and minced
- 1 cup tomato sauce
- 1 cup water
- 2 tablespoons chopped fresh parsley
  Salt and freshly ground pepper, to taste
- 4 waxy medium potatoes (about 1 pound), peeled and cut into 6 wedges
- 4 slices imported feta

1. In a 10-inch deep-sided skillet, heat the oil and sauté the onion over moderate heat until soft and golden. Add the garlic, tomato sauce, water, parsley, and salt and pepper.

2. Bring to a boil, add the potatoes, cover tightly, lower the heat, and cook 30 minutes, or until the potatoes are tender and the sauce is thickened. Serve warm or hot, with slices of feta on the side and good crusty bread.

PAULA WOLFERT

ON OIL. "The Mediterranean cook can do without butter if she must. She can even work without fat. But without olive oil, she is lost. Olive oil is the backbone of the Mediterranean diet."

ON NUTS. "Store all nuts in the refrigerator or freezer."

INSPIRATION IN SITU. "The purpose of my first trip to Southwest France was to seek out the perfect cassoulet. But on that journey I caught sight of something else: a magnificent peasant cookery in the process of being updated. The food was modern, honest, yet still close to the earth—a true *cuisine de terroir*, 'of the soil.'...[These ideas] had to do with a love of logic in recipes in which a dish is built, step by step, inexorably toward a finish that is the inevitable best result of all the ingredients employed. They had to do with simplicity and healthiness and the pleasures of dining upon foods that bear natural affinities, as opposed to wild experimentation, gratuitous gestures, complexity for its own sake, and striking dramatic contrasts and effects."

a wedge of Roquefort, some plump black Mission estate-bottled Sauternes."

[OTHER FACTS—*page 279*]

EGGPLANT CAPONATA

This earthy dish can be served hot from the skillet;
it's also great chilled and used as a relish.

MAKES 3 CUPS

2   teaspoons olive oil
1   eggplant, peeled, if desired,
     and cubed
3   fresh tomatoes, cubed
1   teaspoon sugar
¼   cup red wine vinegar
3   tablespoons capers
¼   cup black olives, pitted and
     chopped
¼   cup chopped fresh parsley or basil
     Salt and pepper

OPTIONAL INGREDIENT

½   red onion, chopped

1. Heat a nonstick skillet over medium heat and add oil. When the oil is hot, add eggplant and sauté for about 5 minutes or until slightly browned.

2. Reduce heat to low. Cover and cook about 20 minutes or until soft.

3. Raise heat to high, add tomatoes, and cook for about 5 minutes. Add remaining ingredients and add salt and pepper to taste. Serve hot, cold, or at room temperature.

"Almost every person has something secret he likes to eat."

M.F.K. FISHER

EGGPLANT

GENDER MYTH. Ideally, you want to pick eggplants with few seeds. But forget anything you may have heard about male eggplants having fewer seeds—eggplants have both male and female characteristics and self-pollinate. Like most vegetables, however, the smaller and younger they are, the better they taste.

SALTING. It's not necessary to salt eggplant, as many recipes recommend. It gets rid of very little liquid, almost no bitterness, and adds unnecessary salt to the dish.

EQUIPMENT NOTE. When cooking with eggplant, it's easy to blacken its white flesh with certain metals; avoid carbon steel knives and aluminum pots.

CALORIE ALERT. An eggplant's flesh is porous and sponge-like. If you deep-fry or sauté eggplant, keep in mind that it absorbs more oil than any other vegetable. (Fried potatoes are dietetic by comparison.)

VALUE. Eggplant is heavily featured in Arabic cooking and is considered so important that eggplant recipes are an essential part of a dowry.

ROASTED EGGPLANT WITH CURRY, CILANTRO, AND RED BELL PEPPER

SERVES 4

1   tablespoon olive oil, plus more
     for pan
1   large eggplant, peeled, if desired,
     and cut in 1–1½-inch cubes
2   cloves garlic
1   tablespoon sherry
1   teaspoon Oriental sesame oil
     (do not use regular sesame oil)
2   teaspoons curry powder
½   teaspoon kosher salt
1–2 tablespoons chopped fresh cilantro
2   scallions, cut diagonally into
     1-inch pieces
½   red bell pepper, diced

OPTIONAL INGREDIENT

¼   cup red wine vinegar (if serving
     cold or at room temperature)

1. Preheat oven to 400° F.

2. Lightly oil a roasting or baking pan. Place the eggplant cubes in pan.

3. Place the garlic, sherry, olive oil, sesame oil, curry powder, and salt in a blender or a food processor fitted with a steel blade and purée until it forms a thin paste.

4. Pour the paste over the eggplant and mix. Place the eggplant in the oven.

5. ⏰ Cook for about 45–60 minutes or until the eggplant is lightly browned. Remove from the oven and sprinkle with the cilantro, scallions, and diced red pepper.

6. If serving cold or at room temperature, add the vinegar.

ROASTED EGGPLANT WITH CURRY, CILANTRO, AND RED BELL PEPPER

ROASTED BELL PEPPERS

ROASTED BELL PEPPERS

Bell peppers prepared this way make a wonderful garnish for baked potatoes and any meat. Even more wonderful when marinated in your favorite vinaigrette.

SERVES 4

4 bell peppers, any color

1. Preheat the broiler or preheat oven to 450° F.

2. Place peppers directly under broiler, in oven or toaster oven, as close together as possible. Singe peppers on all sides.

3. Remove peppers, place in a brown paper bag, and let sweat for about 10 minutes. Peel off burned skin. Seed and stem peppers.

ROASTED BEETS WITH ORANGE AND FRESH MINT

SERVES 4

2 bunches beets, trimmed (if the beets are very small, leave them whole; if they are large, quarter them)
2 tablespoons olive oil
3 tablespoons orange juice
¼ cup balsamic vinegar
1 teaspoon Dijon mustard
Salt and pepper

OPTIONAL INGREDIENT

2 teaspoons fresh mint, finely chopped

1. Preheat oven to 400° F.

2. Lightly rub the beets with about 1 tablespoon of the olive oil. Place them in the oven on a roasting pan and cook for about 1 hour, or until they can be pierced with a fork.

3. Combine the orange juice, vinegar, remaining olive oil, and mustard, and place in a small pan and bring to a boil.

4. Remove the beets from the oven and peel them when they are cool enough to handle. Place them in a bowl.

5. Pour the orange juice mixture over the beets. Add salt and pepper to taste and the fresh mint, if desired.

ROASTED GARLIC

Garlic fans spread this on their favorite bread, on vegetables, or eat it plain.

SERVES 4

1 head garlic
1 tablespoon olive oil or ¼ cup chicken stock (see page 19)

1. Preheat oven to 450° F.

2. Remove as much of the peel from the garlic as possible, while being careful to keep the head intact.

3. Place on a piece of aluminum foil large enough to completely wrap garlic. Drizzle with oil or chicken stock and seal in foil.

4. Cook for about 45 minutes, or until garlic is soft and tender. When cool enough to handle, remove peel; if using it as a purée, mash garlic with a fork.

ROASTED MIXED VEGETABLES

SERVES 4

1 large red onion, sliced, or 4 shallots
1 red bell pepper, sliced
1 yellow squash, sliced
1 zucchini, sliced diagonally, if desired
2 cups cherry tomatoes
4–8 cloves garlic, unpeeled
1 teaspoon dried thyme, basil, or rosemary
¼–½ teaspoon kosher salt
¼ teaspoon black pepper
1 tablespoon olive oil
2 tablespoons balsamic vinegar

1. Preheat oven to 400° F.

2. Put all the ingredients, except for the balsamic vinegar, together in a baking pan and bake for about 1 hour.

3. When finished cooking, remove vegetables from the oven and place them in a serving dish. Sprinkle with the balsamic vinegar.

A L L   H A I L

the Maize Queen, who gives us golden corn to cook. Freshly husked, and squeaky clean, it's as unspoilt as a Kansas

state fair. When corn is cooked in its husk, the flavor is decidedly darker, a more mature synthesis of sun, soil, and rain.

SIMPLE CORN ON THE COB

SERVES 4

4 ears corn

OVEN-ROASTED

Preheat oven to 425° F. Place the un-husked corn directly on an oven rack and bake for 15 minutes.

STEAMED

Bring 4 inches of water to a boil in a large stockpot; add husked corn, cover, and cook about 12 minutes, or until kernels are al dente. TIP: If corn season is not yet at its peak, add a teaspoon of sugar to the water before steaming. ALTERNATIVE: Cover corn with water, bring to boil over high heat, and cook approximately 7 minutes.

MICROWAVE ROASTING

Loosen husks from corn, place ears in an open-ended plastic bag with two tablespoons of water. Lay flat on bottom of microwave, making sure not to crowd the ears. Cook on high setting for 8 minutes; turn ears and cook for an additional 4 minutes.

MICROWAVE COOKING

Place husked corn in a 2–3-quart microwave-proof casserole. Cover and cook on high for 6 minutes. Turn plate around and turn corn over and cook for an additional 6 minutes (total of 3–4 minutes per ear).

GRILLED CORN ON THE COB WITH CAYENNE BUTTER

SERVES 4–8

1/4 pound unsalted butter
1–2 tablespoons cayenne pepper
    Juice of 2 limes
8 ears corn, husked, silk removed
    Salt

1. Melt the butter over low heat in a small saucepan. Add the cayenne and lime juice and mix well.

2. Brush the butter on the corn and place on grill. Baste and turn occasionally until corn is cooked, about 12 minutes.

3. Add salt to taste.

CURRIED CORN WITH RED BELL PEPPER AND HERBS

SERVES 4

1 teaspoon olive oil
1 Spanish onion, chopped
1 red bell pepper, chopped
1 tablespoon curry powder
2½–3 cups corn kernels, fresh or frozen
1/4 cup water or chicken or vegetable broth (see pages 19, 21)
2 tablespoons chopped fresh parsley, basil, or cilantro

1. Heat a skillet over medium heat and add the olive oil. When the oil is hot, add the onion, bell pepper, and curry, and cook until the vegetables are soft.

2. Add the corn and water or broth, and cook until corn is heated and liquid has almost evaporated, about 5 minutes.

3. Add the herb of choice and serve.

NOTE: To make this into soup, add 4 cups chicken stock when you add the corn, bring to a boil, lower the heat, and cook for about 20 minutes more. Purée, if desired.

GRILLED CORN ON THE COB
WITH CAYENNE BUTTER

HUMPTY'S RETURN

WHAT COULD BE MORE PERFECT THAN THE EGG?

IT IS NATURE'S OWN PREPACKAGED FOOD. AT ITS SIMPLEST,

HARD-BOILED WITH A SPRINKLE OF SALT, IT'S DIVINE—WHETHER YOU'RE

sitting at a Parisian bar or basking in the sun on a ski slope. In the kitchen, it is infinitely adaptable, and

no matter what happens to an egg dish, you can always claim it was intentional. Broken yolks become

scrambled eggs, scrambled eggs become omelettes...and if you bungle an omelette, you can mix all the

ingredients together in a pie plate, bake it slowly at a low heat in the oven until browned. The result will

be no accident: a thick, golden disk that's firm enough to be cut into wedges. The dish is so exquisite and

suave it goes by an Italian name, frittata (meaning fried or omelette). Of course, intentional frittatas are

even better and more refined. Get creative with what's on hand in the pantry or the fridge, and make a

frittata with vegetables (whatever you roasted, steamed, or sautéed last night would be just swell), or a

combination of cheeses, meats, and herbs. Within minutes you'll have a simple supper of elegant eggs.

SCRAMBLED EGGS

The secret to scrambled eggs is vigilance. With good timing on your side, you'll produce sunny-yellow, billowing clouds— delectable!

SERVES 2

5   eggs
1–2   dashes Tabasco or hot sauce
1   splash water
½   teaspoon salt
½   teaspoon black pepper
1   teaspoon olive oil

OPTIONAL INGREDIENTS

1   tablespoon fresh tarragon
    Fresh chives, snipped
2   ounces smoked salmon, sliced into thin strips

1. Whisk together the eggs, Tabasco or hot sauce, a splash of water, salt, and pepper in a medium-sized mixing bowl.

2. Heat a large omelette pan or skillet over medium heat and add the oil. When the oil is hot, add the eggs.

3. As soon as the eggs begin to congeal, rapidly push them from the center of the pan, in a back-and-forth or circular motion. As the eggs get hotter, they will cook faster, so work quickly and take the pan off the heat, if necessary. Always transfer them to a plate before they attain the texture you like, since they continue cooking off heat.

OMELETTE

SERVES 1

3   eggs, lightly beaten
1–2   dashes Tabasco or hot sauce
½   teaspoon salt
½   teaspoon black pepper
2   teaspoons olive oil
¼   Spanish onion
1   clove garlic, minced
¾   cup vegetables, chopped

1. Whisk together the eggs, Tabasco or hot sauce, salt, and pepper in a medium-sized mixing bowl.

2. Heat a small pan over medium-low heat and add 1 teaspoon oil. When the oil is hot, add onion and garlic, and sauté for 10 minutes or until onion is translucent. Add vegetables and cook until soft, about 10 minutes. Put mixture in bowl and allow to cool slightly.

3. Heat a large omelette pan or skillet over medium heat and add the remaining oil. When the oil is hot, add the egg mixture and cook over medium-low heat. Shake the pan so the bottom is coated with egg mixture. When the egg is still slightly runny, add the desired filling. While gently lifting the pan from the heat, fold half of the egg over the other, covering the filling.

3. When ready to serve, slowly tip the pan perpendicular to the plate, allowing the omelette to smoothly roll out.

BAKED VEGETABLE FRITTATA

SERVES 4

2   teaspoons olive or canola oil
1   Spanish or purple onion, thinly sliced
2   cloves garlic, finely chopped
3   cups vegetables, coarsely chopped
6   large eggs, lightly beaten
1   cup sour cream, yogurt, or ricotta cheese
2   cups cubed day-old bread, cubed potatoes, or leftover pasta
2   teaspoons salt
1   teaspoon black pepper
1   teaspoon nutmeg

OPTIONAL INGREDIENTS

1   cup grated cheese
    Salsa (see page 55)

1. Preheat oven to 350° F. Lightly grease an 8-inch springform pan or a 10-inch pie plate.

2. See step 2 of Omelette.

3. Combine remaining ingredients, by hand, in a mixing bowl; add cooled vegetable mixture.

4. Place mixture in pan and bake in oven until slightly firm, about 35 minutes. Serve hot, cold, or at room temperature with salsa, if desired.

OTHER CHOICES: If using precooked vegetables, stir them into cooked onion and garlic mixture and continue with recipe.

POTATOES, GRAINS, AND RICE

"I have friends who begin with pasta, and friends who begin with rice, but whenever I fall in love, begin with *potatoes*. Sometime meat and *potatoes* and sometime fish and *potatoes*, but alway *potatoes*. I have made a lot o mistakes falling in love, an regretted most of them, but neve the *potatoes* that went with them

NORA EPHRON, *Heartburn*

BAKED POTATO

You can microwave or boil potatoes, but our favorite potato spends a full hour in a real oven. Slow-cooking heightens it in every way. Its skin metamorphoses into a jacket—crusty, thick, full of flavor. Its insides become soft, sweet, and fluffy. Eat plain or top with just about anything edible, but with a little butter, a little salt, and a bit of pepper, it can be a simple meal in itself.

SERVES 4

4 Idaho or russet potatoes, scrubbed and dried
2 teaspoons butter or olive oil

OVEN-BAKED

1. Preheat oven to 400° F.

2. Prick the potatoes all over with the tines of a fork.

3. Rub the butter or olive oil on the skin to make it slightly crisp.

4. ⏰ Place on a rack in the oven and bake for about 1 hour, or until the inside of the potato feels soft when pricked with a fork. Serve immediately.

MICROWAVE-BAKED

1. Repeat step 2 from above.

2. Place potatoes in a circular arrangement, 1 inch apart, on a paper towel on the floor of a microwave oven. Cook on high for 12–16 minutes (4–6 minutes per potato).

NOTE: If the potatoes feel firm when done, let them stand to soften.

YUKON GOLD

JICAMA

IDAHO

RUSSET

YAMS

YAMS

PERUVIAN PURPLE

NEW WHITE

MAINE

POTATOES

IT'S NO WONDER POTATOES HAD AN ENTIRE FAMINE NAMED AFTER THEM. AMERICANS CONSUMMATE THEIR SPUD-LOVE BY EATING 140 PER HEAD, PER YEAR, AND FOR GOOD reason: Not only are they a high-carbohydrate, low-fat power food, but recipes for their preparation can be as simple as "wash and throw in oven" or "boil, then mash." Potatoes are always satisfying, always apples of the earth—or *pommes de terre*, as they say *en français*.

IDAHO. This member of the russet family is a good all-purpose potato; the skin is slightly thinner than potatoes sold as russets.

JICAMA. This large, bulbous root has thin brown skin and white crunchy flesh. Its sweet, nutty flavor is good both raw in salads and cooked in stir-fries, soups, stews, or boiled and mashed like a potato.

LONG WHITE POTATO. Slender, with pale brown skin and almost imperceptible eyes, these are all-purpose potatoes.

MAINE. This potato is a slightly smaller russet cousin than the Idaho potato. It tends to be waxier; good for boiling.

NEW POTATOES. The youngsters of any variety, they have a crisp, waxy texture and thin, undeveloped, wispy skins. They are excellent boiled or roasted, and because they retain their shape after being cooked and cut, they are the optimal choice for potato salads.

PERUVIAN PURPLE. This small potato with purple skin and flesh has a musty, earthy flavor reminiscent of truffles. Great tasting for all potato uses; just looks strange when mashed.

ROUND RED AND ROUND WHITE. Both round reds and whites are considered waxy and are also known as boiling potatoes, but they can be roasted or fried as well.

RUSSETS. Low in moisture and high in starch, russets are long, with slightly rounded ends, brown skin, numerous eyes, and they are excellent for baking or frying.

SWEET POTATOES. Sweet potatoes and yams look and taste very similar, but while used interchangeably, they are very different species. Both are roots—unlike white potatoes, which are tubers. The smaller ones are best used for baking and the larger ones for roasting, mashing, or boiling.

YAMS. Excellent boiled, fried, or baked, yams make a pleasant change from the more routinely served white potatoes. Yams are sweet with rust-colored skins and orange flesh. Their texture can be creamy, dry, dense, woody, or stringy.

YUKON GOLD. This yellow-fleshed, buttery, waxy potato is a flavorful all-purpose potato. It measures 2–8 inches in length and $\frac{1}{2}$–2 inches in diameter. No matter how it's prepared, you can get away with using less butter.

[POTATOES *first aid—page 264*]

POTATO SALAD VINAIGRETTE

Summertime picnic food at its finest. Great for noshing on while loitering in a lounge chair on the back porch or for accompanying an elegant candlelight-and-wine repast in the gazebo.

SERVES 4

1½ pounds new potatoes, cut in quarters or halves, depending on size and taste
2 tablespoons red wine vinegar
1 tablespoon grainy Dijon mustard
3 tablespoons olive oil
3 scallions, chopped
3 tablespoons finely chopped fresh parsley
2 tablespoons finely chopped fresh dill
Salt and pepper

1. Place the potatoes in a large stockpot and cover with cold water. Bring to a boil and cook until the potatoes are tender, about 15–20 minutes. Drain.

2. While the potatoes are cooking, combine the vinegar and mustard in a large bowl, then whisk in the olive oil.

3. Add the drained potatoes to vinaigrette and mix gently but thoroughly. Set aside to cool to room temperature.

4. Before serving, mix in scallions, parsley, and dill, and salt and pepper to taste.

GARLIC MASHED POTATOES

When garlic is added, this classic comfort food thrills both the squealing child and the sophisticated adult lurking within each of us.

SERVES 4

2 pounds small red potatoes, unpeeled, or Yukon Gold, quartered
2 cloves garlic, smashed
1 teaspoon salt
½ cup chicken stock
Salt and pepper to taste

OPTIONAL INGREDIENTS

½ teaspoon paprika
2 tablespoons grated Parmesan cheese

1. Place the potatoes in a medium-sized pot and cover them with cold water. Add garlic and 1 teaspoon salt. Bring to a boil. Boil for 15–20 minutes, or until potatoes are tender.

2. Drain the potatoes and garlic and return them to pot.

3. Add the stock, paprika, and cheese, if desired, and salt and pepper to taste.

4. Mash all ingredients together. For a creamier texture, use a whisk.

OTHER CHOICES: Substitute or mix stock with milk, buttermilk, or cream. Consider topping with Caramelized Onions (see page 74), a small pat of butter, or a sprinkling of nutmeg.

ROASTED POTATOES WITH LEMON, GARLIC, AND ROSEMARY

Though dried rosemary is almost as tasty, this recipe is an ideal showcase for the graceful spears and heady aroma of fresh rosemary. Serve it with a pair of perfect lamb chops.

SERVES 4

2 pounds new potatoes, unpeeled and cut in eighths
2 tablespoons olive oil
2 tablespoons fresh lemon juice
8 cloves garlic, unpeeled
1 teaspoon kosher salt
2 teaspoons chopped fresh rosemary or ¾ teaspoon dried

1. Preheat oven to 425° F.

2. Place the potatoes in a roasting pan. Add the olive oil, lemon juice, garlic, salt, and rosemary, if dried, and mix by hand until combined.

3. Cook for 35 minutes until browned. For crispy potatoes, cook about 10 minutes longer. If using fresh rosemary, sprinkle it over the potatoes as soon as they're out of the oven.

OTHER CHOICES: Thinly slice ½ Spanish onion. Place in the pan with the potatoes. Or add 2 cans drained whole tomatoes, chopped, or 1 pound cherry tomatoes, halved. Or substitute 2 pounds sweet potatoes or yams for the new potatoes.

POTATO SALAD VINAIGRETTE

TOPPINGS. 1. Butter 2. Sour cream and fresh chives 3. Salt and pepper 4. Yogurt 5. Cheese of choice 6. Olivada 7. Crème fraîche 8. Pesto (see page 180) with Tomato Sauce (see page 178) 15. Grainy Dijon mustard 16. Vinaigrette 17. Caramelized Onions (see page 74) 18. Cherry Tomatoes with a Choice of Herbs (see pa

A DRY SUBJECT

WHY AREN'T PEOPLE MORE IN LOVE WITH GRAINS? WHILE IT'S TRUE THAT FEW SONNETS HAVE BEEN WRITTEN ON THE SUBJECT, MANY GOOD RECIPES HAVE. ARE YOU READY TO LOOSEN YOUR GRIP ON PASTA?

Go ahead, roll in oats, run through the cornmeal, put millet on the menu, or try some wheat neat.

AMARANTH. A mildly spicy seed, it may be cooked in liquid until creamy; when tossed in a hot pan until the seeds burst, it develops a crackle like seasoned popcorn.

BUCKWHEAT. Despite its name, buckwheat is not related to wheat and is not a proper grain. **GROATS** are whole-kernel buckwheat with a slightly nutty flavor and soft texture; when roasted it's known as **KASHA.**

CORNMEAL. Cornmeal is made from ground yellow or white corn kernels that are sweet in flavor and soft in texture. It is used for making polenta, muffins, and bread.

COUSCOUS. While often thought of as a grain and served like rice, couscous is technically a pasta made from ground durum wheat, or semolina.

GRITS. Any grain that's been hulled and ground can be grits, a food high in fiber and protein. Grits are a staple below the Mason-Dixon Line.

HOMINY. Skinned white corn kernels with a firm texture. Often made into grits.

MILLET. This "cereal grass" is rich in some B vitamins, copper, and iron. Protein is enhanced with beans and/or other legumes. Millet may be simmered, steamed, or made into a pilaf.

OATS. ROLLED OATS OR OATMEAL are oat groats with a slightly nutty flavor and soft texture that have been steamed, flattened, and flaked or cut. They're used for cereal and baking. **WHOLE-GRAIN OATS** are crammed with seven B vitamins, vitamin E, and nine minerals, including calcium and iron. Some studies have found that oat bran can help lower cholesterol levels in the blood just as effectively as some drugs.

PEARL BARLEY. These are whole kernels of barley that have been polished. They have a subtle flavor and a soft texture.

QUINOA. Cultivated fruit seeds, which may be prepared whole or blended until creamy. Loaded with proteins, a cup cooked is equal in calcium content to a quart of milk.

WHEAT. BULGAR is cracked, hulled, steamed, and dried berries of wheat. It has a nutty flavor and soft texture and can be used as a side dish (tabbouleh). **BRAN** is the outer coating of the wheat kernel and is primarily used for baking and in cereals. **CRACKED WHEAT** is crushed whole-wheat kernels with a flavor similar to that of wheatberries. It's used in cereals and crackers. **WHEAT GERM** is the seed of the wheat kernel and is used as a supplement and in baking. **WHEATBERRIES** are unprocessed whole-wheat kernels with a chewy texture. They are best used in salads and breads.

"Rice is born in water and must die in wine."

ITALIAN PROVERB

THE QUICK-FIX FAUX GRAIN: COUSCOUS

ANNIE SOMERVILLE

"Accept only that which contributes to the well-being of yourself and others." Such teachings of the

Buddha constituted much of Annie Somerville's early culinary training. At the San Francisco Zen Center,

Somerville was first and foremost a student of Zen; her position as head chef was considered a monastic

position. Yet it was there that she learned her other calling: cooking. In 1979, when Deborah Madison

founded Greens Restaurant in San Francisco, the vegetarian eatery was initially staffed by students whose

common goal was to bring Zen teachings into everyday life. Somerville trained under Madison and

eventually became executive chef. Today only a handful of students remain at the celebrated restaurant, but

Greens is still dedicated to fresh produce, accessible ingredients, and the gentle traditions of Zen Buddhism.

"Stocking your pantry with a few good oils and vinegars, dried mushrooms and
chiles, sun-dried tomatoes, olives, and capers may seem expensive, but just a little of
these fine ingredients will go a very long way to enhance your cooking."

CORN AND BULGUR SALAD WITH CILANTRO AND LIME

SERVES 4–6

½ cup bulgur
½ cup boiling water
1 tablespoon light olive oil
3 ears of corn, shaved (about 3 cups of kernels)
  Salt
¼ medium red onion, diced (about ½ cup)
1 jalapeño pepper, seeded and thinly sliced
1 tablespoon fresh lemon juice
1 tablespoon fresh lime juice
  Cayenne pepper
1 tablespoon coarsely chopped cilantro
1 tablespoon chopped fresh sage (about 5 leaves)

1. Place the bulgur in a medium-sized bowl and pour the boiling water over it. Cover and let sit for 20 minutes.

2. Meanwhile, heat the oil in a sauté pan. Add the corn and ¼ teaspoon salt and sauté over medium heat for 5 minutes. Add the onion and sauté for about 3 minutes, until the corn is tender. Allow to cool, then toss with the bulgur, jalapeño, lemon and lime juices, ½ teaspoon salt, and a few pinches of cayenne. Add salt if necessary. Toss in the cilantro and sage just before serving.

COUSCOUS SALAD WITH APRICOTS, PINE NUTS, AND GINGER

SERVES 4

1 cup instant couscous
2 tablespoons pine nuts, toasted
8 dried apricots, thinly sliced, about ⅓ cup
1 tablespoon dried currants
1 tablespoon golden raisins
2 teaspoons grated fresh ginger
¼ medium red onion, finely diced, about ½ cup
½ cup water
1 cup fresh orange juice
¼ cup light olive oil
  Champagne vinegar
  Salt

1. Pour the couscous grains into a small mixing bowl. Combine the water, orange juice, olive oil, and 2 tablespoons vinegar in a medium-sized saucepan.

2. Bring the liquid just to a boil and stir in the dried fruit, ginger, and ½ teaspoon salt; pour immediately over the couscous. Cover the bowl and let it sit for 20 minutes.

3. Bring a small pot of water to a boil and drop in the red onion for 15 seconds. Drain well; toss the onion with a few splashes of vinegar to draw out its pink color.

4. When the couscous is ready, gently fluff it with a fork and toss with the pine nuts and onion. Add salt to season and an additional splash of vinegar to brighten the flavor.

ANNIE SOMERVILLE

ON TOOLS. "Very clean hands are the best tools for tossing a salad. Toss the greens gently, being careful not to overdress them; you want to be able to taste them and enjoy their fresh flavor."

ON BEANS. "Beans…we never salt the cooking water—in our experience, it constricts the skins and increases the cooking time."

ON FRUIT. "Fresh fruit at its peak is a wonderful way to end a meal, particularly if you're short on time. Dress up a bowl of sliced peaches and berries with a pitcher of crème anglaise or a drizzle of fresh raspberry puree."

ON SALADS. "Our favorite salads are often the simplest, and it's always the freshness of the vegetables that makes them so remarkable."

ON VEGETABLES. "For fresh, clean tastes and textures we cook the vegetables in boiling water until just tender, then quickly rinse them under cool water to retain their vibrant color."

[OTHER FACTS—*page 279*]

TABBOULEH

Served at room temperature, tabbouleh provides the freshness of a salad and the heartiness of rice, which makes it a popular dish in hot Middle Eastern countries.

SERVES 4

1	cup bulgur wheat
1	cup boiling water
1	clove garlic, pressed or finely chopped
1	tablespoon olive oil
1	tablespoon red wine vinegar
2	tablespoons fresh lemon juice (about ½–1 lemon)
2	teaspoons soy sauce
½	medium red onion, chopped
1	bunch parsley, finely chopped (about 1 cup)
1	small bunch mint, finely chopped (about ½ cup)
2	cucumbers, peeled and diced
1	pint cherry tomatoes, cut in eighths Salt and pepper

OPTIONAL INGREDIENTS

⅓	cup currants
1	cup crumbled feta cheese

1. Combine the bulgur and the boiling water in a medium-sized mixing bowl and let sit for about 15 minutes, or until the water has been absorbed.

2. Add the remaining ingredients, except the currants and the feta, and stir gently to combine.

3. 🕐 Refrigerate for at least 2 hours to let the flavors blend. Just prior to serving, add currants and cheese, if desired. Add salt and pepper to taste.

"Anybody who eats three meals a day should understand why cookbooks outsell sex books three to one."

L. M. BOYD

COUSCOUS

This traditional North African food is the national dish of Morocco. Made out of semolina that has been cooked and then dried, it is effortless to prepare —literally, just add water. Though commonly perceived as a grain, couscous is really a kind of pasta. Like rice or Italian pasta, it is completely neutral and adapts well to most flavors. It was originally served alone with butter by the Berbers but later came to be paired with beans, vegetables, meats, chicken, lamb, and, of course, spices. It can be substituted for bulgur wheat and served plain, like rice.

BELL PEPPERS STUFFED WITH COUSCOUS

It's become a summer tradition for Jeffrey Miller, a stylist for Chic Simple, to serve this dish to his friends in Pretty Marsh, Maine. Jeffrey suggests using bell peppers of many colors for visual panache.

SERVES 4–6

1½	cups water or chicken or vegetable stock
1	cup couscous
4–6	red, orange, green, or yellow bell peppers, or a combination
½	cup currants, raisins, or sun-dried cherries
3	scallions, chopped
3–4	tablespoons chopped fresh dill
3–4	tablespoons chopped fresh mint
2	tablespoons fresh lemon juice (about ½ lemon)
2	tablespoons olive oil

1. Preheat oven to 325° F.

2. Place the water or stock in a small saucepan and bring to a boil. Add the couscous, cover, and remove pan from heat. Set aside for 5 minutes.

3. Slice tops off the peppers; reserve the tops. Scoop out the insides and discard. Chop the reserved tops. Stand the peppers in a baking pan just large enough to hold them snugly.

4. Remove the couscous from pan and place in mixing bowl. Add the chopped pepper tops and remaining ingredients and mix well. Divide the couscous mixture evenly among the peppers and place in the oven.

5. Cook for about 45 minutes, or until the peppers are soft.

BELL PEPPERS STUFFED WITH COUSCOUS

POLENTA

IN ITS SIMPLEST FORM

IS A MIX OF WATER AND

COARSE CORNMEAL. IT HAS

a soothing consistency and an

innocent flavor, especially when it's

first cooked, and is warm and soft

like tapioca pudding. But polenta

gets firmer as it cools. That's when it

becomes sophisticated, even racy,

and starts hanging around with wild

mushrooms, hard cheese, fresh

herbs, and other culinary bad boys.

Polenta, after all, is traditional in

Italian cooking. Gather up your

cornmeal and remember *La Dolce Vita.*

POLENTA

*Here are the basic goods, printed with
a warning. Beware: Polenta is
deliciously addictive.*

SERVES 4

4½ cups water or chicken stock
1 cup coarse cornmeal
1 teaspoon salt

OPTIONAL INGREDIENTS

¼ cup chopped fresh herbs,
such as parsley, basil, or
rosemary
¼ cup finely grated Parmesan
cheese, finely grated

1. Place the water or chicken stock in a medium-sized saucepan over high heat and bring it to a boil. Gradually add the cornmeal and salt.

2. Reduce heat to medium low and cook for about 40 minutes, or until the cornmeal becomes quite thick. If desired, add the herbs and cheese.

3. Serve as is or place in a lightly buttered 9-inch pie pan and refrigerate until ready to use.

TIP: Do not use instant polenta mix. Buy coarse cornmeal, if necessary in a specialty or health-food store.

MUSHROOM SAUCE

*You think you've found cornmeal nirvana?
Try this sauce on your polenta! You just
might up and move to Italy.*

SERVES 4

2 tablespoons olive oil
⅓ cup minced shallots (about
2 shallots)
1 large clove garlic, minced
1 pound sliced mushrooms
(shiitake, cremini, oyster,
or any combination)
1 teaspoon minced fresh thyme
Salt and pepper
2 tablespoons minced fresh
parsley, for garnish

1. Heat the olive oil in a large skillet over moderately high heat.

2. Add the shallots and cook, stirring, for 2 minutes, or until softened. Add the garlic and cook, stirring, 1 minute.

3. Add the mushrooms, thyme, and salt and pepper to taste, and cook the mixture over moderate heat, stirring occasionally, for 5–7 minutes, or until the mushrooms are firm and the liquid has evaporated.

3. Spoon the mushroom mixture over the polenta and garnish with parsley.

HOW TO EAT POLENTA 1. Eat it as soon as it's cooked, like mashed potatoes. 2. Put a dollop or two in soup or chili. 3. Let it cool and then make it into croutons (see page 31) and put them on your favorite soup or salad. 4. Let it cool, cut it into sections, and sauté the sections in a small amount of olive oil, like big croutons. 5. Let it cool, then grill or broil it for about 2 minutes per side. 6. Place it in a loaf pan, let it cool, then slice it like sandwich bread. 7. Serve it topped with Chili (see pages 162, 163, and 166), ratatouille, Eggplant Caponata (see page 116), sautéed wild mushrooms, Roasted Mixed Vegetables (see page 119), Tomato Sauce (see page 178), Roasted Bell Pepper Sauce (see page 180), or Spinach with Garlic and Pine Nuts (see page 108).

POLENTA WITH MUSHROOM SAUCE

R I C E

ARBORIO. This is the rice used to make risotto, a classic Northern Italian dish. Arborio is a short-grain, highly glutinous white rice that is grown primarily in the Po Valley of Italy. It has the distinction of absorbing flavors well and merging with liquids yet staying firm. It absorbs five times its weight in liquid, achieving a consistency that can only be described as creamy.

BASMATI. An aromatic rice, basmati is nutlike, buttery, and delicate. It is lower in starch than other long-grain rice and is used mainly in Indian cooking.

BROWN RICE. Higher in fiber, minerals, and other nutrients than any other type of rice, brown rice has been gaining in popularity over the years. It is chewier than white rice and takes quite a bit longer to cook. It can be used interchangeably in any recipe calling for white rice.

GLUTINOUS OR STICKY RICE. This very starchy short-grain rice is used mainly in Asian cooking. Its sticky consistency is perfect for molding into balls, cakes, or rice dumplings.

JASMINE. Available in white and brown, it is similar to basmati, although its texture is a little finer.

WHITE RICE. The most popular and convenient kind of rice, it is also the least nutritious. White rice has been stripped of most of the germ, the husk, and bran—all of which add nutrients and fiber.

WILD RICE. Wild rice is not rice at all, but a grass seed with a nutty and grainy flavor. Because it is expensive and richly flavored, wild rice is often mixed with other rices, especially brown rice.

STEAMED WHITE RICE

MAKES ABOUT 3–4 CUPS

1 cup long-grain white rice
2 cups water or any stock

Place rice and water in a medium-sized pot and bring to a boil. Reduce heat to very low, cover, and let cook for about 15 minutes.

STEAMED BROWN RICE

MAKES ABOUT 3–4 CUPS

1 cup long-grain brown rice
2½ cups water or any stock

Place rice and water in a medium-sized pot and bring to a boil. Reduce heat to very low, cover, and let cook about 45 minutes. For short-grain brown rice, use 2 cups of water; the yield will be 2–2½ cups.

WILD RICE

MAKES ABOUT 3–4 CUPS

1½ cups rice
6 cups water or any stock

Put 1½ cups rice in pot with 6 cups water, bring to boil, cover, and cook, partially covered, over low heat for about 45–50 minutes. Let sit 10 minutes and then cool. If necessary, drain.

OTHER CHOICES: Add all optional ingredients to cooked rice just before serving (except spice powders). **1.** Add fresh herbs, like parsley, basil, cilantro, and oregano. **2.** Add scallions or shallots. **3.** Add slivered almonds, curry powder, currants, and scallions. **4.** Add fresh peas and julienned carrots. **5.** Add diced red, yellow, or green bell peppers, cumin, and oregano. **6.** Mix in any kind of cheese. **7.** Add a whole fresh tomato, diced up, and some shredded basil. **8.** Add cooked black beans, cilantro, diced bell peppers or hot peppers, and chili powder. **9.** Add mushrooms that have been sautéed in wine. Portobellos sautéed in red wine or shiitake mushrooms sautéed in sake are excellent. **10.** Three minutes before cooking is completed add 1 small can of corn kernels or 2 ears of fresh corn kernels, precooked.

RISOTTO

IS NOT MERE RICE. YES, THE WORD MEANS "LITTLE RICE" IN ITALIAN, BUT RISOTTO IS NOT A CONVENIENCE FOOD. IT SHOULD BE LOVINGLY SIMMERED AND WATCHED LIKE A PUBESCENT CREATURE UNTIL THE VERY moment it matures. Then serve it quickly, before the corrupting influence of time is allowed to muddle its delicate nature.

BASIC RISOTTO

SERVES 4 AS MAIN COURSE, 8 AS SIDE DISH

- 1–2 teaspoons olive oil
- 1 medium Spanish onion finely chopped
- 2 cloves garlic, sliced
- 1½ cups Arborio rice (do not substitute any other kind)
- ½ cup white wine
- 4½ cups chicken or vegetable stock (see pages 19, 21) Parmesan cheese, freshly grated Salt and pepper

1. Heat oil in a large heavy-bottomed saucepan over medium-low heat and add onion and garlic. Cook until golden, or about 10 minutes.

2. Add rice and sauté 1 minute.

3. Add wine and simmer until it has been completely absorbed, stirring constantly and slowly.

4. Add stock, ½ cup at a time, until all the stock has been absorbed, continually stirring.

5. Serve immediately with Parmesan cheese. Add salt and pepper to taste.

RISOTTO WITH ASPARAGUS AND SHIITAKE MUSHROOMS

SERVES 4 AS MAIN COURSE, 8 AS SIDE DISH

- 1 pound asparagus, stems and tips separated, stems cut in thirds
- 4½ cups chicken or vegetable stock (see pages 19, 21)
- 1–2 teaspoons olive oil
- 1 small Spanish onion, finely chopped
- 2 cloves garlic, sliced
- ¼ pound fresh shiitake mushrooms (about 8–10), trimmed, wiped clean, and thinly sliced
- 1½ cups Arborio rice (do not substitute any other kind)
- ½ cup white wine Salt and pepper

OPTIONAL INGREDIENT

Parmesan cheese, to taste

1. Place the asparagus stems in a large skillet with ½ cup of the stock. Bring to a boil over high heat. Reduce heat to medium, cover, and cook about 5 minutes, or until the asparagus is bright green and somewhat tender. Place in a food processor fitted with a steel blade and process until puréed. Set the purée aside.

2. Heat the same pan over medium-low heat and add oil. When the oil is hot, add the onion, garlic, and mushrooms. Sauté until onion is golden, about 10 minutes.

3. Follow steps 2 through 4 from preceding Basic Risotto recipe.

4. When you have added all the stock and the rice is still slightly firm but tender, add the reserved asparagus purée and stir well. Add salt and pepper to taste.

5. If desired, add Parmesan cheese.

TIP: Time risotto carefully, it never tastes as good reheated.

RISOTTO WITH ASPARAGUS AND SHIITAKE MUSHROOMS

STUFFED RISOTTO TOMATOES

Joan Didion, whose books include Democracy, Miami, *and* After Henry, *is the author of this delicious solution to the leftover risotto.*

Raw unpeeled tomatoes
Leftover risotto
Chopped fresh mint
Pine nuts
Chopped cloves garlic
Black pepper
Shaved feta cheese

1. Slice the tops off as many raw unpeeled tomatoes as you want. (Small ones will hold together better.) Set the tops aside and scoop out the pulp and seeds. (You can throw the pulp and seeds away, but usually I purée it and freeze it to use when I need extra tomato flavor.) Place the tomato shells in a baking dish wiped with olive oil.

2. Mix the leftover risotto with chopped fresh mint, pine nuts, chopped garlic, black pepper, and shaved feta cheese. Stuff the tomatoes with this mixture, replace the tops, and put the uncovered baking dish in an oven preheated to 400–425° F. for about 30 minutes.

CURRIED RICE

SERVES 4

1 tablespoon olive oil
½ cup finely chopped onion
1 clove garlic, pressed
1 tablespoon curry powder

1 cup long-grain white rice
2 cups chicken stock
(see page 19)
⅔ cup currants or raisins
¼ cup cored and diced Granny Smith apple (leave skin on)
½ cup chopped pecans, almonds, or pistachios

1. Heat a medium saucepan over medium heat and add the oil. When the oil is hot, add the onion, garlic, and curry powder, and cook over medium-low heat, stirring occasionally, until the onion is soft, about 5 minutes.

2. Stir in the rice and broth and bring to a boil. Cover, reduce heat to low, and cook about 20 minutes, or until the broth has been absorbed.

3. Stir in currants or raisins, apple, and nuts. Serve immediately.

TIP: If currants or raisins are dried out, preplump by steeping them in warm water for 30 minutes (while the rice is cooking). Drain and discard water before adding fruit to rice.

WILD RICE AND TURKEY SALAD

Here's a whole new excuse to roast an unreasonably large turkey; the leftovers can contribute to this satisfying salad.

SERVES 4

2 teaspoons olive oil
1 red onion, thinly sliced, or 1 bunch scallions, chopped

4 cups cooked wild rice
(see page 143)
½ pound fresh, smoked, or leftover turkey or chicken, diced or shredded
1 beefsteak tomato, diced, or 1 pint cherry tomatoes, halved
¼ cup chopped fresh parsley

DRESSING

8 sun-dried tomatoes, chopped
2 cloves garlic, chopped or pressed
3 tablespoons red wine vinegar
3 tablespoons balsamic vinegar
1 tablespoon soy sauce
5 tablespoons olive oil

1. Heat a small nonstick skillet over medium heat and add the oil. When the oil is hot, add the onion or scallions and cook about 10 minutes, or until the onion is wilted. Set aside to cool.

2. Combine the wild rice, turkey or chicken, tomato, onion, and parsley in a large bowl and set aside.

3. To make the dressing, place all the ingredients except the olive oil in a blender or a food processor fitted with a steel blade and mix until well combined. While the motor is running, gradually add the olive oil.

4. Add the dressing to the rice mixture and serve either at room temperature or chilled.

WILD RICE AND TURKEY SALAD

THE STAF

Shelves of American supermarkets used to be dominated by bread that was soft, bland, and, predictably, a whiter shade of pale. Machine-made loaves were omnipresent, and so popular that even the soul-singing Supremes had their own brand of white bread. Italian breads and French breads were the exotics—curious long loaves, unapologetically formed by human hands. Over time, organically shaped loaves became the bread of choice at the dinner table; and whole-grain varieties gained new appeal. (Caraway-

"Eggs of an hour, bread of a day.

ITALIA

studded rye and marbleized pumpernickel began to look downright tame in comparison.) Today we've inherited the Earth—that is, wonderfully fragrant and pungent breads from Europe, Africa, and the other Americas. A note to those who still worship commercial white bread: It continues to be the bread of choice in Southern barbecue joints, and for children who strip off the crusts and squeeze it into hard little marbles, and the favorite of high-fashion models, who stuff it into their bras to create pleasing cleavage for swimsuit photos.

wine of a year, a friend of 30 years."

PROVERB

B R E A D

ANADAMA BREAD. Distinctive ingredients of this bread include cornmeal and molasses. Legend has it that a man was left at home to bake bread without a clear recipe from his wife. Frustrated and confused as to what to do, he went about the kitchen, throwing in lots of different flours, cursing her, "Anna, damn her."

BROWN BREAD. Its color is derived from unbleached graham or whole-wheat flour; Boston brown bread contains rye meal, cornmeal, graham flour, molasses, buttermilk, baking soda, and no yeast.

CHALLAH. A loosely braided egg bread, challah is usually associated with the Jewish sabbath. It also makes killer French toast.

CROSTINI. Crostini is simply toasted Italian bread with different toppings, most notably chopped fresh tomatoes, garlic, olive oil, and fresh basil.

FOCACCIA. An Italian flat bread, focaccia is reminiscent of pizza dough and is usually sprinkled with olive oil and herbs, notably rosemary (see recipe, page 207).

FOUGASSE. A flat bread that has been shaped. It is often studded with olives, sun-dried tomatoes, or vegetables.

FRENCH BAGUETTES. Long, thin loaves with crusty exteriors and a light, airy crumb.

ITALIAN BREAD. Traditionally made without salt, this kind of bread is baked in a wood-fired oven.

PAIN DE CAMPAGNE. Country-style French bread, it is usually a large, heavy loaf with a dark, caramelized crust. Although it is made mainly from white flour, it includes some whole-wheat flour as well.

PANINI. Small, Italian-style sandwiches, which have a variety of fillings, including mozzarella and prosciutto; chopped tomatoes and cheese; roasted peppers; black olives; assorted wild greens; or spreads such as pesto. They can be made with baguettes, rolls, or white sandwich bread.

PITA BREAD. These breads are made when rounds of dough puff out and deflate during the baking process. Although they look unleavened, they're not.

POLENTA (see page 140). Made out of coarse cornmeal, polenta can be poured into a loaf pan and refrigerated until it is set. It can then be sliced like bread and either grilled, toasted, or broiled for a few minutes per side.

PUMPERNICKEL. Made with unsifted rye flour, pumpernickel has a rugged texture, a dark brown color, and a strong, bitter flavor. The word derives from an insulting eighteenth-century German term for referring to a flatulent person, presumably someone whose excessive amount of digestive gas is linked to consuming this kind of bread.

RYE BREAD. Made with flour milled from the same common grain used in livestock feed. The grain is also fermented to make rye whiskey.

SEVEN-GRAIN. Bread that includes seven of the following whole grains: soy flour, alfalfa sprouts, corn, wheat, rye, oats, brown rice, millet, sesame or sunflower seeds.

SOURDOUGH BREAD. Sourdough bread is made from a "starter" consisting of flour and water that ferments as it catches airborne yeast, giving the bread its distinctive sourness.

TUSCAN BREAD. A robust, round bread from Northern Italy, Tuscan bread has the texture of sourdough but not the bite.

WHITE BREAD. Made with unbleached flour, sugar and/or corn syrup, it is the most popular bread in the United States.

TUSCAN BREAD AND VIRGIN OLIVE OIL

B E A N S

"Red beans and ricely yours,"

the way **LOUIS ARMSTRONG** *signed his letters*

BEANS AND RICE

*Campfires along the Snake River, student
budget fare, local Spanish diner cuisine: beans
and rice are a delicious staple of many cultures,
and are nutritionally sound enough to stand
solo at suppertime.*

SERVES 4

2 teaspoons olive oil
2 cloves garlic, finely chopped
   or pressed
1 small onion, chopped
¼ teaspoon cayenne pepper
¼ teaspoon cumin
1 teaspoon red wine vinegar
2 cups prepared red kidney or
   black beans, rinsed and drained
1-2 cups water or chicken or
   vegetable stock (see pages 19, 21)
   Salt
3–4 cups white or brown rice,
   cooked (see page 143)

1. Heat a large skillet over medium-low
heat and add oil. When the oil is hot, add
the garlic and onion and sauté for about
10 minutes, or until the onion is golden.

2. Reduce heat to low, add the spices,
vinegar, beans, water or stock and cook
for about 20 minutes, or until the beans
become very soft. Add salt to taste.

3. Serve the beans on top of the rice.

B E A N S

MAYBE WE DIDN'T LOVE THEM BECAUSE THEY WERE SO BORINGLY ECONOMICAL. THEN WE LEARNED THAT THEY'RE PROTEIN-PACKED, LOW IN CALORIES, AND LOW IN FAT. IT STARTED TO DAWN ON US that beans weren't just for starving sailors or plates of franks. We discovered Southwestern chilis, Mexican bean soups, Tuscan bean salads. Our local grocers brought us fava beans, navy beans, cranberry beans. We wised up and learned there was a whole vocabulary of beans out there waiting to be taste-tested.

CANNED BEANS. Because canned beans are packed in liquid, they are conveniently soft enough to eat or cook with as is. One thing to keep in mind, however, is that the degree of softness is predetermined, and some complain that canned beans are too salty. Although they're still very reasonably priced as compared to other foods, canned beans are proportionately more expensive than dried. **COOKING WITH CANNED BEANS.** Canned beans, particularly those that originate in Italy, are usually of such high quality that they can be substituted for dried beans in any recipe. Be somewhat watchful of the cooking time; sometimes they are softer and require less time. Typically, a 16-ounce can of beans, drained and rinsed, will yield 1¾–2 cups of beans.

DRIED BEANS. Some people prefer dried beans because more varieties are available and they are considerably cheaper. They have no additives and last longer than canned beans. However, they are not for the impatient chef. They must be picked over and then soaked or boiled. **COOKING WITH DRIED BEANS.** Before the beans get in the pot, pick over the beans, looking out for any withered ones, pebbles, or debris. To get rid of dust, rinse several times until the water runs clear. Put beans in a bowl of water and discard any that float. Due to their small size, it is not necessary to presoak or precook lentils or split peas. Always discard the soaking or cooking water. Don't fear you're losing nutrients; tests have found that beans cooked up to 75 minutes retained 70–90 percent of most vi-

tamins and minerals. The next time you want to prepare some dried beans but don't want to cope with overnight soaking or with hours' worth of boiling, try this: **THE QUICK-COOK METHOD.** Place the beans in a large pot and cover them with cold water. Bring to a boil, reduce to low, partially cover, and gently simmer for about 1–2 hours, or until soft. Keep checking to be sure you have enough liquid; add water as needed. Always simmer dried beans; boiling will cause the cooking liquid to overflow and the beans will break apart. Salting the cooking liquid for dried beans will slow the cooking and toughen the beans. If salt is desired, add it after the beans are cooked. Some beans, like white cannellini beans, will cook in less time; others, like black turtle beans, will take a little longer. (For **MICROWAVE BEANS,** see page 168.)

[🫘 BEANS *first aid—page 264*]

DRIED KIDNEY BEANS

SPICY BLACK BEAN SALAD

SERVES 4

4 cups prepared black beans, rinsed and drained
3 tablespoons lime juice, freshly squeezed (about 1 fresh lime)
2 tablespoons olive oil
1 tablespoon red wine vinegar
1 teaspoon salt
1/2 teaspoon cayenne pepper
2 scallions, chopped
1/4 cup chopped fresh cilantro
2 fresh or roasted red bell peppers, chopped

1. Place the beans in a medium-sized ceramic or glass bowl and add lime juice, olive oil, vinegar, salt, and cayenne, and mix until well combined.

2. Top with scallions, cilantro, and peppers, but do not combine.

3. Cover and refrigerate for at least 2 hours to let the flavors meld.

4. Toss just prior to serving.

REFRIED BEANS

Refried beans deserve the same attention as risotto. Encourage the beans to get thick. Add the water slowly. And have a beer while you wait.

MAKES 8 CUPS

1 recipe Beans and Rice, without the rice (see page 155)
1 tablespoon olive oil

OPTIONAL INGREDIENT

2–3 tablespoons sour cream
1 fresh or canned tomato, coarsely chopped
1 red bell pepper, diced
2 tablespoons chopped fresh cilantro
Hot sauce, to taste

1. Follow Beans and Rice recipe, step 1, using 1 tablespoon oil.

2. Reduce the heat to low and add the beans, 1/2 cup at a time, each time mashing them with the back of a wooden spoon. In between the beans, add water or stock, slowly, stirring often until the liquid is absorbed. Also add the spices and vinegar.

3. Continue adding and mashing the beans, until the beans have formed a thick paste. Add salt and pepper to taste.

OTHER CHOICES: If calories are not a concern, add the sour cream to the bean mixture before serving. This recipe also makes a great dip, warm or chilled.

BLACK BEAN SOUP

MAKES 10–12 CUPS

1 pound dried black beans, quick-cooked until soft
8 cups water or chicken stock
2 carrots, diced
2 stalks celery, diced
1 small red onion, chopped
1 red bell pepper, diced
4 cloves garlic, finely chopped or pressed
1 slice fresh ginger, the size of a quarter, finely chopped
2 teaspoons chili powder
2 teaspoons ground cumin
2 bay leaves
1/2–1 teaspoon cayenne pepper

TOPPINGS

Limes
Chopped fresh cilantro
Chopped fresh basil
Chopped scallions
Sour cream or yogurt

1. Place all the ingredients (except the optional ones) in a heavy-bottomed 8-quart stockpot and bring to a gentle boil.

2. Reduce heat to low and cook, partially covered, for about 2–4 hours, depending upon consistency desired.

3. If you want a puréed soup or partially puréed soup, simply place at least half the soup, in batches, in a blender or food processor fitted with a steel blade and blend until smooth.

4. Just prior to serving, squeeze the juice of 1/4 lime on each serving and garnish with cilantro, basil, scallions, and sour cream or yogurt.

SPICY BLACK BEAN SALAD

ANAHEIM

POBLANO

RED SERRANO

YELLOW HABANERO

GREEN HABANERO

CUBANELLE

JALAPEÑO

FLAMING HOTS

YEOW!! YOU'VE JUST CUT A CHILE PEPPER AND RUBBED YOUR

EYE WITH A FINGER, AND NOW YOU'RE YELLING, HOPPING AROUND THE

KITCHEN, DOING AN ARM-FLAPPING BUCK 'N' WING. IT WAS THE CAPSAICINOIDS, YOU

know, that just seared your flesh. They're the incendiary substances that make hot peppers hot and that cause your

chilis and salsas to rock 'n' roll. Chile peppers can be used like a spice to provide specific kinds of flavors and specific

levels of heat. If you want a slow, subtle burn, try cayenne in chilis and stews. The high-pitched kick of jalapeño is

ideal for traditional salsas. And if you seek eye-watering, nose-exploding, full-body combustion, go for the habanero peppers.

ANAHEIM PEPPERS (also known as New Mexican). Pale green and tapered, these are the mildest of all the green chiles and are particularly good roasted. They can usually be found stuffed, as in chiles rellenos.

CAYENNE PEPPERS. Red, long, thin, and pointed, these are extremely hot and are most often used in powdered form, as ground cayenne pepper.

CUBANELLES. Light green and tapered, mild and sweet. They can be substituted for anaheims in most recipes.

HABANERO PEPPERS. Also known as Scotch Bonnets, they come in yellow, orange, and green. They are lantern-shaped and fiercely hot.

JALAPEÑO PEPPERS. The most commonly used chile pepper. They are usually dark green, although sometimes red, and are about 1½ inches long and are tapered at the end. They are very hot and can be eaten raw or cooked.

POBLANO PEPPERS. The dark green form of the ancho chile. They are about 5 inches long and tapered at the end. They range from mild to hot. They are often roasted and peeled for chiles rellenos.

SERRANO PEPPERS. They come in red and green, are about 2 inches long, and are considered to be the hottest chile available. They are often used in salsa. You can substitute half a serrano for one whole jalapeño.

THAI PEPPERS. Bright red or dark green, these are about 4 inches long, thin, and pointed. They are extremely hot and can be substituted for serranos. Eat at your own risk.

D E V I L ' S

Legend has it that Kit Carson, as he lay dying, moaned, "Wish I had time for just one more bowl of chili." Most

probably his chili didn't have tomatoes, garlic, onions, oregano, or even beans—a ragged stew of tough,

stringy beef and rip-roaring chile peppers. The peppers were always a form of tenderizer, concealer, and

preservative. Today's chili comes as you like it. Everything has made its debut in the big bowl of red—from

tofu on the West Coast to maple syrup in the Northeast. Chili fanatics are everywhere. It's a regional thing: Texas

BLACK BEAN CHILI

MAKES ABOUT 12–14 CUPS

1 tablespoon olive oil
1 medium Spanish onion, coarsely chopped
1 red onion, coarsely chopped
3–4 cloves garlic, finely chopped or pressed
1 red bell pepper, diced
1–3 tablespoons ground cumin
2 tablespoons dried Greek oregano
1–3 tablespoons chili powder
2 bay leaves
4 1-pound cans whole tomatoes, in their juice, coarsely chopped

6–8 cups water or chicken stock, or more if needed
4 cups dried black beans, quick-cooked (see page 156) or 12 cups canned black beans, rinsed and drained
Salt and pepper

TOPPINGS

Fresh cilantro, chopped
Fresh basil, chopped
Bell pepper, diced
Sour cream or yogurt
Cheddar or Monterey Jack cheese, grated
Scallions, chopped

1. Heat a large stockpot over a medium-low flame and add the oil. When the oil is hot, add the onions, garlic, bell pepper, and spices, and cook, covered, until the vegetables are soft.

2. Raise heat to high, add the bay leaves, tomatoes, water or stock, and beans, and bring to a boil.

3. Reduce heat to low and cook, partially covered, for 2 hours, or until the beans are very soft and the soup has thickened to desired consistency. If necessary, add additional water or stock. Add salt and pepper to taste.

4. Garnish with any or all of the suggested toppings and serve.

OTHER CHOICES: This chili will thicken overnight and become the ideal filling for flour tortillas.

S O U P

aficionados scream at the sight of chopped onions on top; Northerners are appalled by chili that lacks a sprinkle

of cheese. Even the meats have strayed from the early favorites of buffalo, Texas longhorns, and venison to lamb,

pork, and chicken. Unlike other spicy foods, chili is rated on an alarm system. Although it's not a scientific

formula, one can be sure that a three-alarm chili is alarming indeed. (Still, whoever heard of one-alarm chili?)

The great bowls of simmering spice have found fame through sheer bravado and machismo. Chili bites back.

BEEF CHILI WITH BEER

MAKES ABOUT 8 CUPS

- 1 teaspoon olive oil
- 1 medium Spanish onion, chopped
- 4 cloves garlic, chopped or pressed
- 1 pound beef stew meat, cut in 1-inch cubes, or ground beef
- 1–3 tablespoons chili powder
- 2 tablespoons dried oregano
- 1 teaspoon ground cumin
- 1 teaspoon ground cinnamon
- 1 12-ounce bottle beer (any kind will do)
- 2 canned chipotle chiles (smoked jalapeños) in adobo sauce or 2 dried chipotle chiles, chopped
- 1 cup water

OPTIONAL INGREDIENTS

- 1 28-ounce can crushed tomatoes
- 2 16-ounce cans dark red kidney beans or black beans, drained and rinsed
  Salt and pepper

TOPPINGS

(See Black Bean Chili, page 162)

1. Heat the oil in a large skillet over a medium-low flame. When the oil is hot, add the onion and garlic, and cook until golden, about 5 minutes. Add the beef, herbs, and spices, and cook until the beef is well browned. Remove any excess fat from the pan. Add the beer, chipotles, and water, and cook for about 1 hour, or until the beef is tender. Do not let it boil. If a spicy, beef-only chili is desired, it can be served at this point.

2. Add the tomatoes and/or beans, if desired, and cook for 20–30 minutes, or until the beans have softened a bit.

3. Add salt and pepper to taste, and serve with your choice of topping.

BLACK BEAN CHILI

JALAPEÑO CORN BREAD

Corn bread aficionados, like refried-bean fans, are divided into two camps: Some like it sweet. Some like it hot. But with or without an incendiary punch, this corn bread's moist, chewy texture is a sure hit. Also great served in a shallow pool of dark honey.

MAKES 9 GENEROUS SQUARES

1 cup yellow cornmeal
1½ cups unbleached all-purpose flour
2 teaspoons baking powder
1 teaspoon salt
2–3 tablespoons sugar or honey
1 large egg, lightly beaten
1½ cups plain yogurt, buttermilk, or sour cream
1 cup creamed corn (canned)
¼ cup vegetable oil

OPTIONAL INGREDIENTS

1 bunch scallions, finely chopped
1 jalapeño pepper, finely minced
1 teaspoon black pepper

1. Preheat oven to 350° F. Lightly grease an 8-inch-square baking pan.

2. Combine the cornmeal, flour, baking powder, salt, and sugar or honey in a large mixing bowl. In a separate bowl, combine the egg, yogurt, buttermilk, or sour cream, creamed corn, and vegetable oil. Add the egg mixture to the flour mixture and stir until just blended. For a spicy corn bread, stir in the scallions, jalapeño, and/or black pepper.

3. Spoon the batter into prepared pan and bake for 45–55 minutes, or until the bread is just beginning to get golden. Do not let it brown.

VEGETABLE CHILI

This has everything you love about chili—minus the unwelcome fat. Even hard-core carnivores won't miss the beef.

SERVES 8

2 teaspoons olive or canola oil
2 Spanish onions, coarsely chopped
4 cloves garlic, finely chopped
2 bell peppers, any combination of colors, coarsely chopped
1 small eggplant, peeled, if desired, and cubed, or 3 zucchini, cubed
1 tablespoon dried oregano
1–2 tablespoons chili powder
2 teaspoons crushed red pepper flakes
1 tablespoon ground cumin
1 teaspoon cayenne pepper
1 16-ounce can or 2 cups cooked white beans, rinsed and drained
1 16-ounce can or 2 cups cooked black beans, rinsed and drained
4 16-ounce cans dark red kidney beans, rinsed and drained
1 cup dried lentils, washed and picked over for stones
2 20-ounce cans whole tomatoes, coarsely chopped, with juice
Chopped fresh cilantro or basil

1. Heat the oil in an 8-quart stockpot over medium heat. When the oil is hot, add the onions, garlic, peppers, eggplant or zucchini, and spices, and cook until the vegetables are golden, about 10 minutes.

2. Reduce the heat to low and add beans, lentils, and tomatoes, and cook, covered, for 1–2 hours, stirring occasionally.

3. Just prior to serving, add cilantro or basil.

"Dinner, a time when...one should eat wisely but not too well, and talk well, but not too wisely."

W. SOMERSET MAUGHAM

VEGETABLE CHILI AND JALAPEÑO CORN BREAD

MICROWAVE BEANS

SERVES 4

1 pound dried beans (see page 169), rinsed and picked over
4 cups water

OPTIONAL INGREDIENTS

1 ham hock
1 cup coarsely chopped celery
1 small onion, sliced
2 teaspoons salt
1/4 teaspoon black pepper

1. Place the beans and the water in a 3-quart microwave-proof casserole.

2. ⏲ Cover and cook over high heat for 30 minutes or until boiling. Reduce heat to medium and cook for about 1 hour, or until tender, stirring every 30 minutes.

PASTA E FAGIOLI

An old standby in traditional Italian restaurants, this modernized version employs ginger and fresh rosemary for a distinctly up-to-date flavor.

SERVES 4

4 strips thick-cut bacon, chopped, or 1 tablespoon olive oil
1 medium Spanish onion, chopped
2 stalks celery, chopped
2 carrots, chopped
2 cloves garlic, finely chopped or pressed

1 slice fresh ginger (the size of a quarter), finely chopped
1/4–1/2 teaspoon crushed red pepper flakes 🪨
1 28-ounce can "chunk style" tomatoes
3 cups chicken or vegetable stock (see pages 19, 21)
1 teaspoon dried rosemary or 1 tablespoon fresh
2 16–20-ounce cans cannellini or fava beans, drained and rinsed, or about 4 cups cooked white beans
2 cups medium-sized shaped pasta, such as penne, rigatoni, or conchiglie

1. Cook the bacon in a stockpot over medium-low heat until rendered of all fat. Discard all but 1 tablespoon of the bacon fat. Remove the bacon from pan and reserve it for later use. Or, if you are not using bacon, heat oil over medium-low heat.

2. Place the onion, celery, carrots, garlic, and ginger in the pot, and cook until the vegetables are tender, about 20 minutes.

3. Add the crushed red pepper flakes, tomatoes, and stock. If you are using dried rosemary, add it now. Raise heat to medium high and bring to a low boil. Reduce heat to low and cook for 1 hour.

4. Add the beans and reserved bacon and cook until heated through, about 5–10 minutes.

5. While the beans are cooking, bring a large pot of water to boil. Cook the pasta until al dente and drain. Just before serving, add pasta to bean mixture and sprinkle with fresh rosemary, if desired.

6. Serve from the pot or place in a large bowl.

WHITE BEAN SALAD WITH ROSEMARY AND BASIL

SERVES 4

1 16-ounce can small white cannellini beans, drained and rinsed
1/2 small red onion, coarsely chopped
1 tablespoon and 1 teaspoon chopped fresh rosemary
2 teaspoons olive oil
1 tablespoon balsamic vinegar
2 teaspoons red wine vinegar
1 tablespoon chopped fresh basil
5 cherry tomatoes, halved
Salt and pepper

1. Combine all the ingredients in a medium-sized serving bowl.

2. ⏲ Let sit at room temperature for 1 hour while the flavors blend. Add salt and pepper to taste.

3. Serve at room temperature.

BEAN COUNTERS

MIGHT NOT HAVE TOPPLED FROM THEIR MID-'80S PROMINENCE HAD THEY BEEN CALLED "LEGUME TALLIERS." SINCE TIME BEGAN, BEANS HAVE BEEN A SOLID INVESTMENT, AS THEY ARE FOREVER rich—true nutritional portfolio builders. They have twice the protein of grains, and when combined with rice or pasta, beans supply all the amino acids a body needs. A bowl of *Pasta e fagioli*, a plate of black beans and rice, a side of refrieds wrapped with texmati in a tortilla—the bottom line is health and happy taste buds.

BLACK OR TURTLE BEANS. Native to South America. Small, with a shiny exterior and a rich interior. They make a wonderful soup (see page 158) and are excellent boiled, mashed, and served with melting squares of cheese.

BLACK-EYED PEAS. As common in the South as navy beans are in the Northeast, black-eyed peas are medium-sized, pale yellow beans with a black keel and thin skin. Cook them with molasses or with chili; serve them in soups or with rice. They are particularly high in fiber.

CANNELLINI BEANS. A white kidney bean, favored for *pasta e fagioli*, it is available both dried and canned, and is commonly used in Italian cuisine.

FLAGEOLETS. The immature seeds of kidney beans are known as flageolets. The caviar of the bean world, they are removed from the pod when tender and just maturing.

GARBANZO BEANS. These small, hard little nutlike beans (also called chickpeas) are used to make hummus and falafel. Toss them in salads for added texture.

GREAT NORTHERN BEANS. These are the beans used to make Boston baked beans and minestrone-type soups.

HARICOT BEANS. These are the wide variety of legume seeds. The mature seeds come in assorted sizes and may be either creamy white and slightly kidney-shaped (Great Northern, navy, small white, white kidney, cannellini, and yankee beans), or pink to red to reddish brown kidney shapes (kidney red, pink, pinto, and Mexican beans). The following are all haricots.

MEXICAN BEANS. One of the many varieties of pinkish, kidney-shaped beans.

PINK BEANS. These beans are also used in Mexican dishes such as refried beans. They provide a good base for intense spices.

PINTO BEANS. Essential in all Tex-Mex and Mexican dishes, these are the beans that flavor chili and refried bean dishes.

RED KIDNEY BEANS. This large, red kidney-shaped bean is one of the more common beans and a favorite in chili, beans and rice, and pork dishes.

RED LENTILS AND GREEN LENTILS. Probably the oldest cultivated legume, lentils are tiny, lens-shaped, dried pulses (legume seeds). The most widely available variety is grayish brown, though there are also red, green, and yellow lentils. They are great served alone, or added to soups and stews, or dressed with vinaigrette and served as a salad. Green lentils are known as the gourmet lentil; the best variety comes from the South of France.

YELLOW SPLIT PEAS. Field peas are a variety of yellow or green peas grown specifically for drying. These peas are dried and usually split along a natural seam. Most frequently found in split-pea soup.

BLACK (OR TURTLE) BEANS

RED LENTILS

BLACK-EYED PEAS

RED KIDNEY BEANS

CANNELLINI BEANS

PINK BEANS

YELLOW
SPLIT
PEAS

GREAT
NORTHERN
BEANS

GREEN LENTILS

MEXICAN BEANS

FLAGEOLETS

PASTA

In a month's time (if *the winds* are not *against* you) you will arrive on the affluent island of Sicily, where you will eat some of those macaroni that have taken their name from [the Greek word] "beatify": they are usually cooked together with fat capons and fresh cheese, dripping butter and milk on all sides, and then, using a wide and liberal hand, sprinkled with sugar and cinnamon of the finest that can be found. Oh dear, how my mouth waters just remembering them.

ORTENSIO LANDI, *Secretary to Lucrezia Gonzaga, sixteenth century*

SPAGHETTI WITH GARLIC
AND OLIVE OIL

*Pasta can be lavished with cheeses, meats, and
sauces, but the simplest pasta
dishes start with garlic and olive oil as
the common denominator.*

SERVES 6–8

1 pound spaghetti
½ cup olive oil
6 cloves garlic, thinly sliced or
   crushed in a press
   Kosher salt and coarsely
   ground pepper, to taste

OPTIONAL INGREDIENTS

¼ teaspoon crushed red pepper flakes
⅓ cup toasted pine nuts (see page 181)

1. Bring a large pot of water to boil. Add the spaghetti.

2. Heat a large skillet over medium-low heat and add the oil. When the oil is hot, add the garlic and crushed red pepper flakes, if desired, and sauté until the garlic is golden, about 3 minutes.

3. Cook the pasta until it is al dente. Drain cooked pasta and add it to the garlic and olive oil mixture in skillet. Add salt and pepper to taste. Mix well and serve immediately. Just prior to serving, add the pine nuts, if desired.

OTHER CHOICES: For an equally delicious but reduced-fat version, reduce the olive oil to ¼ cup and when adding pasta to the skillet, add ½ cup chicken stock.

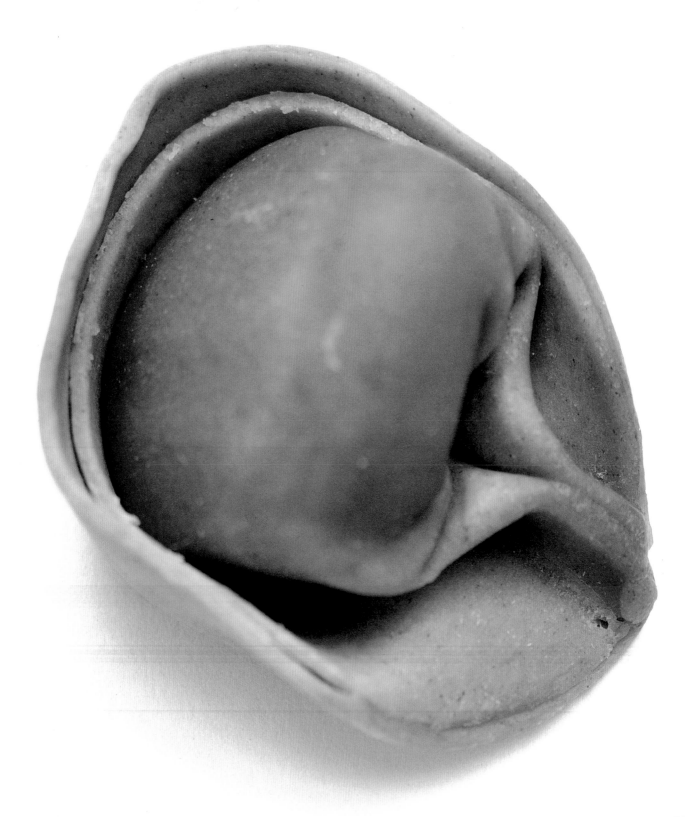

SPINACH TORTELLINI

PASTA

WAS IT MARCO POLO WHO, TREKKING FROM FARTHEST CHINA, BROUGHT PASTA ALL THE WAY TO THE SHORES OF ITALY? OR SHOULD WE THANK THAT YOUNG WOMAN WHO STOPPED TO DALLY WITH her lover? They say, you know, that she was carrying a basket of uncooked dough. While the couple was enjoying nonculinary delights, the dough seeped through and formed spaghetti. No. We have our favorite story about the origin of pasta. It's an uncomplicated tale—simply that it was created by a magician in Sicily. Pasta is magic, after all. Everyone from grandmas to babies loves it; marathon runners need it; cooks have been endlessly inspired by its easy possibilities. Noodles, shells, alphabets, orzo, angel hair. Pasta is the staples of staples, magic.

FIRMNESS. We like our pasta cooked al dente, which leaves pasta slightly underdone with a chewy consistency—pleasurable "to the tooth," as any Italian will tell you. To check if your pasta is done, lift out one strand and break it with your fingernail. If it feels too hard, keep that pasta pot boiling. You can also tooth-test for the right firmness.

FRESH VS. DRIED. Imported dry pastas are easier to cook al dente than domestic and fresh pastas. Soft, fresh pasta is usually used for butter-based and cream-based sauces; dried for oil-based and shellfish sauces. Because it holds its shape well, dried pasta is a better choice for heavy, chunky vegetable sauces. Ridged and shell-shaped pastas are good for meat sauces because they trap the bits of meat in the ridges and hollows.

PASTA COURSE. Pasta may be used in every course of the meal, from the first course to dessert. Sweet dishes include kugel noodles baked with cottage cheese, eggs, sugar, raisins, and cinnamon. In France, vermicelli is simmered in cream with sugar, spices, lemon peel, and eggs, then baked like a soufflé.

"Everything you see I owe to spaghetti."
SOPHIA LOREN

[PASTA *first aid—page 264*]

TOMATO SAUCE

This 15-minute sauce requires no special ingredients, yet its clean, bright flavor can enliven almost everything—try it on polenta, broccoli, fish, spaghetti squash, and, of course, pasta.

MAKES 3 CUPS

1	tablespoon olive oil
4–6	cloves garlic, coarsely chopped
3	shallots, finely chopped
1	35-ounce can whole plum tomatoes, drained and pulp squeezed dry
1	tablespoon dried basil
1	28-ounce can crushed tomatoes
¼	cup red wine
8	fresh basil leaves, chiffonade (see page 272) Shavings of Parmesan cheese

1. Heat a large skillet over medium heat and add oil. When the oil is hot, add the garlic and shallots. Sauté until garlic is golden, about 2–3 minutes.

2. Add the whole plum tomatoes and mash until the tomatoes are coarsely chopped. If you are using dried basil, add it now.

3. Mix in the crushed tomatoes and red wine. Cook until sauce simmers, approximately 5 minutes. Reduce heat to low for another 5 minutes.

4. Top each serving with fresh basil and Parmesan shavings.

TOOLS

WHAT. Colander

WHY. This upstanding sieve should be sturdy enough to endure the heat and weight of draining a batch of pasta—stainless steel models are preferred to plastic.

SAUCE ETIQUETTE

Some like to toss the pasta in with the sauce and others prefer to serve the sauce on top of a virginal "bed" of pasta. Pro-mixers swear that by mixing the sauce into the pasta right after it has been drained, the pores of the pasta absorb the sauce's flavor and hence enhance the flavor of the dish. Some recipes make the decision for you. Cream sauces are generally incorporated into the pasta when served. Long pasta, like spaghetti, should get a light sauce, whereas short, shaped pasta warrants a heavier sauce. Tiny pastas, like orzo, are best in a soup.

MEAT SAUCE

A traditional Italian native takes on a French accent with subtle marjoram, white wine, and fennel.

MAKES 10-12 CUPS

2	teaspoons olive oil or chicken stock
1	medium Spanish onion, chopped
4	cloves garlic, chopped
1	tablespoon dried marjoram
2	teaspoons dried basil
2	teaspoons fennel seed
¼–½	teaspoon crushed red pepper flakes
1–1¼	pounds lean ground beef
2	28-ounce cans crushed tomatoes
½	cup white wine

1. Heat a large skillet over medium heat and add the oil or chicken stock. When the oil is hot, add the onion, garlic, herbs, and red pepper flakes, and cook, stirring occasionally, until the onion is golden, for 3–5 minutes.

2. Add the beef and stir until it loses its raw color.

3. Add the tomatoes and white wine and cook, uncovered, over lowest heat, for about 3 hours. Stir occasionally. If the sauce becomes too thick, add small amounts of water or stock 1 tablespoon at a time.

"Ragú. Now, that's Italian!"

RAGÚ COMMERCIAL FROM THE 1970S

TOMATO SAUCE

S A U C E

Simple or sinful, sauce makes the dish. If it's really good, you'll want to skip the entrée and drench a loaf of fresh warm bread in it or, when no one's looking, lick the plate clean with your fingers to savor every last drop. Think of eating your favorite dishes without it. Fettuccine without Alfredo? Mussels without marinara? Macaroni without cheese? Just dreadful.

PESTO

Pesto is so intense that, like hot fudge, a little goes a long way. When creating a pasta dish, toss it with pesto so that the noodles are evenly coated. For a memorable salad, coat pieces of cheese and grilled meat with pesto, then add to crunchy greens.

MAKES 1 ¾ CUPS

2 cloves garlic
1 large bunch fresh basil, leaves only (about 2–2½ cups, packed)
¼ cup pine nuts, pecans, or walnuts
¾ cup grated Parmesan cheese
½ cup olive oil

1. Place garlic in the bowl of a food processor fitted with a steel blade and chop until fine. Add basil, pine nuts, pecans, or walnuts, and process until fully blended.

2. Add Parmesan cheese and very, very slowly add olive oil, gradually increasing the amount.

NOTE: Pesto freezes well and has a refrigerator life of about 3 days. Be sure to add a thin layer of olive oil on top of pesto before storing. Pesto can also be frozen in ice-cube trays and then defrosted and used as needed.

ROASTED BELL PEPPER SAUCE

Roasted peppers add color in more ways than one. They smell wonderful, and those cooks with gas stoves can have the added fun of roasting peppers directly on the stovetop's blue flame.

MAKES 2 CUPS

6 red, orange, or yellow roasted bell peppers (see page 119)
2–4 cloves garlic
2 tablespoons olive oil
½–1 cup water from cooked pasta or chicken stock

1. Place roasted peppers, garlic, and olive oil in a food processor fitted with a steel blade. Purée.

2. Add water from cooked pasta or stock to pepper purée and mix thoroughly.

PASTA GARNISH

The whole point of garnish is that it's supposed to be pretty. Pasta dishes benefit from a bit of gussying up now and then, but they've got to taste right. Count on these toppings to lend a little cachet to your *capelli d'angelo.*

1. Shredded cheese 2. Parsley 3. Basil 4. Chives 5. Other fresh herbs 6. Toasted nuts 7. Zests 8. Bacon bits 9. Chopped olives 10. Prosciutto 11. Pimiento or roasted red peppers

SEASONAL SAUCE

Let the seasons inspire your sauces. Think of chilled pasta with a pesto topping for a late summer lunch or the filling warmth of a hearty Alfredo sauce in the dead of winter. Seasonal sauces create a mood that you will crave year-round.

REDUX

Once you've got a really good sauce in your repertoire, you'll find that it's destined to graduate from the pasta bowl and go on to grace a whole variety of dishes. When thickened, a sauce becomes a spread for sandwiches; when whipped, it's a dressing for crudités; when thinned, it becomes a dipping sauce for cold meats and warm bread.

PINE NUTS

are also known as pignoli because they come from cones of several pine trees, including the piñon. They are creamy and sweet and should be used sparingly because they are both high in fat and very expensive.

SAUCE & SANDWICH COMBOS

1. Tomato, Basil, Mozzarella, and Pesto Sauce on Focaccia Bread 2. Grilled Eggplant and Roasted Pepper Sauce Purée on French Bread

PUTTANESCA SAUCE

This traditional mixture borrows its name from the Italian word for "slutty"—a reference, perhaps, to its pungent flavor. Or maybe to its unholy yet very sensual mingling of ingredients.

SERVES 6–8

1	pound cooked pasta
1	teaspoon olive oil
4	cloves garlic, chopped or pressed
2	28-ounce cans plum tomatoes, drained and coarsely chopped
2–3	tablespoons capers, drained and rinsed
1–2	teaspoons dried oregano
1	teaspoon dried basil
1/4–1/2	teaspoon crushed red pepper flakes
1/2	cup Greek or French olives (see page 187), pitted and chopped
1/2–1	cup water from cooked pasta or chicken stock
1/2	cup coarsely chopped fresh parsley

1. Heat a large skillet over medium-low heat and add olive oil. When the oil is hot, add garlic and sauté until golden, or about 2 minutes.

2. Add remaining ingredients except pasta water or chicken stock and parsley. Bring to a boil. Reduce heat to low and cook for about 20 minutes.

3. Stir in reserved pasta water or stock. Garnish with fresh parsley.

TOASTED PINE NUTS

These unpresuming little nuts, precious kernels from a pine-cone cob, are worth the extra effort. Toasting them until golden will gently coax forth their wonderfully subtle flavor to its fullest extent.

1. Preheat oven or toaster oven to 300° F.

2. Place the pine nuts on an ungreased baking sheet or toaster rack and toast until they turn golden, about 5 minutes. As it's easy to burn pine nuts, keep an eye on them. Set aside to cool.

VARIETY

HOW MANY SHAPES AND SIZES OF PASTA ARE THERE?

MAYBE 60, MAYBE 100? WRONG: A CONSERVATIVE ESTIMATE IS 650,

INCLUDING ORECCHIETTE ("LITTLE EARS"), FARFALLE ("BUTTERFLIES"), LINGUINE

("little tongues"), ravioli ("little turnips"), tagliatelle ("little ribbons"), and vermicelli ("little worms").

ACINI DI PEPE. "Peppercorns." Tiny peppercorn-shaped pasta.

AGNOLOTTI. "Priests' caps." Small, crescent-shaped pastas.

CANNARONI. Wide tubes; also called zitoni.

CAPELLINI OR CAPELLI D'ANGELO. "Angel's hair." Long, extremely fine strands.

FARFALLE. "Butterflies." Bow- or butterfly-shaped pasta.

FARFALLINE. Small farfalle.

FETTUCCINE. "Little ribbons." Thin, flat egg noodles about ¼ inch wide.

FUSILLI. "Little springs." Traditional fusilli comes in spaghetti-length spiral-shaped noodles. Cut fusilli are about 1½ inches long.

LASAGNA. Long, very broad noodles (2–3 inches wide); straight or ripple-edged.

LINGUINE. "Little tongues." Very narrow (⅛ inch or less) ribbons.

ORECCHIETTE. "Little ears." Tiny disk shapes.

ORZO. Pasta grains, the size and shape of rice.

PENNE. "Pens" or "Quills." Diagonally cut tubes with either smooth or ridged sides.

RADIATORE. "Radiators." Short, chunky shapes (about 1 inch long and ½ inch in diameter) that resemble tiny radiators with rippled edges.

RAVIOLI. Square-shaped stuffed pasta.

RIGATONI. Large grooved macaroni about 1½ inches wide.

ROTELLE. "Little wheels." Small, spoked-wheel shapes.

SHELLS. Actual name: conchiglie, or "conch shells." Shell-shaped pasta.

SPAGHETTI. Long, thin, round strands.

TAGLIATELLE. Long, thin, flat egg noodles about ¼ inch wide.

TORTELLINI. "Little twists." Small stuffed pasta, similiar to cappelletti.

ACINI DI PEPE

LASAGNA

ORECCHIETTE

SHELLS

PENNE

FARFALLE

ORZO

RIGATONI

AGNOLOTTI

RADIATORE

SPAGHETTI

ROTELLE

RAVIOLI

FETTUCCINE

TORTELLINI

FARFALLINE

FUSILLI

TAGLIATELLE

LINGUINE

CANNARONI

CAPELLINI

PASTA WITH BROCCOLI RABE AND WHITE BEANS

BROCCOLI RABE

IMAGINE IF ALL THE LEAFY VEGETABLES IN THE WORLD WERE REDUCED TO THEIR ULTIMATE INTENSITY AND MADE INTO ONE ALL-POWERFUL VEGETABLE: BROCCOLI RABE WOULD BE THE RESULT.

So add this nutritious bouquet of dark, leafy stalks to any variety of dishes and savor its sharpness.

PASTA WITH BROCCOLI RABE AND WHITE BEANS

Broccoli rabe with white beans, pasta, and a simple sauce. With the added crunch of toasted pine nuts, this becomes a one-dish wonder.

SERVES 4

2 teaspoons olive oil

4 cloves garlic, chopped or pressed

1 large bunch broccoli rabe, heavy stems removed and flowers coarsely chopped

1/4–1/2 teaspoon crushed red pepper flakes

2–4 cups prepared white beans, rinsed and drained

1/2 pound medium-sized, shaped pasta, such as penne, rigatoni, or conchiglie

1 cup pine nuts, toasted (see page 181)

1. Bring a large pot of water to boil.

2. Heat a large nonstick skillet over a medium flame and add olive oil. When the oil is hot, add garlic, stirring until just turning golden.

3. Add broccoli rabe to skillet; stir and cook for about 3–5 minutes, or until the rabe begins to brighten.

4. Raise heat under skillet to high, add red pepper flakes and white beans, and cook until the beans are heated through, about 3 minutes. Reduce heat to low.

5. Add pasta to boiling water and cook until al dente.

6. Drain pasta, reserving 1/2 cup of the pasta water. Add pasta water to broccoli rabe mixture and stir to combine.

7. Add pasta to broccoli rabe mixture and stir. Just before serving, add toasted pine nuts.

BROCCOLI RABE

Broccoli rabe (pronounced *rah-bay*), also called rapini and broccoli di rape, is an intense, bitter green popular in both Italian and Chinese cooking. High in vitamins A and C and low in calories, it is available all year long and can be kept, wrapped, for several days in the refrigerator. Broccoli rabe should be purchased only when it is dark green and its leaves are tightly packed. If the flowers have started to turn light green or yellow, this bunch is not for you.

PICHOLINE OLIVES

STUFFED OLIVES

NIÇOISE

SICILIAN-
STYLE
OLIVES

BELLA DE
CERIGNOLA

MOROCCAN
OLIVES

KALAMATA OLIVES

CRACKED
PROVENÇAL
OLIVES

OLIVES

THERE, IN GLASS JARS ON THE COUNTER AT THE MARKET, ARE WHAT WE CAME FOR: OLIVES. LAWRENCE DURRELL WROTE THAT BLACK OLIVES HAVE "A TASTE OLDER THAN MEAT, OLDER THAN WINE. A TASTE AS OLD as cold water." Perhaps we don't eat them by the dozen, fetchingly spitting the pits into our gloved hands as Justine once did. But we can sure cook with them. Their presence will enhance our dish. Whether we choose the fat Italian Alfonso, or the Greek Kalamata with its smooth purple skin, or Moroccan olives packed with twigs and leaves, we honor the olive-curer's artistry by choosing that olive as the dominant flavor of our savory sauce.

There are hundreds of varieties, each with a distinct flavor and color. Initially, olives are separated by color, green or black (with various shades of tan and purple in between). All olives start out green and, unless they are harvested early, ripen to black. They are too bitter to be eaten straight from the tree and must be cured to leach out bitterness before being eaten. Curing is traditionally done by soaking olives in a lye solution or brine. Once they are cured, they are preserved in brine (very salty water) or olive oil, then often dressed in wine or olive oil flavored with herbs. California "black olives" are picked partially ripe, bleached in a weak lye solution, then turned black using a chemical colorant.

BELLA DE CERIGNOLA. Large, meaty olive with a mild, almost fruity flavor. Brine-cured. From Italy.

BLACK-CURED OLIVES. Green olives that have been left on the tree to ripen. Too bitter to eat raw, they are cured with water, oil, brine, salt, or lye to dissipate their bitterness and preserve them.

CRACKED PROVENÇAL OLIVES. Mildly flavored with herbes de Provence and packed in brine.

GAETA. Slightly bitter flavor. Brine-cured. From Italy.

KALAMATA OLIVES. Very meaty with a tangy flavor. Brine-cured. From Greece.

MOROCCAN OLIVES. Mediterranean olive flavored with garlic and rosemary. Oil-cured.

NIÇOISE. Mildly flavored. Brine-cured.

PICHOLINE OLIVES. Firm texture with a salty flavor. Brine-cured.

SICILIAN-STYLE OLIVES. Large, meaty, and very spicy.

STUFFED OLIVES. Sweet olives stuffed with pimiento.

PASTA WITH BROCCOLI, CAULIFLOWER, PINE NUTS, AND RAISINS

SERVES 6–8

- 2 teaspoons canola or olive oil
- 1 small Spanish onion, coarsely chopped
- 2–3 cloves garlic, finely chopped or pressed
- ½ head cauliflower, core removed, florets chopped
- ½ head broccoli, stem discarded or saved for another use, florets chopped
- 1 cup chicken or vegetable stock (see pages 19, 21)
- 1 pound medium-sized, shaped pasta, such as penne, rigatoni, or conchiglie
- ½ cup pine nuts, toasted (see page 181)
- ½ cup raisins or currants
- ½–1 cup freshly grated Parmesan cheese
- ½ cup chopped fresh parsley
- 2 tablespoons balsamic vinegar

1. Bring a large pot of water to boil.

2. Heat a large skillet over medium heat and add oil. When the oil is hot, add onion and garlic and sauté until onion is golden, about 5 minutes.

3. Add cauliflower and broccoli florets, stirring occasionally for 5 minutes. Add stock and bring to a boil.

4. Reduce the heat to medium and let simmer until the florets are almost tender—about 5 minutes.

5. Add the pasta to boiling water and cook until al dente.

6. While the sauce is cooking, place toasted pine nuts, raisins or currants, Parmesan cheese, parsley, and balsamic vinegar in a bowl. Set aside.

7. Add the sauce to the cooked and drained pasta and top with pine nut mixture. Serve immediately.

PASTA WITH SMOKED SALMON AND FRESH DILL

These pasta cravats are further spiffed up with strips of succulent smoked salmon, sweet bell peppers, zippy vinaigrette, and the essential fresh dill. The end result? Light, clean-tasting—sublime.

SERVES 6–8

- 1 pound pasta bow ties (farfalle)
- 2 cloves garlic
- 1 red bell pepper, julienned
- 2 tablespoons Dijon mustard
- ¼ cup red wine vinegar
- ¼ cup fresh lemon juice
- 6 tablespoons olive oil
- 1 pound smoked salmon, cut in strips (see Other Choices)
- 1 yellow bell pepper, julienned
- ⅓ cup chopped fresh parsley
- ⅓ cup chopped fresh dill
  Coarsely ground black pepper

OPTIONAL INGREDIENTS

- 2 tablespoons sour cream or heavy cream
- 2–4 tablespoons capers
- 1 small red onion, chopped
  Freshly grated Parmesan cheese

1. Bring a large pot of water to boil. Add pasta and cook until tender. Drain immediately. Transfer pasta to a large mixing bowl.

2. While the pasta is cooking, make the dressing. Place garlic and half of 1 red pepper in a blender or in a food processor fitted with a steel blade; pulse until chunky.

3. Add mustard, vinegar, and lemon juice, and process until combined. Gradually add olive oil and sour cream or heavy cream, if desired.

4. Pour dressing over pasta. Add salmon, peppers, parsley, dill, and, if desired, capers and red onion. Mix together.

5. Add pepper to taste. Top with parmesan, if desired

OTHER CHOICES: This dish is particularly good if you grill the smoked salmon. Grill the salmon on an open flame for about 2 minutes on each side. After grilling, you can wrap salmon in aluminum foil and refrigerate up to a day in advance. Slice the fish into strips just before you're ready to use it.

PASTA WITH SMOKED SALMON AND FRESH DILL

PINO LUONGO

First Pino Luongo learned discipline. (He spent years in military school in accordance with his father's wishes.) Then he learned dramatic expression. (He became an actor, much to his father's chagrin.) It was during his proverbial starving-artist days that Luongo began to cook for his friends, in order to bring "quality and style" to his life on a limited budget. His imagination was captured by the great Tuscan dishes of his childhood—the cuisine that, according to Luongo, "has never become an institution"—and he discovered that the generosity of his spirit was well expressed in the act of cooking. "For me, cooking is about creating magic from something very real," says the author of *Tuscan in the Kitchen*. It is a "way to do something for someone else that will be enjoyed." Patrons of his four New York restaurants heartily agree.

"Keep the meal simple and spontaneous; it leaves room for more complicated experiences."

PASTA WITH TOMATOES, MOZZARELLA, AND BASIL

Freshness is what counts in this basic pasta concoction; as such, it is a perfect summertime supper. If the mozzarella is particularly good, use more; if tomatoes are at their beautiful peak, let them work their influence. And who can have too much fresh-picked basil?

Fresh or buffalo mozzarella
Fresh tomatoes, chopped
Fresh basil
Farfalle (or other pasta)
Extra virgin olive oil
Black pepper

1. Cut the mozzarella into small cubes. Mix the tomatoes and basil together. Set aside.

2. Cook the pasta in boiling water until al dente, drain well, and put each portion on a warmed plate.

3. Place the mozzarella in the center of each serving of pasta and put the tomato-basil mixture around the edge.

4. Sprinkle with olive oil and black pepper and serve.

PINO LUONGO

ON OLIVE OIL. "The classification of 'extra virgin' is the most important consideration when you're shopping for olive oil. It's a guarantee that the olives were hand-picked from the trees and that the oil has been pressed in the traditional way, with stone wheels and without the use of heat. Olive oil can be used for cooking, of course, but its main purpose is to add flavor, so it's best left the way it is—raw and natural. Olive oil can always be added to top off a soup or stew: It's like a heavenly coat."

ON GARLIC. "Once the garlic has been browned, get rid of it, especially if you are preparing something delicate. The garlic flavor should be there, but not there."

BAKED PEACHES STUFFED WITH WALNUTS AND CHOCOLATE

When peaches are heavy and summery ripe, this simple dessert can cause spontaneous swooning. Good chocolate is always good, but very good chocolate is always something more than very good.

Sugar
Large, firm peaches
Baker's sweet chocolate
Walnuts, shelled and chopped

1. Preheat the oven to 350° F. Heat equal amounts of water and sugar over low heat until the sugar is melted. Set aside.

2. Cutting through the top, remove the pit from each peach, leaving a cavity for stuffing. Set peaches aside.

3. Melt the chocolate in the top of a double boiler until it is just melted but not runny. Stir in the walnuts. Fill the cavities of the peaches with this mixture, then moisten the top of each peach with a spoonful of the sugar syrup.

4. Bake in the oven until peaches are tender. Check for doneness after 15 minutes.

SOME RECIPES AREN'T RECIPES AT ALL; THEY'RE COMBINATIONS OF FLAVORS THAT IN ALMOST ANY AMOUNT WILL COMPLEMENT ONE ANOTHER AND BECOME A PERFECTLY BALANCED DISH. HERE CHEF LUONGO GIVES SOME INGREDIENTS FOR SUCCESS. THE DETAILS ARE YOURS TO IMPROVISE.

[🐾 OTHER FACTS—*page 279*]

RED FRUIT

WE YEARN TO CALL IT A VEGETABLE. IT ISN'T SWEET, AFTER ALL, AND IT'S SEEDED LIKE A CUCUMBER, THIN-SKINNED LIKE A PEPPER, AND GROWS ON A VINE LIKE A GREEN BEAN. ALAS, EXPERTS TELL us it's a fruit. But we can pretend it's a vegetable and continue making pasta sauces from it, celebrate its summer ripeness with black pepper and fresh basil, then dry it in the sun to enliven our winter fare.

FRESH. Tomatoes should be stored at room temperature, never in the refrigerator. To speed ripening, place tomatoes in a brown paper bag with an apple, which will cause them to emit ethylene gas, helping them ripen.

CHERRY. Very sweet, these tiny tomatoes require minimal preparation; they are wonderful raw and whole in salads.

BEEFSTEAK. The largest and meatiest of all tomatoes, they are great for slicing. A local, in-season beefsteak will have better flavor than a Holland.

HOLLAND. They are actually from Holland. These tomatoes always look perfect and are a good bet off-season.

ROMA OR PLUM. These are great cooking tomatoes and are usually ideal for use off-season, when Hollands are expensive and beefsteaks are pale and bland.

PEAR. Similar in flavor to cherry tomatoes, they come in red and yellow and are chosen more for their appearance than for any distinctive taste difference.

YELLOW CHERRY. All yellow tomatoes, large and small, are less acidic than red ones, and therefore less likely to cause heartburn.

CANNED. Although fresh, seasonal ingredients are always best for cooking, tomatoes have their place of honor in the world of canned goods. Canned peeled tomatoes, packed at the height of ripeness, are excellent for cooking, as they're reliable in both flavor and texture.

WHOLE. Peeled, whole unseasoned tomatoes in their own juice are the best substitute for fresh tomatoes—sometimes better to use than fresh when fresh have little flavor.

PURÉE. Unseasoned tomato pulp with some tomato juice. Bland in taste. May be used as basis for a smooth sauce when spices are added and it's cooked down.

CRUSHED. Crushed whole tomatoes with tomato purée. Bland in taste. May be used as a basis for sauce. Also good for soups, stews, etc.

PASTE. Tomato paste is highly concentrated tomato purée. It is used in small quantities when a hint of tomato flavor is desired.

HOLLAND

PLUM

CHERRY

YELLOW CHERRY

PEAR

PENNE WITH ASPARAGUS

For Jeff and Kim, Penne with Asparagus is an addiction. Every week they go to the same restaurant (Lucky Strike in SoHo) and order the same dish (you guessed it). "We eat it in five minutes," says Kim, "and basically lick the bowl with our bread." Jeff and Kim agree that it's "just perfect."

SERVES 6-8

1 tablespoon olive oil
2 garlic cloves, finely chopped or pressed
3 tablespoons fresh lemon juice
1 pound asparagus, woody stems discarded, remainder cut into quarters
3/4 cup chicken stock
1 pound penne, cooked
1/3 cup toasted pine nuts (see page 181)
1/4 cup shaved Parmesan cheese or more to taste
1 small bunch chives, chopped into 1-inch pieces
Salt

OPTIONAL INGREDIENT

1/4 teaspoon crushed red pepper flakes

1. Bring large pot of water to boil.

2. Heat a large saucepan over low heat and add oil. When the oil is hot, add the garlic, and crushed red pepper flakes, if desired, and cook until golden, about 3 minutes.

3. Add lemon juice, asparagus, and chicken stock and raise heat to bring to a boil. Reduce heat to low and cook until asparagus is al dente, about 3 minutes.

4. Add pasta to boiling water and cook until al dente. Drain cooked pasta and add to asparagus mixture. Just prior to serving, add pine nuts, Parmesan cheese, and chives. Salt to taste.

PASTA WITH BELL PEPPERS, MUSH-ROOMS, AND BACON

SERVES 4

1/2 pound bacon
2-3 cloves garlic, finely chopped or pressed
3 bell peppers, any color, thinly sliced
3/4 pound button mushrooms, wiped clean and thinly sliced
3 tablespoons chopped fresh oregano or 1 tablespoon dried
3/4 pound spaghetti
Salt and pepper
Parmesan cheese, freshly grated

1. Fry bacon in a large skillet over medium-low heat until rendered of all fat. Discard all but 1 tablespoon of the bacon fat. Remove bacon from pan, blot it with paper towels, and crumble or chop it. Reserve it for later use.

2. Place garlic, peppers, and mushrooms in the skillet (if you are using dried oregano, add it now), and sauté until the vegetables are tender, about 15 minutes.

3. Bring a large pot of water to boil. Add the pasta and cook until tender.

4. Drain the pasta, reserving 1/2 cup of the pasta water.

5. Add pasta water to pepper mixture and stir to combine. Add the pasta to the skillet, add salt and pepper to taste, and serve immediately.

6. Garnish with fresh oregano and Parmesan cheese.

PANCETTA

Pancetta is Italian bacon that has been air-dried and salt-cured. It is leaner than bacon. Unlike bacon, it is not smoked; unlike prosciutto, it must be cooked. For a smoky taste you can substitute bacon.

PROSCIUTTO

Prosciutto is a dry-cured Italian aged ham. Its unique salty flavor makes it a good match for melon and fresh figs. Make sure it's sliced paper-thin for pasta and fruit, thicker for other cooking needs.

BACON

American bacon is not only cured but smoked as well. It's the breakfast meat that is also good for lunch as a salad garnish.

HAM

Like American bacon, American ham is cured and smoked, but in addition, it contains water and sugar.

COOKED SPAGHETTI

LINGUINE WITH CLAMS

LINGUINE WITH CLAMS

SERVES 4

1	tablespoon olive oil
4	cloves garlic, finely chopped
4	tablespoons chopped fresh parsley
2	teaspoons anchovy paste
4–6	dozen baby clams, soaked in water and scrubbed
¾	cup white wine
¾	pound spaghetti or linguine

OPTIONAL INGREDIENT

1	tablespoon unsalted butter

1. Bring a large pot of water to a boil.

2. Heat a large saucepan over a low flame and add oil. When the oil is hot, add the garlic. Cook for about 5–10 minutes, or until the garlic begins to look translucent. Do not brown. Add the parsley and anchovy paste and cook for 2 minutes, stirring constantly.

3. Raise the heat to medium high and add the clams and white wine; bring to a boil. Cover the pan and steam the clams for about 7–10 minutes, or until they open up.

4. At this point, add the pasta to the pot of boiling water.

5. When the clams have opened, remove them from the pot and shuck all but 16 of them. Return the shucked clams to the pot, and set aside the remaining 16.

6. Cook the pasta until tender. Drain and add to the pot with the clams. If desired, add the butter. Toss well and divide among 4 plates. Garnish each with 4 clams in the shell.

WARNING: Use washable insulated mitts for shucking the meat from the hot shells, which may contain scalding liquid.

PENNE WITH CABBAGE AND SAUSAGE

This savory and hearty dish comes from the kitchen of writer and film director Nora Ephron. We recommend eating it with (her book) Crazy Salad *on the side. And don't worry about* Heartburn.

SERVES 4

6	hot Italian sausages, skin removed and broken into pieces
1	medium Spanish onion, sliced
⅓	cabbage, outer leaves removed, cut into small slices and chunks
½	jar Rao's marinara sauce (see Note)
1	pound penne

1. Sauté sausage bits in a large skillet until some fat is rendered. Add the onion and cook until the onion is golden and the sausage has browned. Add cabbage and stir to coat with the oil.

2. Cover and cook about 6–7 minutes, or until the cabbage is nicely wilted. Add the Rao's sauce and cook until heated through.

3. Meanwhile, boil penne in salted water. Drain and add to sauce.

NOTE: Rao's sauce can be purchased in 33-ounce jars at Zabar's, 2245 Broadway, New York, NY 10024, 212/787-2000. If you can't find Rao's, you can use 16 ounces of any really good marinara sauce. Rao's sauce is distributed by Rao's Specialty Foods, 445 East 114th Street, New York, NY 10029, 800/466-3623.

ON CLAMMING UP

Clams, like all other bivalves, should be bought live, whole, and shut tight. Any that are open or cracked are dead and should be discarded. But after cooking, the converse is true. Any that are still closed tight are dead and should be discarded.

SAFETY OF THE FRUITS OF THE SEA

Low in calories and cholesterol, high in protein and iron, mollusks are smart foods to consume—cooked. (Crustaceans like shrimp or crayfish can have twice as much cholesterol as a similar serving of beef.) Because most mollusks filter 15–20 gallons of water a day, they can be repositories for dangerous bacteria. As warmer weather encourages bacterial growth, avoid eating raw shellfish May through August. A good rule to use is the old adage about eating oysters only in the months containing the letter "R."

P I Z Z A

"For the cafe picnic, [Nathalie] bought *fougasse* with anchovies and olive oil, some pizza with wild mushrooms, and two or three *pains bagnats*—a *pain bagnat* being, more or less, a *salade niçoise* in a bun. For dessert she bought some chèvre and some *brousse,* which is a kind of cheese made with ewe's milk. To avoid problems about bringing her own lunch to a cafe, Nathalie had picked a place that did not serve food. As we all tore into the picnic, the waiter didn't look irritated—just envious."

CALVIN TRILLIN, *Travels with Alice*

CHEESE, TOMATO, AND HERB PIZZA

It's only four simple ingredients, but just out of a hot oven, it tastes like everything a king or a pauper could ever want. Learn this one first, and then go crazy with your favorite variations— you may never visit a pizza parlor again.

MAKES FOUR 7-INCH PIZZAS

PIE

1   recipe Simple Pizza Dough (see page 206) or ready-made pizza dough (available at supermarkets or local pizza parlors), divided equally into 4 balls

TOPPING

$2^2/_3$ cups grated mozzarella cheese
4   beefsteak tomatoes, thinly sliced
$^1/_4$ cup chopped fresh basil or
2   tablespoons dried oregano

1. Preheat oven to 500° F. Grease a cookie sheet with olive oil. (If using a pizza stone, see page 203.)

2. Place prepared and shaped pizza dough on a cookie sheet (see page 203). Depending on the size of your baking sheet, you may only be able to fit 2 pizzas at a time.

4. Sprinkle $1^2/_3$ cups of the mozzarella evenly among the 4 pizzas. Place tomatoes in a circle on top of the mozzarella, then fill in with more slices. Sprinkle the remaining mozzarella and fresh basil or dried oregano.

5. Lower heat to 475° F. and cook pizza for 7–10 minutes, or until dough is golden.

PIZZA

THEY SAY PIZZA WAS INVENTED IN THE 1920S IN
NEW HAVEN, CONNECTICUT, BY THE FAMOUS MR. FRANK PEPE. HE
CALLED HIS CREATION THE "TOMATO PIE," AND IT WAS SUCH A HIT THAT, AS
the story goes, it even caught on in Italy. Whether you believe the legend or not, it is true that big, thin-
crusted pizzas slathered with cheese and sauce have become an essential part of our culture—as American
as hamburgers and Harleys. In recent history pizza has scaled down and become personal. Home cooks,
inspired by Wolfgang Puck and other inventive chefs, have pounced on pizza's potential with creative glee.

We know why. Pizza making is good fun, and even without the help of a pizza stone or a pizza peel, the
process is easy, easy, easy. All it takes is an oven and an idea. Sliced duck and rosemary pizza with
dried apricots? Sure. Wild greens and goat cheese? Sounds wonderful. Grilled eggplant and
prosciutto? Save a few slices for us. If you can imagine it, you can make it.

TIPS: 1. Pizza must be baked in a very hot oven, so it's important to preheat it at 500° F. for at least 20 minutes. If using a pizza stone, place stone in cold oven before heating. Reduce heat to 475° F. after placing pizza in oven. 2. Place cornmeal on peel and on pizza stone just before adding pizza to ensure easy removal. 3. Experiment by adding a little bit of cornmeal or other kinds of flour to the dough to create interesting tastes and textures, or try adding various herbs, fresh or dried, to the dough. Some favorites: rosemary, basil, oregano. 4. Have a variety of ingredients readily available for unique and spontaneous creations. 5. To ensure a crisp crust and a good moisture balance, don't weigh your pizza down with a lot of topping. For one 7-inch pizza, 1–1½ cups of topping is plenty. Because pizza toppings become significantly drier in hot ovens, try to integrate a sauce into your creation. 6. Most nonmeat toppings need not be precooked, with the exception of pork and beef. Be sure to slice meats and vegetables very thin. If using fish, slice approximately ¼ inch thick and add 3–5 minutes to the cooking time. If using fresh herbs, add them during the last 5 minutes of baking, since they will lose their flavor if overcooked. 7. Leftovers make great pizzas. Moo shu pork pizza, with a splash of soy sauce, is divine; thick black bean soup, with grated mozzarella or Monterey Jack cheese, is a natural high. 8. Oven temperatures vary notoriously. Pizzas should cook between 7–15 minutes, or until the crust is golden brown. Monitor the first pizzas you cook, and you will come to know the cooking time required in your oven.

PIZZA STONES AND TILES. Although you can make great pizzas without fancy equipment, pizza stones or baking tiles allow the home cook to replicate the work of a commercial brick oven. Twenty minutes before you start baking, place a pizza stone in a cold oven and then set the oven to 500° F. This way you can re-create the heat of the wood fire that cooks the pizza rapidly and evenly, producing a crust that is crispy without overcooking the pizza.

PIZZA PEELS are large wooden paddles that are a great help in getting pizza in and out of the oven.

GRILLING. Prepare a fire in your grill and set your rack 3–4 inches above the coals. Transfer formed dough from a greased pan or a pizza peel to a hot grill. Cook until lightly browned, about 1–2 minutes. Turn pizza over, and place toppings on the cooked side. Do not leave pizza directly over the hot coals. Rotate the crust with tongs so that the topping cooks through and any cheese melts, about 5–10 minutes.

"Americans eat 75 acres of pizza a day."

BOYD MATSON

[🍕 **PIZZA** *first aid—page 265*]

GREEK PIZZA

SALAD PIZZA

SIMPLE PIZZA DOUGH

MAKES FOUR 7-INCH PIZZAS

1   package active dry yeast
⅔   cup warm water (110°–115° F *)
     Pinch of sugar
2   cups unbleached all-
     purpose flour
¼   cup cornmeal
1   teaspoon kosher salt
1½ tablespoons olive oil

OPTIONAL INGREDIENT

½   cup fresh rosemary or
     ¼ cup dried

EQUIPMENT

Food thermometer needed

1. Place yeast in small bowl. Stir in the water and the sugar. Let stand for about 10 minutes, then mix.

2. In a large mixing bowl or work bowl of a food processor, combine flour, cornmeal, rosemary, if desired, and salt. Add yeast and olive oil, and mix well.

3. Set dough mixture on a work surface dusted with flour. Knead dough vigorously for about 5 minutes. Divide dough into 4 equal parts and shape into balls.

4. Lightly oil a baking sheet. Transfer dough onto sheet and lightly brush each ball with olive oil. Cover baking sheet with plastic wrap and let sit in a warm place until dough has doubled in size (about 1½ hours).

5. Dough can be frozen at this point, if desired. Place dough balls in plastic freezer bags and freeze. To defrost, let thaw completely at room temperature before rolling out.

6. Flatten dough ball with heel of hand on lightly floured work surface. The smaller the dough ball, the easier it is to work. Lift and pinch each disk from center outward in a circular motion until dough is thin. Don't worry about the shape and occasional holes.

7. Place dough on a pizza paddle (a "peel," see page 203) that has been liberally sprinkled with cornmeal.

8. Place toppings on dough.

9. Slide pizza onto preheated stone that has been just sprinkled with cornmeal (see page 203) by giving a slight, quick jerking movement forward and then backward. Or put it on an oiled baking sheet.

FUTURE TIME-SAVER

Bake pizza dough without topping for about 10 minutes. Let cool. Wrap with plastic wrap and freeze. It is not necessary to defrost before final cooking. When ready to cook, add toppings, then cook as directed.

POLENTA DOUGH

Instead of pressing the cooked polenta (see page 140) into a 9-inch pie pan, press it into 2 pans. Refrigerate until ready to use and proceed by adding the topping of your choice.

P E R

BAR-B-Q. Top pizza with Bar-B-Q sauce (see page 64), cooked chicken or duck, dried apricots, chopped scallions, and Gouda cheese.

BEANS AND GUACAMOLE. Top pizza dough with Refried Beans (see page 158), top with slivers of precooked chorizo sausage and grated Cheddar cheese or Monterey Jack, chopped tomatoes, chopped red onions. After baking, top with sour cream or guacamole (see page 55) or salsa (see page 55).

BRIE & TWO-GRAPE. Artfully scatter bite-size pieces of Camembert and Brie with lengthwise-sliced grapes over Simple pizza dough. Brush lightly with oil before baking—it makes the grapes shine. Or brush with melted orange marmalade before baking for dessert.

CALZONE. Place filling over half the dough and fold over, pressing sides together. Be sure you are working with pizza dough that's not so big as to become unmanageable. Follow pizza baking instructions (see page 203).

CARAMELIZED ONION, TOMATO, AND ARUGULA. Cover dough with caramelized onions (see page 74), grated mozzarella cheese, and chopped tomatoes. When it comes out of oven, sprinkle with 2 bunches of chopped arugula.

SONAL PIES

CLAMS DIABLO. Mix crushed red pepper flakes into tomato sauce (see page 178). Spread sauce on pizza dough and begin baking. One to two minutes before pizza has finished cooking, sprinkle with cooked clams and Parmesan cheese. When it's done, top with chopped fresh oregano and serve.

DEEP-SEA. Top pizza dough with olivada or pesto (see page 180), and thin slices of red onion. Add thinly sliced tuna, and fresh tomatoes for the last 1–2 minutes of cooking time.

EGGPLANT CAPONATA. Cover dough with Eggplant Caponata (see page 116), mozzarella, and ricotta cheese. Sprinkle with fresh basil when it comes out of oven.

ENGLISH DESSERT. Top dough with shredded Monterey Jack cheese. Quickly sauté sliced pears in a little Calvados, add to topping. Cover with prosciutto and chopped walnuts. Melt a little Stilton cheese with some Calvados and drizzle over pizza topping. Serve with Calvados or port.

FOCACCIA. Brush pizza dough with extra virgin olive oil. Squeeze 2 cloves of garlic and spread over dough. Sprinkle with kosher salt and dried rosemary.

FONTINA AND SPINACH. Cover dough with shredded Fontina and Spinach with Garlic and Pine Nuts (see page 108), then sprinkle with Parmesan cheese.

GREEK. Cover dough with Spinach with Garlic and Pine Nuts (see page 108). Add crumbled feta cheese, chopped fresh tomatoes, and Kalamata olives. After cooking, sprinkle with fresh oregano or rosemary (shown on previous spread).

MAIZE. Top pizza dough with chopped fresh tomatoes, fresh kernels of corn, diced red onion, diced red bell pepper, shredded Parmesan and Fontina cheese, and drizzle with olive oil. Sprinkle with chopped fresh basil before serving.

MEXICAN. Cover dough with salsa (see page 55), Black Bean Soup (see page 158), grated Monterey Jack cheese, and jalapeño peppers. After baking, sprinkle with chopped fresh cilantro and a dollop of sour cream.

NEW YORK BREAKFAST. Bake pizza dough, then top it with a thin layer of cream cheese, smoked salmon, fresh chives and capers, add a squeeze of lemon, and serve.

PESTO PRIMAVERA. Cover dough with pesto (see page 180). Top with thin slices of zucchini or summer squash, chopped blanched broccoli, shredded mozzarella, and sprinkle with 4 chopped fresh tomatoes.

PORTOBELLO MUSHROOMS. Top pizza with crushed tomatoes, thinly sliced portobello mushrooms, pressed garlic, thinly sliced eggplant, and shredded Fontina cheese.

ROASTED GARLIC AND CARAMELIZED ONION. Spread dough with roasted garlic (see page 119), caramelized onions (see page 74), and thyme. Sprinkle with Parmesan cheese.

ROASTED PEPPERS AND BLACK OLIVES. Cover dough with roasted bell peppers cut in strips or puréed (see page 180), thin slices of red onion, grated Fontina, and sprinkle with black olives.

ROASTED VEGETABLE AND GOAT CHEESE. Cover dough with Roasted Mixed Vegetables (see page 119) and top with crumbled goat cheese. When the pizza comes out of the oven, sprinkle with chopped fresh basil or oregano.

SALAD. Cover the dough with tomato sauce (see page 178) and bake. Top with a favorite green salad already tossed with vinaigrette (shown on previous spread).

SHRIMP AND GARLIC. Place chopped tomatoes on pizza dough and bake. Sauté the shrimp and garlic in olive oil and put on top of cooked pizza just before serving.

SUN-DRIED TOMATOES WITH GARLIC. Sauté chopped garlic and chopped sun-dried tomatoes in olive oil. Sprinkle dough with mozzarella and thinly sliced red onions. Sprinkle with thyme and Parmesan cheese.

C H E E S E

COWS HAVE THE KINDEST EYES. MAYBE THAT'S WHY

CHEESE IS SO MILD WHEN IT'S FRESH FROM ITS BOVINE MOTHER.

BUT GOATS' EYES ARE NOT SO KIND. MAYBE THAT'S WHY THEIR CHEESE

has such a kick. Cheese has been popular since Neolithic times, the result of milk that fermented and thickened

into a completely new food. Today the cheese that graces our tables is chosen to complement various dishes.

If we need salty, we can choose Parmesan. If we want a tangy cheese, we may choose Romano. But that's just

the beginning. Traditionally only softer cheeses were used on pizzas; now we embrace the whole gamut.

"Many's the long night I've dreamed of cheese—toasted, mostly."

ROBERT LOUIS STEVENSON

Firm/Hard

DRY JACK CHEESES. These grating cheeses may be hard to find, but they are well worth the search. Slip some into a sandwich or eat with your favorite fruit.

PARMESAN (Parmigiano-Reggiano). This traditional topper for pasta is sweet and nutty with a slightly grainy texture. Invest in a big chunk with a decent rind. A vegetable peeler makes elegant shavings.

ROMANO. A staple ingredient in Southern Italian cooking, this cheese is very hard, dry, salty, tangy.

Semifirm

CHEDDAR . Though there are many kinds of Cheddar, stick with the white farmhouse varieties that have been aged for at least 6 months. Best bets for snacking are a Vermont Cheddar and Tillamook Cheddar. Black Diamond Cheddar, when served with fresh fruit and nuts, makes for a delectable dessert.

GRUYÈRE. Full-flavored and nutty, this cheese is made only in the summer from cow's milk in the French town where it originated. It's the perfect addition for quiches or vegetable tarts.

Semisoft

FONTINA. This cheese gets richer as it ages. Its distinct nutty flavor and creamy texture makes it superb for both pasta or served cold with fresh fruit and wine.

GOUDA AND EDAM. Holland's best-known cheeses; they are smooth and mild in flavor. As they age, their flavor becomes distinctively sharper. Shred them over omelettes or use them for grilled cheese sandwiches.

HAVARTI. This mild, rindless cheese from Denmark. It comes plain or flavored with chives, caraway seeds, dill, and other spices. Try serving at brunch with fruit and crackers.

MUENSTER. This orange-rinded cheese is mild when young and gets sharper with age. Choose either variety for a winning club sandwich.

PROVOLONE. A mild cheese that comes in many sizes and shapes, Provolone makes a good match with roasted red bell peppers or crusty Italian bread.

Soft-ripening

BRIE. Of all the French cheeses, brie is perhaps the one Americans are most familiar with. If perfectly ripe, it will ooze at room temperature. Toss it with hot pasta or smear it on your favorite wheatmeal cracker. Delicious when stuffed with either pesto and sun-dried tomatoes or with honey, dates, and pecans and baked alone or in phyllo dough.

CAMEMBERT. This cheese with red-speckled rind reaches peak maturity at six weeks old—creamy enough to use as a spread on sandwiches, crackers, or fruit.

Chèvres/Sheep's-milk

FETA. No Greek salad could be without this salty, crumbly cheese made from sheep's milk. Try it as a piquant alternative to Parmesan on pasta.

GOAT CHEESES. When goat cheese comes from France, it goes by the French word for goat, *chèvre*. Its many varieties of flavors and textures are wonderful on pizza, in vegetable tarts, and on bread.

Fresh

CREAM CHEESE. Famous for its creamy quality, this bland cheese mixes well with herbs, vegetables, and smoked fish to be spread on your favorite bagel.

MOZZARELLA. Originally made from buffalo's milk, it's now made from a cow's (for a lot less money). Slip some into the sandwich or melt it over pizza. Better still, make an *insalata caprese* by alternating slices of mozzarella with ripe tomato, whole leaves of fresh basil and dress with dark virgin olive oil and salt and pepper.

RICOTTA. This soft white cheese is made from whey and is similar to cottage cheese. It's light, creamy, and delicate—perfect for lasagna or fruit. The best ricotta is available in Italian specialty stores.

Blue

BLEU D'AUVERGNE. Less salty than Roquefort, this blue is choice for salad dressings.

GORGONZOLA. Rich and piquant in flavor, Gorgonzola is sweet and creamy-smooth when young and becomes increasingly sharper as it ages. End a heavy dinner with gorgonzola, pears, and a nip of port.

ROQUEFORT. This magnificent cheese acquires its unusual hue after being aged for 2 months in the limestone caves of Cambalou in Southern France. Crumble it over fresh bread or combine with walnuts and fruit—its taste is simply magnificent.

CHIVES

H E R B S

YOU CAN HEAL WITH THEM, BATHE WITH THEM, OR BURN THEM TO DRIVE AWAY EVIL SPIRITS, BUT IT'S IN THE KITCHEN WHERE HERBS ARE PERHAPS BEST USED AND BEST LOVED. EACH HAS ITS OWN distinct personality, texture, flavor, and aroma. While conventional culinary wisdom pairs certain dishes with certain herbs, we suggest you experiment on your own. Once you're acquainted with the properties of herbs, your spice cabinet and window-box garden can become a world of delectable possibilities.

BASIL. With its sweet, robust flavor and lovely pungent smell, basil is particularly good in tomato dishes and fresh salads.

CHIVES. Chives are part of the onion family, often used as garnish. Use fresh chives in soups, salads, eggs, with sour cream or cream cheese, and in simple sauces.

CILANTRO. The leaf of the coriander plant (also known as Chinese parsley) has a surprisingly fresh, unfamiliar taste, distinctly different from the seed. Cilantro is used in Mexican, Indian, Chinese, Vietnamese, and Thai cooking.

DILL. Fresh dill has become increasingly easy to find in local markets lately, and while it has a mildly sweet flavor, it should be used sparingly. An integral component of Scandinavian and Russian cuisine, it is used with fish and cucumbers.

MINT. While dried mint is all right, fresh mint is worth looking for. Its distinct, sweet flavor makes it popular in teas, but it is equally tasty with fruit, peas, and even in some cold soups.

OREGANO. Dried oregano is much more pungent than fresh. It has a wide variety of uses, from meats and poultry to soups and sauces.

PARSLEY: ITALIAN AND CURLY. Parsley should always be used fresh. A common garnish, it helps to bring out the other flavors in a dish. Italian parsley has a flat leaf (closely resembling cilantro) and a strong flavor. Curly parsley is milder and more decorative. Can be used in salad with lettuce or as a substitute for lettuce, and freshens the breath when eaten after a meal.

ROSEMARY. Its strong, aromatic perfume is perfect with pork, lamb, beans, potatoes, and in stuffings.

SAGE. Extremely pungent. In America it is commonly used in stuffings, sausages, and with pork. Too tough to be eaten raw.

TARRAGON. With a subtle lemon and licorice flavor, tarragon is wonderful in dishes where flavors do not compete, and in some sauces with poultry, fish, veal, and eggs.

THYME. This pungent herb goes well with soups, stews, and roasted poultry.

NOTE: All fresh herbs lose their oomph when cooked for long periods of time. Add fresh herbs right before serving.

[HERB *first aid—pages 266, 271*]

BASIL

TARRAGON

MINT

ITALIAN OR FLAT-LEAF PARSLEY

"I believe that if ever I had to practice cannibalism, I might manage if there were enough tarragon around."

JAMES BEARD

ROSEMARY

THYME

"Doth not rosemary and Romeo both begin with a letter?"

SHAKESPEARE

CURLY PARSLEY

OREGANO

SAGE

WOLFGANG PUCK

Austrian-born Puck started his formal cooking career at age 14, when he went to work as a chef's apprentice. Unlike those chefs whose childhoods were spent in comforting home kitchens, Puck lacked the support of his family. His father told him he'd "never amount to anything." His father was wrong. In 1973 Puck came to California. "It took me nearly eight years to break away from the traditions of my European training and feel free to experiment with new ways," he remembers. But when he shook off his past and opened Spago, the result was liberating for all of American cooking. One of its best successes was gourmet pizza, an invention that established Puck's fame as a culinary spin-doctor. Puck's signature style—the open kitchen centered around a grill, the healthful food prepared and presented with panache—has set new standards for chefs around the world. His creativity is from the heart and is evident in his advice for fledgling chefs: "Think of cooking as an outlet for your ideas, a release for the artist in you."

[OTHER FACTS—*page 279*]

ON TURNING UP THE HEAT. "A very hot oven is essential to produce a crust that is crisp on the outside and chewy within. Even without a brick oven, the home cook can get excellent results with a pizza stone, which distributes the heat evenly and does not scorch the crust as a baking sheet might do."

ON CHEESE. "Fresh cheeses, such as mozzarella, Fontina, and the mild goat cheeses, are what you need for your pizza; avoid the hard, salty types."

ON ATTITUDE. "Don't let the new seriousness about pizza scare you away from making it at home. It's just as easy as it was in the old days."

SPICY CHICKEN PIZZA

Wolfgang Puck's modern pizza employs moist, marinated chicken, an intriguing mix of vegetables, and two fresh cheeses—but none of the toppings are allowed to swamp the all-important crust.

SERVES 4

3 cups (about 1 pound, skinned and boned) cubed chicken

MARINADE

$\frac{1}{2}$ cup plus 1 tablespoon olive oil
$3\frac{1}{2}$ tablespoons lime juice
2 teaspoons chopped jalapeño pepper 🌶
   Pinch of chopped fresh cilantro
   Salt

TOPPINGS

3   cups grated mozzarella cheese
2   cups grated Fontina cheese
1   pound (about 6) plum tomatoes, ends removed, cut into thin slices
$\frac{1}{2}$ cup cubed eggplant, sautéed or grilled
$\frac{1}{2}$ cup grilled onion, chopped
4   teaspoons grated Parmesan cheese
3   cups marinated chicken, sautéed
   Chopped fresh chives

1. Prepare Simple Pizza Dough (see page 206).

2. ⏲ Arrange the cubed chicken in a medium bowl and toss with the marinade ingredients, using $\frac{1}{2}$ cup of the olive oil. Season lightly with salt. Let marinate for about 1 hour, refrigerated.

3. In a skillet large enough to hold the chicken in one layer, heat the remaining 1 tablespoon oil. Sauté the chicken just to brown on all sides.

4. Place a pizza stone in the oven and preheat oven to 525° F.

5. To prepare each pizza, place a ball of dough on a lightly floured surface. Press down on the center, spreading the dough, or roll into a 7- or 8-inch circle, with the outer border a little thicker than the inner circle. Brush lightly with oil and arrange the topping or toppings of your choice only over the inner circle.

6. Arrange the pizza on the baking stone and bake 15–20 minutes, or until the pizzas are nicely browned. Transfer to a firm surface and cut into slices with a pizza cutter. Serve immediately.

"I am happiest when spending a few hours behind the stove in one of my kitchens. I think it is important to enjoy yourself [when cooking], whether it is peeling potatoes, seasoning a roast, whisking a sauce, or creating an elegant dessert."

SALADS

"
It's certain that fine
women eat
A crazy salad with
their meat.

WILLIAM BUTLER YEATS

"

GREEN SALAD WITH LEMON DRESSING

Every chef has a swift, simple salad
in his or her bag of tricks. A plate of crunchy
greens refreshes the senses, cleanses the
palate, and complements almost any dish.
Add substantial ingredients—tomatoes,
fruit, nuts, avocado, cheese grilled tuna—
and you've got yourself a meal.

SERVES 4

SALAD

2   heads Boston lettuce, torn
    Salt and coarsely ground
    pepper

DRESSING

2   tablespoons fresh lemon juice
3   tablespoons olive oil
1   garlic clove, finely chopped
    or pressed

1. Whisk lemon juice, olive oil, and garlic together.

2. Sprinkle over lettuce. Add salt and pepper to taste.

OTHER CHOICES: Substitute balsamic vinegar for the lemon juice.

S A L A D S

ALLOW YOUR MOUTH TO ROMP THROUGH AN IMAGINARY GARDEN OF YOUR OWN INVENTION. LIKE THE GARDEN ITSELF, A SALAD IS SUBJECT TO SEASONS. THE BEST SALADS ARE STUDIES of opposites: bland iceberg lettuce becomes forgivable when it's paired with something as intense as blue cheese. For crunchy versus soft, there is green beans and mushrooms; for the raw and the cooked, there's romaine and croutons; and who can resist the sweetness of pears tossed with peppery watercress?

ETYMOLOGY. The word salad comes from *sal,* the Latin word for salt—the first salad dressing.

MIXING SALADS. Salads should be composed of contrasts—mild with strong, crunchy with soft, sweet with bitter, salty with sweet.

SERVING SALAD. Greens are more pleasing torn, not shredded. In the U.S., lettuce is served in bite-size pieces. In France, whole leaves of lettuce are served and left to be eaten with a fork, never cut. Allow 8 cups of lightly packed lettuce for 4 servings. Apply dressing at the last possible moment, to prevent wilting of delicate greens.

OPTIMIZING SHELF-LIFE. It's best to buy fresh greens the day you intend to eat them, but if it's more convenient to get them in advance, cleaning them will prolong crispness. You can wash and store lettuce optimally for 3 days—up to a week with heartier varieties like romaine. **WASH-ING: Manual method.** Soak greens in cold water, swishing the salad with your hands to shake off any tenacious dirt. **Salad-spinner method.** Put the salad in the basket nested in the outer bowl, add water, lift the basket up and down. Remove the basket from bowl to dispose of the sandy water and repeat soaking if necessary. **DRYING:** It's imperative to get the greens as dry as possible, either with a dish towel, paper towels, or with a spinner's centrifugal force—excess moisture accelerates spoiling. Once the salad is clean and dry, wrap it loosely in paper towels and place in a plastic bag with lots of room to breathe. Store the greens in the crisper drawer of your fridge. Tying up the corners of a large dish towel also works well and has the environmental advantage of being washable and reusable. Never store salad that's already been dressed.

EDIBLE FLOWERS. When lettuces and herbs go to seed, the leaves may be past peak, but the re-sulting delicious blossoms redeem the plant. Look too for arugula, borage, day lilies, honey-suckle, marigolds, nasturtium, pansies, rose petals, violets, or the flowers from any herb. Use flowers with caution; buy from a reputable nursery or grow your own.

ORGANIC PRODUCE. Legal definitions may vary, but the difference is down in the dirt. In an organic field, the earth is cultivated as carefully as the crops it produces. Organic farmers believe that soil is healthiest when rich with organic matter. To this end, they don't use synthetic fertilizers and pesticides because these artificial chemicals interfere with the decaying process of vegetable and animal matter. When left alone, natural degeneration replenishes the earth with nutrients. Though organic produce is costlier, there are people who swear its improved taste and healthiness justify the extra expense.

[SALADS *first aid—page 265*]

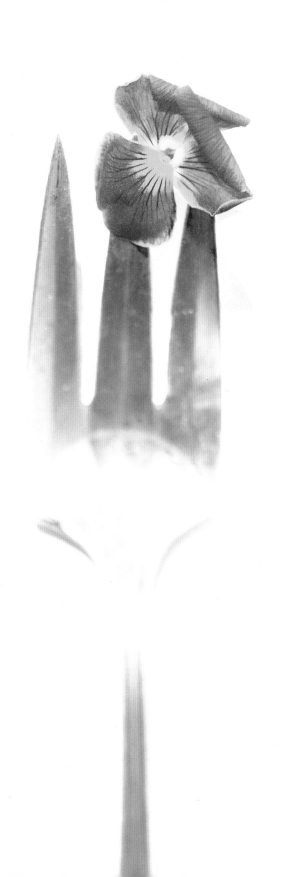

PANSY

BOSTON

ROMAINE

RED
OAK-LEAF

ARUGULA OR
ROCKET

ENDIVE

GREEN
OAK-LEAF

ICEBERG

RADICCHIO

CHICORY

BIBB

LEAFY GREENS

ARE NOT STRICTLY GREEN ANY MORE—THEY SPAN THE WHOLE SPECTRUM.

LEAFY REDS, CURLY YELLOWS, CRISPY PURPLES, and crunchy whites have come into their own, allowing an endless variety of salads with extraordinarily diverse shapes, textures, and flavors.

ARUGULA OR ROCKET. This peppery leaf is popular in Italian cuisine—a few leaves spice up any green salad. The initiated enjoy whole salads of the stuff.

BELGIAN ENDIVE. Bitter and crunchy, it pairs well with strong, creamy cheeses, or simply paired with beets and a vinaigrette.

BIBB. A prized lettuce for green salads, its mild and sweet leaves work well with light vinaigrettes but can handle stronger dressings.

BOSTON. Buttery, with very soft leaves and a tender heart, its subtle flavor combines well with a light vinaigrette.

CHICORY. The spiky, curly-edged leaves have a pleasing, bitter taste; they make a good counterpoint to milder greens.

GREEN OAK-LEAF. A loose-leaf lettuce with a grassy flavor, it wilts quickly and should be used as soon as possible.

ICEBERG. This all-purpose lettuce is available everywhere, anytime. It is mild and crisp and best mixed with other greens and crunchy salad companions.

MÂCHE OR LAMB'S LETTUCE. Its delicate, slightly nutty flavor offsets more bitter greens in a salad.

RADICCHIO. Its slightly peppery, bitter taste is good in green salads, but it is also delicious grilled, braised, or steamed with meat dishes.

RED OAK-LEAF. Similar to the green oak-leaf, this loose-leaf lettuce adds color to any mixed green salad.

ROMAINE. Its nutty, crunchy, and slightly sweet leaves is a good match for more assertive dressings.

WATERCRESS. Its spicy, peppery taste works well with other greens and astringent fruits like oranges or grapefruit. Try substituting watercress for lettuce in sandwiches.

WATERCRESS SALAD

It's nothing short of elegant. Three easy ingredients contribute three entirely different flavors, colors, and textures, and they all come together with a glistening vinaigrette.

SERVES 4

1 bunch watercress, torn
½ head romaine lettuce, torn into bite-size pieces
1 pear, diced

DRESSING

2 tablespoons olive oil
2 tablespoons red wine vinegar
Shavings of Parmesan cheese

1. Combine watercress, romaine, and pear in a large serving bowl and toss.

2. Sprinkle oil and vinegar over lettuces. Garnish with Parmesan cheese and serve.

ARUGULA SALAD WITH MANGO AND BLUE CHEESE

SERVES 4

4 bunches arugula, torn
½ cup (about 3–4 ounces) crumbled blue cheese
1 ripe mango, peeled and diced
Salt and pepper
½ cup dry-roasted sunflower seeds (salted, if desired)

DRESSING

1 lime, zest finely grated and lime then juiced
3 tablespoons rice vinegar
4–5 tablespoons olive oil

1. Combine arugula, blue cheese, and diced mango in a bowl. Add salt and pepper to taste. Toss.

2. Whisk together dressing ingredients. Dress and garnish servings with a generous handful of sunflower seeds.

NOTE: Blue cheese is salty; salt salad sparingly.

OTHER CHOICES: 2 peaches or nectarines may be substituted for the mango.

SALAD OF MIXED GREENS

"You fussed!" they'll say. Indeed, as salads go, this is an ambitious undertaking for those who dread washing, chopping, peeling, and tearing. But the results are spectacular.

SERVES 4–6

1 bunch watercress, torn
1 bunch arugula, torn
1 head romaine lettuce, torn into bite-size pieces
½ bunch fresh basil, chiffonade (see page 272)
1 head radicchio, coarsely chopped
1 small log Montrachet cheese, torn apart in chunks

DRESSING

2 tablespoons grated Parmesan cheese
3–4 tablespoons olive oil
3–4 tablespoons balsamic vinegar

1. Combine all salad ingredients in a large bowl.

2. Whisk together the dressing ingredients in another bowl. Toss salad and dressing together and serve.

MESCLUN

Mesclun means "mixed up" and refers to a mixture of greens, usually including several kinds of delicate baby lettuces, such as red oak-leaf lettuce, romaine, arugula, radicchio, and mizuna, among others.

"According to the Spanish proverb, four persons are wanted to make a good salad (dressing): a spendthrift for oil, a miser for vinegar, a counsellor for salt and a madman to stir it all up."

ABRAHAM HAYWARD

(1801–84)

SALAD OF MIXED GREENS

VINAIGRETTE

If cooking were music, vinaigrette would be a jazz standard. You can make it a jangling, double-time bebop, like Chet. You can cool it down like Miles. Or, like Ella, you can smooth the edges and send it soaring. Vinaigrette is the same song with the same basic structure, but everybody improvises, personalizing the tangy result.

KIM'S SWEET AND SOUR VINAIGRETTE

SERVES 8

6 tablespoons olive oil
2 tablespoons balsamic vinegar
2 fresh cloves garlic, pressed
2 teaspoons grainy Dijon
   mustard
   Large pinch of Sweet'n Low
   or 2 pinches of sugar, for a
   sweet and pungent kick

Whisk all ingredients together.

GEORGIA'S TARRAGON MUSTARD VINAIGRETTE

SERVES 8

1   clove garlic, minced
     Salt to taste
$^1/_3$–$^1/_2$ cup extra virgin olive oil
2   tablespoons tarragon vinegar
2–3 teaspoons Dijon mustard
1   tablespoon fresh lemon juice
     Freshly ground black
     pepper, to taste
     Pinch of sugar
1–2 tablespoons minced fresh
     tarragon

1. In a bowl, crush the garlic with salt and 1 tablespoon of the olive oil until the mixture forms a paste.

2. Add the tarragon vinegar, mustard, lemon juice, pepper, and sugar.

3. Add the remaining oil in a stream, whisking the dressing until it is combined well. Just before serving, stir in the fresh tarragon.

SALLY'S ORANGE VINAIGRETTE

SERVES 8

4–5 tablespoons olive oil
3   tablespoons sherry vinegar
     or 2 tablespoons red wine
     vinegar with 1 tablespoon
     sherry
2   tablespoons orange juice
     Zest of 1 orange, minced
     (about $^3/_4$–1 tablespoon)
     Salt and pepper

Place all ingredients in a jar, blender, or food processor and combine. Add salt and pepper to taste.

JEFF'S HOT AND CRUNCHY VINAIGRETTE

SERVES 8

4   tablespoons sesame oil
2   cloves garlic, sliced thin
$^1/_4$ teaspoon Inner Beauty
     Real Hot Sauce (see
     Gourmet America, page 274)
1   tablespoon raw sunflower
     seeds
3   shallots, cut up very thin
2   tablespoons chopped fresh
     cilantro
2   tablespoons red wine vinegar

OPTIONAL INGREDIENT

$1^1/_2$ teaspoons light brown sugar

1. Heat oil in saucepan and add slices of garlic. Sauté until brown and then remove garlic.

2. Still on medium heat, add Inner Beauty Real Hot Sauce, sunflower seeds, shallots, and 1 tablespoon of the cilantro.

3. Let everything get hot, add vinegar, stir, and, if desired, add brown sugar. Then add the second tablespoon of cilantro and pour into serving bowl.

"I am a vegetarian not for my health, but for the health of the chickens."

ISAAC BASHEVIS SINGER

EUROPEAN

KIRBY

228

SLICING CUCUMBERS. These familiar cucumbers have a thick, deep emerald skin, and since they are often waxed for longer shelf life, they are usually peeled before eating.

EUROPEAN CUCUMBERS. Another variety of "slicing" cucumbers, they are also known as English or greenhouse cucumbers. They are milder, thinner, longer, and virtually seedless, with soft skins. As they are not waxed, they need not be peeled.

KIRBY. Dill pickles are made with this smaller cousin of slicing cucumbers. Though often categorized as a "pickling" cucumber, Kirbys can be eaten fresh.

SLICING

COLD CUCUMBER SALAD

SERVES 4

1 large cucumber (long European soft-skinned preferred), with skin scored or removed if hard or waxy, sliced paper-thin, deseeded to avoid excess water
½ small-to-medium red onion, sliced paper thin
¼ cup any clear vinegar
1 teaspoon sugar
¼ cup chopped fresh dill
1 teaspoon kosher salt
Freshly ground pepper, to taste

⏲ Combine all ingredients in a bowl and chill for 1–2 hours, stirring occasionally.

OTHER CHOICES: Replace vinegar with ¼ cup fresh lime juice, and dill with ¼ cup chopped fresh mint.

TIP: An old-fashioned vegetable slicer is the safest and easiest way to slice cucumbers really thin.

AVOCADO AND HEARTS OF PALM

This recipe is inspired by the Insalate Tropicale served at Bice, a restaurant in Milan. The key is to use flavorful avocados, the best olive oil, and fresh Pecorino Romano or Parmesan with a bite.

SERVES 4

- 2 large ripe Haas avocados, peeled and pitted
- 1 16-ounce can hearts of palm, drained and rinsed
- 1 teaspoon olive oil
- 2 teaspoons red wine vinegar
- 10 large shavings of Pecorino Romano or Parmesan cheese
  Salt and pepper

1. Cut avocados and hearts of palm into similar sizes, either lengthwise or into bite-size pieces. Mix together gently.

2. Divide into 4 parts and place on individual plates.

3. Whisk together oil and vinegar. Pour over avocado and hearts of palm.

4. Sprinkle shavings of cheese over the salad. Add salt and coarsely ground pepper to taste.

TUSCAN BREAD SALAD

SERVES 4

- 2 cups cubed day-old French or sourdough bread
- 2 medium tomatoes, diced
- 1 cucumber, peeled and thinly sliced
- 1/4 cup coarsely chopped fresh chives
- 1 bell pepper, any color, cubed
- 1/4 cup coarsely chopped fresh basil
- 1 tablespoon finely chopped fresh oregano
- 1/2 cup fresh coarsely chopped parsley
- 1-2 cloves garlic, finely chopped or pressed
- 1-2 tablespoons red wine vinegar
- 1/2 teaspoon salt
- 1/4 teaspoon black pepper
- 1-2 tablespoons olive oil

1. Combine bread, vegetables, and herbs in a large mixing bowl.

2. Place garlic, vinegar, salt, pepper, and oil in a small bowl and mix well. Drizzle over bread mixture, then toss.

TOMATO AND BASIL SALAD

Simply the best of summer. Fresh basil and tomatoes are essential for this salad. If you're lucky, you need not go farther than your garden.

SERVES 4

- 4 beefsteak tomatoes, sliced or diced
- 12 basil leaves, chiffonade (see page 272)
- 1 tablespoon red wine or balsamic vinegar
- 1 tablespoon olive oil
  Salt and pepper

1. Place tomatoes in a large shallow plate or bowl and sprinkle with basil leaves. Sprinkle with vinegar and oil. Add salt and pepper to taste.

OTHER CHOICES: Add sliced or diced mozzarella to the mix.

AVOCADO

Like tomatoes, avocados are worth waiting for. Haas avocados have pebbly skin; in the summer they're what make guacamole holy. Smooth-skinned varieties are available year-round, yet they pale in comparison to the rich flavor of a creamy, dreamy Haas in season.

"What peaches and what penumbras! Whole families shopping at night! Aisles full of husbands! Wives in the avocados, babies in the tomatoes!— and you, García Lorca, what were you doing down by the watermelons?"

ALLEN GINSBERG, from *"A Supermarket in California"*

AVOCADO AND HEARTS OF PALM

A L I C E

It is possible that Alice Waters was born with sophisticated taste. "I wanted green beans and rare charcoal-grilled steaks, every birthday dinner," she recalls of her precocious childhood wishes. Today Chef Waters has redefined culinary sophistication. Her mastery is evident in her five cookbooks and in the dishes she serves daily at Chez Panisse, her world-famous restaurant in Berkeley, California. Yet, while Waters' inventive cookery is based on French cuisine made with fresh, healthy ingredients, she has never lost sight of the ritual of mealtimes and the pleasures of serving fine food. "I opened a restaurant so that everybody could come and eat," she explains. "Remember that the final goal is to nourish and nurture those who gather at our table. It is there, within this nurturing process, that I have found the greater satisfaction and sense of accomplishment."

"My obsession with salads must have had its beginnings the local park's party and contest when I was three and a half. and vegetables from my

WARM GREEN BEAN SALAD WITH ROCKET AND GARDEN LETTUCES

Chef Waters' special talent is that her recipes enhance the goodness of vegetables—our definition of a great cook. This salad is a Waters classic.

SERVES 6

6	handfuls mixed garden lettuces and rocket (arugula) (include small red-leaf lettuce for color)
1¼	cups shelled walnut halves
1½	tablespoons finely diced shallots
¾	cup virgin olive oil
¼–⅓	cup balsamic vinegar
¼	cup Niçoise olives
½	pound haricots verts
	Salt and pepper

1. Wash and dry the mixed garden lettuces and rocket. Pinch the ends from ½ pound haricots verts.

2. Spread 1¼ cups walnut halves on a baking tray. In an oven preheated to 350° F., bake the nuts for 10–15 minutes until they are well-toasted. Remove from the oven and set aside.

3. Make the vinaigrette by combining 1½ tablespoons finely diced shallots, ¾ cup olive oil, about ½ cup balsamic vinegar, and salt and pepper to taste.

4. Blanch the beans for 2 to 3 minutes in plenty of boiling salted water, or until they are crisp but tender and bright green. Drain the beans.

5. Toss the warm beans, the greens, the walnuts, and ¼ cup Niçoise olives in enough vinaigrette to coat lightly but thoroughly. Arrange the salad on slightly warm plates and serve.

ALICE WATERS

ON QUALITY NOT QUANTITY.
"I personally cannot eat massive quantities of food, so to me, heaped-up plates are truly offensive. A heavily laden plate allows one course to dominate and the risk is that it will overwhelm the entire framework of the meal. I do like platters of food in the middle of the table, family style; a more appealing presentation can be made and those at the table can help themselves to precisely the amount they want. This encourages everyone's involvement in the food, eases serving complications in the kitchen, and evokes a communal sense about dining."

in the costume my mother created for me to wear to Dressed as the queen of the garden, I was adorned with the fruits parents' Victory garden."

[OTHER FACTS—*page 279*]

DESSERT

"Claudine, squatting cross-legged in a dressing-gown before the marble chimney piece, [was] completely absorbed in roasting one side of a bar of chocolate kept upright between a pair of tongs. When the surface exposed to the fire softened, blackened, cracked and blistered, I lifted it off in thin layers with my little knife.... Exquisite taste, a mixture of grilled almonds and grated vanilla! The melancholy sweetness of savoring the toasted chocolate...."

BAKED APPLES

*The apple is infinitely adaptable. As a
dessert, it can be eaten right off the tree,
but any variety becomes somehow
elegant when baked.*

SERVES 4

1 tablespoon maple syrup,
  light brown sugar, or honey
½ teaspoon ground cinnamon
¼ cup raisins
¼ cup coarsely chopped walnuts
2 strips lemon zest, grated or
  chopped
4 Granny Smith apples, cored,
  the top third cut off and
  discarded
6 tablespoons white wine

1. Preheat oven to 375° F.

2. Combine maple syrup, brown sugar
or honey, cinnamon, raisins, walnuts,
and lemon zest in a small bowl. Divide
mixture into four parts and stuff inside apples.

3. Place apples in a small baking dish,
so that they are touching (the mutual
support helps keep them together)
and pour the wine around them.

4. Bake for about 1 hour, or until the
apples are soft.

HEAVEN

CALL IT A MOMENT OF LAUGHTER AND FORGETTING.

THE WORLD SHRINKS TO A PINPOINT: THERE IS NOTHING, NOTHING

BUT AN ANGEL-TASTE MELTING ON YOUR TONGUE. AH, THE SWEETNESS OF

sweets after a fine meal. That army of endorphins conquering your senses. Childhood dreams of sugarplums are re-

placed by more complicated pleasures: perhaps we swoon for lemon mousse, banana cake with a bittersweet glaze. Oh,

honey: is heaven only for the good? Or is there a special place reserved for the rich, the sinful, the smooth and the devilish?

BROWN SUGAR. When granulated sugar is mixed with molasses, it becomes brown sugar, a good example of a product being better because of the sum of its parts. The darker the sugar, the richer the flavor. The molasses content makes baked goods even moister. By storing brown sugar with a slice of apple, a piece of stale bread, or a piece of paper towel, you can prevent it from crystallizing.

CONFECTIONERS' SUGAR. Cornstarch is added to granulated sugar to produce this powdery rich sugar. A dark pudding or cake becomes dazzling with a dusting—but sprinkle only just before serving (through a doily if you want to be fancy), since the pudding's moisture will spoil the effect if allowed to sit.

GRANULATED (WHITE) SUGAR. This dry, loose sugar comes in fine or superfine grains. At teatime you might want it in cubes.

HONEY. The smooth taste of this bee-made natural sugar syrup comes from any number of flowers and plants, each with a distinctive flavor: heather, raspberry, spearmint, thyme, orange flower, or buckwheat. Oil your measuring cup or spoon before measuring out honey. The oil will allow all the honey to stream out smoothly.

[DESSERTS *first aid—page 269*]

STRAWBERRY RHUBARB CRISP

GUILTLESS PLEASURE

Crisps, crunches, and cobblers are old-fashioned desserts. Simpler than pie—which requires special skills, not the least of which is deft rolling-pin operation—a simple fruit crunch or crisp is easy to make and easier to eat.

FRUIT CRUNCH

This topping gets its crunch with the addition of chopped nuts.

SERVES 4

Fruit—see center column for seasonal options
- ⅓ cup plus 1 tablespoon unbleached all-purpose flour
- ⅔ cup pecans, coarsely chopped, or hazelnuts, finely chopped
- 2 tablespoons sugar
- ¼ cup light brown sugar
- Pinch of salt
- ½ teaspoon ground cinnamon
- 3 tablespoons unsalted butter, chilled

1. Preheat oven to 300° F.

2. Combine the fruit with 1 tablespoon of flour in an ungreased 8 x 8-inch baking pan.

3. Combine the remaining ingredients in a large mixing bowl, and mix, by hand or with two forks, until the mixture is crumbly and consistent.

4. Place the mixture on top of the fruit and place pan in oven. Bake for 30 minutes and then raise heat to 350° F. and bake 15 minutes longer.

FESTIVAL OF FRUIT

Since the tastiest fruits are both fresh and local, your best source is the local farm market. We've made some seasonal suggestions, but don't be shy. Almost all fruits go well with other fruits, so you can mix and match to your heart's content.

AUTUMN. Apple: 5–6 Granny Smith apples, peeled, cored, and thinly sliced.

WINTER. Pear Ginger: 6 ripe pears, quartered and thinly sliced. Add 2 teaspoons finely chopped fresh gingerroot. Substitute nutmeg for the cinnamon.

SPRING. Strawberry Rhubarb: 1 pound rhubarb, halved lengthwise and thinly sliced and 1 quart strawberries, berries cut into quarters. Omit ground cinnamon and increase sugar to taste.

SUMMER. Peach Blueberry: Mix 5 ripe peaches, quartered and thinly sliced, with 1 cup blueberries.

FRUIT CRISP

This more traditional fruit crisp has a topping made from oats—which is a perfect excuse to eat it for breakfast.

SERVES 4

Fruit—see center column for seasonal options
- ⅔ cup unbleached all-purpose flour
- ⅔ cup rolled oats
- 3 tablespoons light brown sugar
- 3 tablespoons sugar
- ¾ teaspoon ground cinnamon
- 1–1¼ teaspoons ground nutmeg
- ¼ teaspoon salt
- 4 tablespoons unsalted butter, melted

1. Preheat oven to 350° F.

2. Place the fruit in an ungreased 8 x 8-inch baking pan.

3. Place the remaining ingredients in a medium-sized mixing bowl and mix, by hand or with 2 forks, until the mixture is crumbly.

4. Place the mixture on top of the fruit and place pan in oven. Bake for about 35 minutes, or until top is golden brown.

FUJI

EMPIRE

GALA

ROME

IDA RED

GOLDEN DELICIOUS

EMPIRE lean toward the crisp and tart side. FUJI are a good dessert apple, crisp with a sweet but tart flavor. GALA are sweet, red, and similar to the Royal Gala but smaller in size. GOLDEN DELICIOUS are fine, sweet all-purpose apples, tasting good fresh off the tree or cooked. GRANNY SMITH are an old Australian variety, crisp, tart, and excellent for cooking, as the apple holds its shape well. IDA RED are crisp with a sweet but tart flavor. MACOUN are slightly sweet. MCINTOSH are tart red-to-green

MACOUN

MCINTOSH

apples, good for eating and for making pies and apple sauce. **RED DELICIOUS** are a sweet, crisp apple, good for eating out of hand. **ROME** are a firm-fleshed red apple, good for baking. **ROYAL GALA** are crisp with a sweet but tart flavor and tender skin.

GRANNY SMITH

ROYAL GALA

RED DELICIOUS

"I love fruit, but I'd just as soon eat a piece of cake."

SHIRLEY MACLAINE

TOOLS

WHAT. The Bundt pan.

WHY. With a Bundt pan, a hurried cook can make a grandly tall cake without using multiple layer pans. As to why Bundt pans are always textured like cut crystal, we haven't a clue. The secret, of course, is that funnel—it allows a cake to cook from the inside.

GLAZED APPLE CAKE

The glaze makes this cake irresistible; this one's made with buttermilk, which has less fat than whole milk.

SERVES 16

1½ cups sugar
3 large eggs, at room temperature
1 cup canola or corn oil
¼ teaspoon salt
¼ cup apple or orange juice
3 cups unbleached all-purpose flour
1 teaspoon baking soda
1 teaspoon ground cinnamon
1 teaspoon vanilla extract
2 Granny Smith apples, peeled and finely chopped

OPTIONAL INGREDIENTS

½ cup shredded coconut, unsweetened
½ cup coarsely chopped walnuts

BUTTERMILK GLAZE

2 tablespoons unsalted butter
¼ cup sugar
½ teaspoon baking soda
½ cup buttermilk

1. Preheat the oven to 325° F. Lightly grease and flour a 10-inch Bundt pan.

2. Combine the sugar, eggs, oil, salt, juice, flour, baking soda, cinnamon, and vanilla in a large mixing bowl and blend well. This can be prepared in a mixer or by hand.

3. By hand, add apples, coconut and walnuts, if desired, and mix until combined.

4. ⏰ Place batter in prepared Bundt pan and bake for about 50–60 minutes, or until a tester inserted comes out clean. Let cake cool in pan about 15 minutes.

5. While the cake is baking, place the butter, sugar, baking soda, and buttermilk in a small saucepan. Stir and bring to a boil. Pour the glaze over the cake while both are still warm.

BANANA CAKE

SERVES 16

2 cups sugar
1 cup canola or vegetable oil
3 large eggs
1 tablespoon vanilla extract
4 overripe bananas, mashed with a fork
3 cups unbleached all-purpose flour
1 teaspoon baking soda
½ teaspoon baking powder
1 teaspoon salt
½ teaspoon ground cinnamon
½ teaspoon ground nutmeg

1. Preheat oven to 325° F. Lightly grease and flour a 10-inch Bundt pan.

2. Beat the sugar, oil, and eggs together in a large bowl. Add vanilla and bananas and mix until just combined.

3. In a separate bowl, combine the remaining ingredients and add to banana mixture.

4. ⏰ Mix until just combined. Pour into Bundt pan and cook 1 hour.

OTHER CHOICES: Top warm cake with Chocolate Glaze (see page 249).

GLAZED APPLE CAKE

LEMON CAKE

SERVES 10-12

- ¼ cup unsalted butter, at room temperature
- 1 cup granulated sugar
- 2 large eggs
- ½ cup milk
- ¼ cup fresh lemon juice (about 1–2 lemons)
  Grated zest of 1 lemon
- 1¼ cups unbleached all-purpose flour
- 1 teaspoon baking powder

OPTIONAL INGREDIENT

- ⅔ cup chopped pecans

GLAZE

- ¼ cup fresh lemon juice
- ¼ cup confectioners' sugar

1. Preheat oven to 350° F. Lightly grease an 8 x 4-inch loaf pan.

2. Beat the butter and sugar in a large mixing bowl (an electric mixer will make it easier). Add the eggs, milk, lemon juice and zest. Mix until combined.

3. Combine the flour and baking powder and add to batter. Mix until well combined. If desired, add pecans and stir by hand.

4. ⏰ Place batter in loaf pan and bake about 50 minutes, or until top is lightly browned.

5. While the cake is baking, prepare the glaze by combining the lemon juice and confectioners' sugar in a small bowl. Mix until well combined.

6. When cake has finished baking, remove from oven. Pour glaze evenly over hot cake and let both cool before removing from pan.

LEMON SQUARES

MAKES 9 SQUARES

CRUST

- ¾ cup unbleached all-purpose flour
- 1½ tablespoons confectioners' sugar
- ¼ teaspoon salt
- 6 tablespoons unsalted butter

FILLING

- 2 large eggs
- 1 large egg yolk
  Zest of 1 lemon
- ⅔ cup fresh lemon juice
- ½ cup granulated sugar

TOPPING

- ¼ cup confectioners' sugar, for sprinkling

1. Preheat the oven to 350° F. Lightly butter an 8 x 8-inch baking pan.

2. Combine the flour, confectioners' sugar, and salt in a large bowl or food processor fitted with a steel blade. Add butter, 1 tablespoon at a time, and mix until all butter is incorporated.

3. Pack well into the prepared baking pan and bake for about 20–25 minutes, or until slightly golden. Cool completely.

4. Place the eggs, egg yolk, lemon zest, lemon juice, and sugar in a large bowl or food processor fitted with a steel blade. Mix until the ingredients are completely incorporated.

5. Pour over cooled crust and bake for about 15–18 minutes, or until the custard sets. Do not overbake.

6. ⏰ Cool to room temperature, cover and refrigerate for at least 1 hour. Sprinkle with confectioners' sugar.

FRESH LEMON MOUSSE

Jacqueline de la Chaume, the culinarily gifted woman behind this excellent dessert, grew up in France and worked for eight years with Gregory Mosher, the former artistic director of Lincoln Center.

SERVES 4

- 3 lemons, zest minced; juice from 1 lemon
- ¾ cup sugar
- 4 large eggs, separated
- 6 tablespoons butter
  Raspberries, for garnish

1. Place lemon zest, lemon juice, sugar, and egg yolks in a double boiler and cook, over low heat, until thickened (the mixture should be able to coat the back of a spoon). Add small amounts of butter at a time.

2. Beat the egg whites until they form stiff peaks. Gently fold the egg whites into the lemon mixture.

3. Refrigerate until well chilled and serve with raspberries.

CHOCOLATE

YOUR HEAD IS LIGHT.

CIRCLED IN DIZZINESS,

YOUR BODY UNCOILS, THE

edges of your vision blur ever so

slightly as your pupils dilate, and your

skin begins a slow flush. You want to

have a cigarette....Was it good for you?

Don't ask—it's chocolate. Even the

Aztecs, who first harvested the fruit of

the Theobromo cacao, recognized it

as a natural aphrodisiac. And you've

got to love its convenience—ever try

to bring oysters to the movie theater?

CHOCOLATE MACAROONS

MAKES 12

3 egg whites
Pinch of salt
¾ cup sugar
13 ounces coconut, grated
¾ cup unsweetened cocoa powder

1. Preheat oven to 350° F.

2. In a medium-sized bowl, beat egg whites until stiff, gradually adding salt and sugar. By hand, blend in coconut. Gradually fold in cocoa.

3. Drop large tablespoons of dough onto an ungreased cookie sheet. Bake for 20 minutes.

4. Cool on waxed paper.

CHOCOLATE GLAZE

When frosting is too heavy-handed, this sophisticated bittersweet glaze is tops for drizzling over cakes and brownies.

FOR 1 CAKE OR 1 BATCH OF BROWNIES

3 ounces semisweet chocolate
3 tablespoons heavy cream
3 tablespoons water
½ teaspoon vanilla

1. Melt chocolate in microwave or in double boiler.

2. Stir in heavy cream, water, and vanilla when chocolate has melted.

OTHER CHOICES: Substitute dark rum for water and vanilla.

BROWNIES

MAKES 16

4 ounces unsweetened chocolate
½ pound unsalted butter
1¾ cups sugar
4 large eggs
1 tablespoon vanilla extract
1 cup unbleached all-purpose flour
½ teaspoon salt

OPTIONAL INGREDIENTS

1 cup walnuts or pecans, coarsely chopped, or chocolate chips, peanut butter chips, or caramel chunks

1. Preheat oven to 325° F. Lightly grease and flour a 9 x 12-inch baking pan.

2. Over the lowest possible heat, melt chocolate and butter in a small saucepan, stirring occasionally. Set aside to cool to room temperature.

3. Combine the sugar, eggs, and vanilla in a medium-sized mixing bowl. Whisk together until slightly frothy. Add cooled chocolate mixture and mix until just combined. Add flour and salt and mix until well combined.

4. Add nuts, if desired, and mix.

5. Place batter in pan and bake for about 25–30 minutes, or until a tester comes out clean.

CHOCOLATE BREAD PUDDING

We didn't find this recipe. This recipe found us. In fact, it followed us home. It isn't exactly chic and it isn't exactly simple, but for those of us who love the texture of pudding and the kick of chocolate, it is, exactly, a must-have.

SERVES 6 GENEROUSLY

- 6 cups bread cubes (standard crouton size) from fresh anadama, oatmeal, challah, cinnamon, or white bread
- 1 cup heavy cream
- 6 ounces semisweet chocolate, grated
- 2 ounces unsweetened chocolate, grated
- 1/2 cup sugar
- 5 large eggs, separated
- 1/3 cup unsalted butter, at room temperature
- 1 tablespoon vanilla extract
- 1/2 teaspoon ground cinnamon
  Pinch of salt

1. Preheat oven to 350° F. Lightly butter an 8 x 8-inch baking pan.

2. Place bread cubes in a large mixing bowl.

3. Heat the cream over low heat in a small saucepan. Add chocolates and cook, stirring occasionally, until completely dissolved. Place mixture in a food processor fitted with a steel blade. Add sugar, egg yolks, butter, vanilla, and cinnamon, and process until smooth. Pour mixture over bread cubes.

4. Place egg whites and a pinch of salt in a separate bowl and whisk or beat with an electric mixer until the whites form stiff peaks.

5. Gradually add whites, by hand, to chocolate mixture and gently combine until incorporated. Place in baking dish.

6. Place the baking dish in a roasting pan filled with enough water to surround the pudding dish halfway up its size. Bake for 35 minutes, or until pudding just begins to set.

7. While bread is warm, scoop out individual servings. This is great with whipped cream (recipe follows).

WHIPPED CREAM

Mr. Wizard couldn't have impressed us more than by showing us the magic of whipping cream. The transition from white liquid to foamy confusion, to sleek decadence...we could have eaten a whole bowlful. Then Mr. Wizard showed us the magic of Irish coffee...

MAKES ABOUT 1 3/4 CUPS

- 1 cup heavy cream, chilled
- 1 teaspoon vanilla extract

OPTIONAL INGREDIENT

- 2 teaspoons confectioners' sugar

Place the cream in a chilled glass mixing bowl. Using a whisk or an electric beater, beat until it forms soft peaks. While beating, gradually add vanilla and, if desired, confectioners' sugar.

MATCH MADE IN HEAVEN

Chocolate and fruit—each delicious, but even better together. This is one of the sweetest rewards for finishing all that good-for-you stuff. Waiting on your plate is a bite-size morsel of chocolate-covered fruit.

Melt bittersweet chocolate in a double boiler. Mount a chunk of fresh pineapple, a slice of banana, a raspberry, a tangerine section (you get the idea?) on a toothpick and dip it into the sweet, murky pool of chocolate. Hold the fruit over the pot a moment to allow for the hot drippings to fall. Then put coated fruit on a waxed paper–covered plate and remove the toothpick. Allow chocolate to harden on the fruit in the refrigerator— the resulting brittle shell is worth the wait.

CHOCOLATE BREAD PUDDING

GINGERSNAPS

These are the American equivalent of France's madeleines. It takes only one spicy mouthful for the molasses to work its magic—be prepared to lose yourself in blissful reveries.

MAKES 4 DOZEN

½ cup unsalted butter, at room temperature
1 cup sugar, plus more for rolling
1 large egg, at room temperature
3 tablespoons dark molasses
1½ teaspoons vanilla extract
2 cups unbleached all-purpose flour
2½–3½ teaspoons ground ginger
1½ teaspoons baking soda
1 teaspoon ground cinnamon
¼ teaspoon salt

1. Preheat oven to 350° F. Lightly butter a cookie sheet.

2. Combine the butter and 1 cup of the sugar and mix until light and fluffy. Add the egg, molasses, and vanilla, and continue beating until smooth. Gradually beat in dry ingredients.

3. To form the cookies, break off small pieces and roll into balls about an inch in diameter. Roll them in sugar and place on cookie sheet. Flatten each ball into a flat disc.

4. Place the cookies in the oven and bake for 15–17 minutes, or until cookies begin to brown. If you like your cookies slightly soft, decrease the time and remove from the sheet as soon as they come out of the oven. If you like them crisp, let them cool on the cookie sheet.

COOKIES

DOUGH. Most cookie doughs can be frozen for up to 1 year if they are in airtight freezer bags. Roll the dough in a log before freezing. When you want just a few oven-fresh cookies for dessert, all you need to do is saw off a few rounds of frozen dough and bake them while you eat your main meal. Cooked cookies can be frozen for 4–6 months. Make sure to separate the layers of cookies with plastic wrap or waxed paper.

SUBSTITUTING. Never use diet margarine or anything labeled "spread" as a substitute for butter. Because they are low in fat and have a lot of water, they will make very unyummy cookies.

BAKING. A cookie sheet needs to be a good heat conductor. The best ones are made of shiny, heavy-gauge aluminum and have a non-stick coating

MOISTNESS. Here is a trick for keeping soft cookies moist, or re-invigorating them if they have become dry. Place several apple quarters in the storage container, cover tightly, and wait 1–2 days.

OATMEAL COOKIES

Ah, when rough oats are kissed by brown sugar, it's wholesome romance at its finest. Whether in a bowl at breakfast or with milk as a snack, this old-fashioned couple will be sure to cure whatever ails you.

MAKES 4 DOZEN

½ pound unsalted butter, at room temperature
1 cup dark brown sugar
½ cup granulated sugar
2 large eggs, at room temperature
1 tablespoon vanilla extract
1 tablespoon water
1¾ cups unbleached all-purpose flour
1 teaspoon baking soda
½ teaspoon salt
2½ cups rolled oats

OPTIONAL INGREDIENTS

2 cups semisweet chocolate chips
1 cup chopped pecans, walnuts, or almonds
1 cup coconut
1 cup raisins
1 teaspoon ground cinnamon

1. Preheat oven to 375° F.

2. Cream butter and sugars in a large mixing bowl. Add eggs, vanilla, and water, and mix until thoroughly incorporated.

3. In a separate bowl, combine flour, baking soda, salt, and rolled oats. Add to butter mixture and blend well. Add up to 2 cups optional ingredients, if desired, by hand.

4. Place heaping teaspoonfuls of dough on cookie sheet. Bake for about 12 minutes. Cool sheet between batches.

CHOCOLATE CHIP COOKIES

A classic. A bold beauty, chips studding the dough universe in a galaxy of black holes. Einstein would love these.

MAKES 4 DOZEN

1/2	pound unsalted butter, at room temperature
1	cup light brown sugar
3/4	cup granulated sugar
2	large eggs, at room temperature
1	generous teaspoon vanilla extract
2	cups unbleached all-purpose flour
3/4	teaspoon baking soda
1	teaspoon salt
2	cups semisweet chocolate chips

OPTIONAL INGREDIENT

1–2	cups chopped walnuts, pecans, or cashews

1. Preheat oven to 340° F. (You don't have to measure this; just set your thermometer between 325° and 350°). Grease a cookie sheet lightly.

2. Cream butter and sugars until light. Add eggs and vanilla, being careful not to overbeat.

3. Sift in dry ingredients and mix well. Stir in chips and, if desired, nuts.

4. Drop large tablespoons of dough onto cookie sheet. Bake 12 minutes, or until the cookies are brown at the edge but soft in the middle. Cool cookie sheet between batches.

TOOLS

WHAT. Flour sifter

WHY. A flour sifter mixes dry ingredients as it passes them through its sieve.

IN A WORD, COOKIE

The term "cookie" was introduced to the U.S. in the late eighteenth century by Dutch immigrants; it is an Americanized spelling of the Dutch word *koekje*, a diminutive form of the word *koek*, "cake." In Britain, cookies are called "biscuits." British food writer John Ayto says, "To be sure, [the term] is used in the U.S.A. and Canada for 'biscuits,' but only sweet biscuits; and it also includes slightly leavened biscuits that attain a partially raised shape which would almost qualify them in Britain for the word 'cake.' "

PEANUT BUTTER COOKIES

The concept of peanut butter cookies caused a war of the wills: Sally said they were superfluous. Jeff said that they rank among the Important Foods of the World. Wayne, our art director, broke the tie by announcing that peanut butter cookies were his favorite. Which proves Todd's theory: Men love nuts. (But women fall for them.)

MAKES 4 DOZEN

1/2	pound unsalted butter, at room temperature
1	cup granulated sugar
1	cup light brown sugar, packed
2	eggs
2	teaspoons vanilla extract
1 1/2	cups smooth peanut butter
3 1/3	cups unbleached all-purpose flour
1 1/2	teaspoons baking soda
1/2	teaspoon salt
3/4	cup coarsely chopped peanuts,

1. Preheat oven to 300° F. Grease a cookie sheet lightly.

2. Cream butter and sugars until light. Add eggs, vanilla, and peanut butter, being careful not to overbeat.

3. Sift in dry ingredients and mix well. Stir in peanuts.

4. Drop heaping teaspoonfuls of dough onto cookie sheet and flatten with fork tines. Bake 15–18 minutes, or until the cookies are brown at the edge but soft in the middle. Let cookie sheet cool between batches.

"Milk and cookies keeping you awake, eh?"

MR. TYRRELL, *Blade Runner*

CHOCOLATE CHIP COOKIES

SEASONAL MENUS

OUR BODIES WANT DIFFERENT FOODS AT DIFFERENT TIMES OF THE YEAR, AND NATURE SUPPLIES US, MOST SERENDIPITOUSLY, WITH THE PERFECT INGREDIENTS AT JUST THE RIGHT TIME. THESE MENUS consider both the seasonal freshness of produce and the weather (in July we favor grilling outside over hot ovens inside). Foods have been selected and grouped for their natural harmonies, but like much else in this book, it is your personal taste, your creative variations, that will make these meals truly memorable. **THE WINES**. Wine consultant Richard J. Shiekman, vice president of the Parliament Import Co., provided wine suggestions for the menus below. The wines he lists are not formal selections but general inspirational guidelines. After all, as Mr. Shiekman observes, "Chardonnay" is open to interpretation: Within varieties of wine there is a vast range of prices, regions, vintners, and flavors. He suggests that simple wines be drunk with complex foods, and vice versa. Beyond that tip, he only advises to "Drink what you like." Cheers and *bon appetit*.

Pasta with Smoked Salmon 188
and Fresh Dill
Green Salad with Lemon 219
Dressing
Tuscan Bread 150

RICH REDS/RICH WHITES

Chardonnay
Sauvignon Blanc
Pinot Noir
☞

Curried Vegetable 31
Soup with Fresh Gingerroot
Salad of Mixed Greens 224
Brown Bread 150

SIMPLE WHITES

Alsace
Gewurztraminer
Sauvignon Blanc
☞

Salmon on a Bed of Leeks 93
and Carrots
Watercress Salad 224
Baked Potato

BIG REDS/BIG WHITES

Chardonnay
Pinot Noir
Sauvignon Blanc
☞

Penne with Asparagus 194
Crostini 150

LIGHT REDS

Dolcetto d'Alba
Chianti Classico
Sangiovese
☞

Chicken Paillards with Balsamic 46
Vinaigrette and Wilted Greens
White Bean Salad with 168
Rosemary and Basil

BIG WHITES

Chardonnay
White Burgundy
White Bordeaux
☞

Risotto with Asparagus 144
and Shiitake Mushrooms
Watercress Salad 224

BIG REDS

Bordeaux
Burgundy
Chianti Classico
☞

SUMMER MENUS

Shrimp and Garlic Pizza 207
Arugula Salad with Mango 224
and Blue Cheese

LIGHT WHITES

Chardonnay
Frascati
Sauvignon Blanc
☞

Spicy Gazpacho 31
Wild Rice and Turkey Salad 146
Pain de Campagne 150

LIGHT WHITES

Gewurztraminer
Riesling
Sauvignon Blanc
☞

Grilled Chicken Breasts with 64
Bar-B-Q Red Sauce
Roasted Mixed Vegetables 119
Spicy Black Bean Salad 158

LIGHT REDS

Beaujolais
Cabernet Sauvignon
Chianti Classico
☞

Shish Kebab with Yogurt 79
and Mint Dipping Sauce
Curried Rice 146
Cherry Tomatoes with Herbs 108

BIG REDS

Cabernet Sauvignon
Merlot
Rhône Reds
☞

Grilled or Broiled Fish 89
Steaks with Pesto 180
Grilled Yellow Squash and 110
Zucchini with Balsamic Vinegar
Curried Corn with Red Bell 120
Pepper and Herbs

BIG WHITES

Chardonnay
White Burgundy
White Bordeaux
☞

Linguine with Clams 197
Tomato and Basil Salad 230
French Baguette 150

CRISP WHITES

Frascati
Pinot Grigio
Sauvignon Blanc
☞

Moroccan Burgers 74
Cold Cucumber Salad 229
Grilled Corn on the Cob with 120
Cayenne Butter

ALL LIGHT REDS

Cabernet Sauvignon
Merlot
Beaujolais
☞

AUTUMN MENUS

Pasta with Broccoli Rabe and 185
White Beans
Salad of Mixed Greens 224
Italian Bread 150

LIGHT REDS

Dolcetto
Chianti Classico
Merlot
☞

Veal Scaloppine 82
Green Salad with Lemon 219
Dressing
Pasta with Roasted Bell 180
Pepper Sauce

BIG REDS

Chianti Classico
Merlot
Cabernet Sauvignon
☞

Chicken Soup with Lemon Zest, 22
Thyme, and Potatoes
Avocado and Hearts of Palm 230
Toasted Pita Bread 150

LIGHT WHITES

Chardonnay
Sauvignon Blanc
Gewurztraminer
☞

Fajitas with Salsa 55
and Guacamole
Steamed Broccoli 103
Refried Beans 158

LIGHT WHITES

Chardonnay
Chenin Blanc
Sauvignon Blanc
☞

Provençal Fish Stew 96
with Rouille
Salad of Mixed Greens 224
Focaccia Bread 207

BIG WHITES

White Burgundy
Chardonnay
Loire Whites
☞

Pasta e Fagioli 168
Green Salad with
Kim's Sweet Sour Vinaigrette 226
Fougasse Bread 150

BIG WHITES

Pinot Grigio
Chardonnay
White Rhône
☞

Spice-Rubbed Roasted Turkey 44
with Fruit and Nut Stuffing
Wild Rice 143
String Beans sweated in
Chicken Stock 19

BIG REDS

Bordeaux
Cabernet Sauvignon
Rhône
☞

first aid.

No one says you need to become a *cordon bleu* chef. But the basic techniques of good, healthy, uncomplicated cooking should be part of everyone's repertoire. If you know the ingredients you can design the menu. Improvise on your own and feed yourself. Give the delivery guys a night off.

"I can't believe I ate the whole thing."

ALKA-SELTZER AD SLOGAN

Rules of Thumb

1. Wash hands before cooking!
2. Keep a fire extinguisher handy in case of kitchen fires.
3. Never throw water on a grease fire. Use salt, baking soda, or, if the area is a small one, a metal lid.
4. When pan-frying or sautéing, keep a colander handy to place over the pan should the fat begin to spatter.

FIRST AID

For a minor cut during food preparation, wash the wound, apply an antiseptic cream and bandage. For anything more severe, seek medical help.

Soup

STORING. Freezing. Homemade chicken stock is best stored in the freezer. To avoid the cumbersome, messy hassle of chiseling at a frozen block of chicken stock, wait until the soup has cooled to room temperature and freeze it in a variety of quantities (either in plastic containers or paper cups lined with small plastic bags).

PREPARING. For a Creamy Soup. After a soup has nearly finished cooking, you can add heavy cream, sour cream, half-and-half, or plain yogurt to any soup, as desired. Be careful not to boil because the dairy products will separate. Also, be aware that you're adding more calories. **For a Smooth Soup.** Depending on your soup aesthetic, you may enjoy many soups puréed—although some people feel that it makes soup seem like baby food. **Fish-stock Alternatives.** Many recipes substitute canned chicken broth for fish broth. You can also substitute vegetable broth lightly flavored with clam juice, fish paste (found in Asian food markets), or anchovy paste.

HEALTH. Merits and Myths. Homemade chicken soup does have its benefits though it is not medicinal per se. Depending on how it's prepared, chicken soup can be a low-calorie, low-sodium meal. The heat of the soup will improve nasal drainage, which will help relieve head-cold misery. The pleasant smell and taste can't hurt, either. However, there still is no cure for the common cold.

Poultry

BUYING. The most economical way to purchase poultry is to buy a whole bird and cut it up yourself.

STORING. Fresh poultry can be kept, securely wrapped, in the refrigerator for two days. If you are keeping it longer than that, freeze it. Frozen poultry should be kept no longer than 6-9 months. You can freeze and defrost chicken in its marinade.

PREPARING. Thawing. It's best to thaw poultry in the refrigerator. Allow 3–4 hours of thawing time per pound; poultry parts may take less time. **Salmonella Alert.** In order to prevent the possible spread of salmonella, make sure you wash your hands and all surfaces and cutting utensils with hot, soapy water after cutting up raw poultry and before you prepare other foods. **Doneness.** You can tell that a roast chicken is done when the juices run clear from the breast and the legs move easily. If juices are still rosy-colored, you may still have a risk of salmonella. If you are using a thermometer, place it deep in the inner thigh: the chicken is done when the internal temperature reaches 160° F.

HEALTH. Cholesterol Alert. Chicken liver is not high in calories or fat, but 3½ ounces contain 631 milligrams of cholesterol, twice the maximum daily amount recommended. **For a Slimmer Roaster.** Roast chicken on a rack to reduce fat content. Serve poultry skinless to cut down even more calories. **The Bottom Line.** Three ounces of skinless chicken breast has approximately 24 grams of protein, 1.5 grams of fat, and 116 calories.

QUICK BAR-B-Q HOW-TO

1. Organize your work area. Have all the tools you need within easy reach. Clean the grill. Cooking residue will interfere with other flavors and can also cause food to stick.
2. Lay the coals on the grill.
3. Start your fire.
4. Wait for coals to turn uniformly gray, covered with a layer of fine gray ash. For hot fires, light coals 35 to 40 minutes before you plan to cook; for medium fires, 40 to 45 minutes; for low fires, 45 to 50 minutes.
5. If food has not been marinated or brushed with oil, now is the time to brush oil on the grill.
6. Place food on grill, cook and baste on first side as recipe directs. Remember to grill first the side of the food to be presented.
7. Turn food over and baste again. Cook and turn again as recipe directs until desired doneness.
8. Remove food to warm plate and serve!

ADDITIONAL TIPS: • Be sure to bring foods to room temperature 30 minutes to 1 hour before grilling. • Chimney flues are easy to use, and don't require lighter fluid. Hardwood lump charcoal is recommended.

FIRE FLARE-UPS IN GRILLING. Fat and meat juices dripping onto hot coals can cause sudden flare-ups. Reduce flare-ups by either raising the grill rack, covering the grill, spacing the hot coals farther apart, or removing a few coals to cut down on the heat. As a last resort, remove the food from the grill to prevent it from getting coated with ashes, and mist the fire with a pump-spray bottle filled with water.

"I have known many meat eaters to be far more nonviolent than vegetarians."

MAHATMA GANDHI

Meat

BUYING/BEEF. Considerations to keep in mind: **Color.** Look for bright pink-red flesh, light-colored bones, and creamy-white fat. Exposure to oxygen turns meat a cherry red, called bloom. If meat is vacuum-packed, it will be purple because no oxygen has entered the packaging. As the meat ages, oxygen will turn the meat brown, which doesn't mean it's spoiled, but does mean it should be cooked immediately. **Texture.** Look for fine flesh, moist-looking bones, and crumbly exterior fat. The best beef rarely makes it into your local supermarket, but it is identifiable by a delicate network of fat running through the flesh called "marbling." The marbling dissolves during cooking, providing an automatic internal basting that enhances the meat's flavor. Since all cuts of beef have the same nutritional value, it's a good idea to experiment with different cuts and methods of preparation so you can take advantage of sales at the market or butcher. **Tender Cuts.** When choosing cuts of meat, remember that the most tender cuts—such as rib, short loin, and sirloin—come from the least-exercised region of the animal's body—the upper back. Frequently used muscles, such as the shoulders (chuck) and the thighs (round), are less tender.

BUYING/GROUND BEEF. Low Grade. The cheapest grade is usually just called ground beef and contains fully 30 percent fat. Though it's often identified as chuck, other parts may be included in the grind. The grade may be used in dishes such as spaghetti sauce, where the meat is browned first and the fat poured off; however, considering the loss of nearly a third of the meat's volume, it's not really economical. It can also be used in meat loaf recipes that contain a high proportion of bread crumbs (which will absorb fat) if calories and cholesterol are not a problem. **Middle Grade.** Often labeled lean ground beef, lean ground chuck, or ground round, it contains about 20 percent fat, and is the normal grade used for hamburgers, meat loaf, meatballs, and more elaborate ground-beef dishes. **High Grade.** The leanest grade—usually identified as ground sirloin or extra-lean ground beef—contains approximately 15 percent fat. Although somewhat dry when cooked, it's the dieter's choice.

STORING. Freezing. Although it's fine to freeze meat for up to three months, you will lose some flavor, and the texture will tend to toughen. Burgers can be formed and then frozen. To cook at a later date, simply defrost in the refrigerator and cook as directed. Burgers with cheese can also be frozen.

PREPARING. Cutting. For most cuts of meat, cutting against the grain will yield the best flavor. It will also make tougher cuts easier to eat.

HEALTH. Though beef can contain high amounts of fat and cholesterol, it is a good source of iron, zinc and vitamin B_{12}—nutrients hard to come by in vegetarian diets. **To Reduce Fat in Cuts of Beef.** Carefully trim off all excess fat and eat small portions. Be sure to marinate or to baste lean meat frequently, otherwise the results could be tough to cut, much less to swallow. **To Reduce Fat in Ground Beef.** Cook it; place in a sieve; rinse with warm water; towel dry; return meat to recipe.

BEEF STOCK

MAKES ABOUT 10 CUPS

3–4 pounds meaty beef bones
1 Spanish onion, quartered
2 carrots, sliced
2 stalks celery, including greens, sliced
8 sprigs parsley
1 tablespoon dried thyme
2 bay leaves
1 6-ounce can tomato paste
12 cups cold water

1. Preheat the oven to 400° F.

2. Place the bones in a large roasting pan and cook until the bones are browned, about 1–1½ hours. Discard the rendered fat.

3. Place the bones in a large stockpot and add the remaining ingredients. Bring to a boil over high heat. Reduce heat to low and cook, partially covered, for 4–5 hours.

4. Strain the soup and discard the solids. Add salt to taste.

5. Cover and refrigerate until ready to use. Discard the solidified fat.

Fish

BUYING. If you can, purchase fish from a reputable local fishmonger the day you're going to eat it. Studies show that at least 10 percent of the fish available in supermarkets is spoiled. Fresh fish should be firm and moist, and should smell sweet rather than fishy. **Frozen.** Fish that is immediately frozen on the ship just after it's been caught is flash-frozen. Sometimes, because of time and distance, fish that's flash-frozen is fresher and will taste better than that labeled "fresh."
STORING. If fish was very fresh when purchased, it can be stored for a day in the refrigerator. Whole or drawn fish lasts better than cuts of fish; lean fish, better than fatty. First, rinse and dry the fish (even if it has been prepackaged); wrap pieces (no larger than 2 pounds) snugly in freezer paper or PVC plastic wrap; overwrap in a freezer bag or foil. Freeze fish at 0° F, fatty fish up to 3 months, lean fish up to 6 months.
PREPARING. Thawing. Frozen fish should be thawed in the refrigerator. **Doneness.** Fish is safely cooked when it loses its translucence and becomes opaque. If you like your fish raw or nearly raw, be very careful (see health warning below).
HEALTH. Considering the state of the world's waters and the amount of bacteria fish normally carry, many people believe that eating raw fish under any circumstances is foolhardy. Curing, salting, and pickling can preserve fish but they cannot kill all dangerous organisms. Freezing at –4° F. for 72 hours will kill all parasites but may ruin some fish, or at least affect its texture. Anything salt-cured will have a high sodium content.

Vegetables

A few general guidelines: buy vegetables that are firm and seem heavy for their weight. Avoid anything discolored, wrinkled, withered, bruised. Except where noted, vegetables are fat-free, low in sodium, low in calories, and have no cholesterol—that's why we should eat so many of them. Vegetables are most nutritious in their raw state but if unavailable, frozen vegetables are the second-best option. Canned vegetables often have a lot of preservatives and can be very high in sodium.

ASPARAGUS

BUYING. Best in April through May, the greener the better. Compact tips; thinner ones are most tender.
STORING. Must be kept in the refrigerator, where it can last one week.
PREPARING. Cut off stalk end and peel stalk if thick. **Cooking.** Steam or stir-fry for 3 to 10 minutes depending on thickness; asparagus should remain bright green and crisp.
HEALTH. Asparagus is a good source of vitamins A, C, and folacin. After eating asparagus, many people's urine takes on a strange odor—don't be alarmed, it's a benign reaction.

AVOCADOS

BUYING. The most flavorful are the ones grown in California, called Haas, with pebbled black skin—they look like leathery pears. In fact, botanically speaking, avocados are considered a fruit, but because they contain so much fat and are not sweet, they're treated like a vegetable. When they are ripe, the skin should be purplish black and they should yield slightly to the touch. If they're very soft or have bruises, they are already rotting. Smooth-skin varieties (also known as "Florida avocados") are larger than Haas avocados and have bright green skin. They are not as flavorful.
STORING. Avocados should be stored in a warm place until they're ripe, at which point it's okay to refrigerate them. To speed the ripening process, place avocados in a brown paper bag. Some people find that putting a tomato (which releases ripening ethylene gas) in the bag with the avocado accelerates the ripening process. Once ripe, avocados can be put in the refrigerator, where they can remain for 4–5 days. Cut avocados should be refrigerated with the pit inside, and covered with plastic wrap. A squirt of lemon juice will help prevent discoloration.
PREPARING. Cut an avocado from tip to tip, lengthwise around the pit. If it is properly ripe, the pit and skin should come off easily—though it might be green and slimy.
HEALTH. Avocados are high in beta carotene

(higher than apples, bananas, or grapefruit) and in potassium (60 percent more than a banana). Florida avocado varieties have half the fat and two thirds the calories of Haas avocados. Though exceptionally high in fat, avocados' fat is monounsaturated (as in olives), which is believed to lower blood cholesterol.

BEANS, FRESH FAVA AND LIMA

BUYING. Buy young, fresh beans; when beans are old, their sugar turns to starch.
STORING. Keep in a plastic bag, refrigerated for no longer than 3 days.
PREPARING. Cooking. Strip beans from their shells and boil for 10 minutes. Drain water and serve. Add butter and dried or fresh herbs to beans before serving, if desired.
HEALTH. Fresh beans are high in protein, potassium, and iron, but in lower levels than dried beans. Fresh beans are higher in vitamin C than dried beans.

BEANS, GREEN (STRING)

BUYING. Green beans should be very thin with the interior seeds barely visible through pod. They should snap when bent.
STORING. Green beans can stay fresh in the refrigerator up to 3 days.
PREPARING. Great raw, for crudités. **Cooking.** Snap off both ends and boil or steam for 5–10 minutes. (Steaming preserves more nutrients.) Beans should remain bright green.
HEALTH. Good source of fiber and vitamins C and A; high in iron, potassium, and carbohydrates.

BEETS

BUYING. Buy small, deep red beets with their green tops still attached. If cooking whole, pick ones of similar size so they cook in the same time.
STORING. Don't trim the greens or long root until ready to cook. Store beets, unwashed, in the refrigerator, in a plastic bag with air holes, for up to 3 weeks.
PREPARING. Don't scrub or peel beets when washing. Be careful with beets—if the skin is broken, they'll bleed and lose their color and sweetness.

HEALTH. Rich in complex carbohydrates, vitamin C, and potassium.
STAINS. Remove beet stains by rubbing your hands with salt and then washing with soap and water. Bleach will remove beet-juice stains from cutting boards and utensils.

BELL PEPPERS

BUYING. Sweet bell peppers, whether green, orange, red, or yellow, should be bright and should have firm, unblemished skins.
STORING. Bell peppers can last in the refrigerator 1 week. **Tip.** To store roasted peppers that have been peeled, drizzle them with olive oil and refrigerate—up to 1 week.
PREPARING. Wash bell peppers thoroughly before seeding. Cut peppers in half by slicing them vertically from one side of the stem to the other. Break the halves apart and pop out the seed core. Cut away the white membranes, which are often bitter. You can also remove the seed core by holding the pepper firmly and smacking the stem side on the countertop. The jolt loosens the seed core, which you can pull right out. Many enjoy eating bell peppers raw.
HEALTH. By weight, bell peppers have twice as much vitamin C as citrus fruit. (Red peppers have 3 times as much as green; hot red peppers have nearly 14 times as much.)

BROCCOLI

BUYING. Look for tight green heads on firm stalks. Florets should not be yellowed.
STORING. Store unwashed broccoli in a plastic bag, with holes, in the crisper drawer of the refrigerator up to 4 days.
PREPARING. Rinse before cooking; peel stalks so they cook in same time as florets.
HEALTH. Very high in vitamin C and calcium as well as vitamins A, E, and K. Very low in calories (26 per cup). Frozen varieties usually have higher concentrations of florets, which are richer in beta carotene than the stalks. However, frozen varieties also have half the amount of calcium, iron, thiamin, riboflavin, niacin, and vitamin C.

BROCCOLI RABE

BUYING. Look for stalks with the smallest stems and crisp leaves.
PREPARING. Too bitter to eat raw. Rinse before cooking. No matter how cooked (boiled, steamed, stir-fried or sautéed), it only needs 3–5 minutes or else it gets mushy.
HEALTH. The green leaves are especially nutritious, high in vitamins A and C, calcium, iron, and folacin.

CABBAGE (GREEN, RED)

BUYING. Look for a bright color, and a firm and heavy head.
STORING. Never wash before storing in refrigerator. Will keep for up to 2 weeks.
PREPARING. Remove tough outer leaves; remove core before cooking or shredding. To avoid strong cooking odors, don't overcook.
HEALTH. High in vitamin C (especially red cabbage) and folacin.

CARROTS

BUYING. Buy smooth, firm, small carrots for sweetness and tenderness.
STORING. Cut off green tops before storing in refrigerator. They'll last up to 2 weeks. Scrub small carrots under running water; peel larger ones. Should be cooked until just tender.
PREPARING. Cut off greens and eat raw, or sauté, steam, or roast.
HEALTH. Very high in vitamin A, also B_1 and B_2. High in fiber and carbohydrates. One carrot has only 20 calories. Thought to reduce cholesterol levels. Eat too many and your skin will turn yellow—a harmless condition remedied by reducing consumption levels.

CAULIFLOWER

BUYING. Buy tight, heavy heads with white or cream-colored florets.
STORING. Keep head whole in refrigerator up to 4 days.
PREPARING. Remove core before cooking. Soak in cold, salted water to get rid of any bugs.
HEALTH. High in vitamin C, folacin, fiber, and carbohydrates.

CELERY

BUYING. Look for bright green leaves and firm light-green stalks. (Darker celery is older and stringier, though higher in nutrients.)

STORING. Keeps refrigerated for up to 10 days. It freezes easily, so keep away from colder parts of the refrigerator. If slightly wilted, crisp up stalks by soaking in cold water for 10 minutes.

PREPARING. Cut off ends and dark greens of outer stalks. Tender interior leaves can add flavor to salads and soups.

HEALTH. Unfortunately, that rumor about celery having "negative calories" really is too good to be true. It is very low in calories, though, and is high in fiber and folacin.

CORN

BUYING. Look for husks that are green, moist, and tightly wrapped. Stems should be moist and yellow—kernels at top should be firm and plump. **Peak Season.** Spring and summer, with some variations from state to state. Since the sugar in corn begins turning to starch as soon as the ears are picked off the stalk, corn should be purchased the day you intend to cook it.

STORING. Keep in the refrigerator. Eat within a day.

PREPARING. See page 120.

HEALTH. Good source of vitamins A, B, C, and potassium.

CUCUMBERS

BUYING. They should be refrigerated in stores, kept in the shade if at a roadside stand. Beware of the bulge; if the middle is distended, it's probably very seedy and has a watery, tasteless flesh. Skin should be a deep emerald without any soft, dark green spots.

STORING. Uncut, they should last a week in the crisper drawer of a refrigerator. Cut cucumbers should be wrapped tightly in plastic wrap and be used within 2 days.

PREPARING. Skins can stay on fresh cucumbers so long as they are washed.

HEALTH. Cucumbers are about 96 percent water, and the average cucumber has only 10 calories. Slices of cucumber feel refreshing on eyelids but have no topical medicinal qualities.

EGGPLANTS

BUYING. Gently squeeze to check for firmness. If it gives a bit, then it's ripe. Eggplants are highly perishable; buy shiny, dark, smooth eggplants and use them within a day or two. Dented or discolored eggplants will be bitter.

STORING. Keep refrigerated no more than 4–5 days.

PREPARING. To Peel or Not to Peel. Depends upon the dish. When using whole slices, leave peels on to hold the slice together. If intended for dips or soups, peel skins off. **A Tip Before Frying.** Salt eggplant slices—it reduces amount of the oil required by two thirds. Cut slices, spread them on paper towels, sprinkle moderately. Let sit for 30 minutes, then rinse and dry.

HEALTH. Low in calories and fat—unless fried.

GARLIC

BUYING. Fresh garlic should have a plump, firm appearance. Thanks to the staggered harvest, fresh garlic is available year round. Garlic heads should be firm and tight, with tissuelike skin; do not buy garlic that is bruised, shriveled, sprouting, or soft. Buy loose garlic heads instead of those packed in a box—they're fresher. Though decorative, garlic braids are impractical—the last bulbs will probably spoil before you get around to using them.

STORING. Keep garlic in a loosely covered container in a cool, dark spot (not in the refrigerator or freezer). Depending on conditions, garlic can be kept for up to 2 months. When garlic sprouts, it loses much of its flavor; the sprouts themselves, however, can be used like mild-flavored chives.

PREPARING. Peeling. The easiest way to skin a clove is to place it on a chopping board, lay the broad side of a butcher knife on it, and pound the knife with your fist. This will split the skin without smashing the clove. If you need to peel several cloves at once, cover them with boiling water for 1 minute, then cool them under running water. The same trick can be accomplished by placing them in a microwave oven for 5 seconds; in either case, the skins will easily slip off. **Intensity.** The strength of garlic flavor is the direct result of how much oil is released when a clove is cut. Whole, roasted garlic is the sweetest and least pungent, whereas crushed or pressed raw garlic is at maximum strength. Sliced or chopped garlic is somewhere in the middle. If a recipe requires sautéing garlic in oil, and you want a very mild garlic taste, remove garlic after it turns golden and before proceeding with recipe.

HEALTH. Garlic and onions both contain a substance that is suspected to prevent the formation of blood clots and reduce cholesterol. While garlic consumption has been recommended as a folk remedy for heart disease for ages, thus far there is no definitive medical evidence to support this claim. Both garlic's circulatory and anti-carcinogenic properties are currently under medical scrutiny. Anecdotally, garlic is famous for its ability to fend off evil spirits and lily-livered lovers.

LEEKS

BUYING. Should be no thicker than 1½ inches in diameter. Tops should look bright green. Avoid those that look yellow.

STORING. Refrigerate no more than 5 days.

PREPARING. Rinse before using—they're usually packed with sand. Cut off tops and root tendril bottoms. Cutting into smaller pieces will make them easier to clean. If you wish to cook them whole, cut lengthwise down the middle and then make a perpendicular cut; then fan the ends and swish in water until the water comes clean.

HEALTH. High in folacin, iron, and vitamin C.

MUSHROOMS

BUYING. Should be firm and dry. Avoid mushrooms that are wet or slimy. Buy them on the day you need to cook them.

STORING. Mushrooms are highly perishable and should be stored unwashed in brown paper bags or baskets in the refrigerator. Prepackaged mushrooms should be refrigerated and used within the week.

PREPARING. Cleaning. Just prior to use, wipe with a damp towel or a mushroom brush, rather than rinsing with water. (They're like sponges and absorb water quickly.) Discard the stems only if they are woody.

HEALTH. Mushrooms contain glutamic acid, the naturally occurring version of MSG. They are high in folacin and riboflavin.

ONIONS

BUYING. Scallions or chives: Look for smooth, unwilted bright green stalks. All other onions: Look for dry, hard, smooth, flaky skins.

STORING. Refrigerate unwashed scallions or chives for up to 5 days. All other onions should be kept in a dry, cool space in open containers, e.g., open netting or baskets. Keep up to 4 weeks. Once cut, onions have a short life. Refrigerate cut onions in a tightly sealed plastic bag and use within two days.

PREPARING. Onions lose their pungent flavor once peeled or cut, so don't slice or peel them until you're ready to use them. Cut a thin slice from the top, peel, then cut in half through the root end. Using a very sharp knife will help hold back your tears because it will slice without releasing as much of the onions' juices.

HEALTH. Scallions are the most vitamin-packed of the onion family—4 times as much vitamin C and 5,000 times as much vitamin A as other onions.

PEAS (FRESH SHELL)

BUYING. Look for bright, shiny pods. Eat one—if it's sweet, it's fresh. Avoid dry or yellowed pods.

STORING. Refrigerate up to 4 days. Store in plastic bags.

PREPARING. Snap off stem and run your thumb down the pod to remove the peas.

HEALTH. Shelled peas are higher in B vitamins and protein than snow peas.

PEAS, SUGAR AND SNOW

BUYING. Look for a bright green color and avoid dry or yellow-looking pods.

STORING. Refrigerate up to 4 days. Store in plastic bags.

PREPARING. To prepare peas, snap off stem end; otherwise leave whole. If pods are large, some people like to slice them diagonally, especially for frying. If snow peas get a little droopy after cooking and you wish to serve them cold, soak them in ice water for 30 minutes to zap them back to life.

HEALTH. Peas in pods supply less protein than shelled peas because they are eaten before their seeds are mature. Pod peas are nutritionally redeemed, however, by their calcium content, which is twice as high as that of shelled peas; they also contain higher iron and vitamin C levels as compared to shelled peas.

> "An onion can make people cry, but has there never been a vegetable invented to make them laugh?"
>
> **MAY IRWIN (ATTRIB.)**

SPINACH

BUYING. Leaves should be crisp, dark green, and have no signs of wilting. Spinach sold in bundles is usually younger and fresher than that prepackaged in plastic bags.

STORING. Before storing, cut or pull the leaves off the stem and wash thoroughly in a container full of cold water. Dry the leaves, wrap them in paper towels, and place them in a sealed plastic bag in the refrigerator, where they can be stored for up to 3 days.

PREPARING. Never cook spinach in an aluminum pan, never serve it in silver, and make sure to use a stainless steel knife to keep them both from turning color.

HEALTH. Just 28 calories per cup, and loaded with vitamins A, B, and C if eaten raw.

SQUASH

BUYING. Go for smaller sizes. Look for firmness. Avoid squash that is soft or bruised.

STORING. Refrigerate unwashed up to 5 days.

PREPARING. Don't peel. Rinse with water to remove dirt.

HEALTH. Summer squash must be eaten with its skin to get the beta carotene nutrients. Winter squashes are more nutritious, higher in complex carbohydrates and vitamin A.

TOMATOES

BUYING. Tomatoes are, according to a botanist, considered fruits. Optimally, tomatoes should feel firm, but not too hard. Look for a red-to-deep-red coloration. During winter use cherry tomatoes—they taste better year-round than other tomatoes. Avoid inferior tomatoes; the result is never worth the effort. **Peak Season:** Tomatoes are available year-round and peak from May to October.

STORING. Store at room temperature. To speed ripening, put in a brown paper bag. (Like apples, they emit ethylene gas, which accelerates ripening.)

PREPARING. To avoid losing the tomatoes' seeds and juice, it is best to use a stainless steel serrated knife when slicing. To peel: Place in a pot of boiling water for 1–2 minutes, then drop them in ice water.

HEALTH. Good source of vitamins A, C, and beta carotene.

Potatoes, Grains, and Rice

POTATOES

BUYING. Look for a well-shaped, firm, heavy potato. Be wary of cracks, discoloring, and sprouting eyes. Avoid green-tinted potatoes; they'll taste bitter and may make you sick.
STORING. Potatoes need to stay dry, so make sure they're stored in a well-ventilated, cool, dry place. Do not store in plastic bags.
PREPARING. Scrub and peel, if desired, right before cooking. When peeling potatoes, make sure to put them in a bowl of cold water to keep them from browning if you are not using them right away.
HEALTH. Loaded with vitamin C, especially in the skins—high in potassium, fiber, and complex carbohydrates.

"Bread that must be sliced with an axe is bread that is too nourishing."

FRAN LEBOWITZ

BREAD

STORING. A great way to store whole, fresh loaves of bread in the freezer is to cut the loaf into slices and then freeze it. (It's really difficult to slice bread once it's frozen.) Don't store bread in the refrigerator; it's the best way to encourage staleness. To preserve freshness in freshly made bread, slice the whole loaf, put it in a plastic bag, and then take from the middle of the loaf. Except for bread made without any fat, like French or Italian baguettes, most bread can be stored at room temperature for 3–4 days.
HEALTH. White bread is not naturally as nutritious as whole wheat, but some white bread is fortified with calcium and iron.

Dried Beans

HEALTH. Beans take a long time to digest, which allows for a gentle rise in blood sugar, a dietary boon for diabetics. In fact, consuming enough beans can greatly reduce a diabetic's dependence on artificial insulin.

Pasta

BUYING. Pasta made from semolina (durum wheat) is a premium pasta that absorbs little water, retains its firmness when cooked, and has a mellow flavor.
STORING. Dried pastas will keep for months in an airtight container in a cupboard. Fresh pasta will last for a week in the refrigerator for a couple days. Adding extra oil to cooked pasta will prevent clumping.
PREPARING. The best way to cook pasta is to bring a large pot of water to a rolling boil (about 4 quarts of water per pound of pasta). Add pasta and let it simmer until done—about 10 minutes for dry pasta and about 3 minutes for fresh. Stir occasionally. Pasta should be cooked until it is al dente, not mushy. **Reheating.** To reheat cooked pasta: Add some water and quickly sauté over medium heat. Or microwave in a bowl.
HEALTH. High-protein pastas are enriched with soy flour, wheat germ, yeast, or dairy products; cook carefully to keep from sticking. Be aware that fresh pasta is made with egg and therefore has higher cholesterol.

OLIVES

Olives are a fruit native to the Mediterranean, with cultivation going back to at least 3500 B.C. on the island of Crete.
STORING. Olives should be refrigerated in their brine and may be kept for several weeks. If they become soft, discard them. Oil-cured olives should be well coated with oil, stored in an airtight jar, and refrigerated.
PREPARING. Serving. Some ways that olives are served are as part of a relish tray, in puréed paste form as a spread for crusty bread and cheese (tapenade), in salads, baked into breads, layered and baked with other vegetables, such as potatoes, onions, and herbs, and as a flavorful addition to pasta or other main dishes.
HEALTH. Olives contain traces of iron, protein, and vitamins A and B, and are low in calories. However, they are fairly high in fat and sodium. Black olives have a higher fat content than green ones.

SUN-DRIED TOMATOES

BUYING. Sun-dried tomatoes are available today in many more varieties than the original red, including: yellow tomatoes; those packed in flavored oils; packed in cellophane; and even puréed into paste and packed in tubes. Sun-dried tomatoes that have not been packed in oil should be somewhat leathery but still chewy and not overly dry. When added to soups, stews, and chilis, sun-dried tomatoes impart a slightly beefy, smoky flavor.
PREPARING. To Reconstitute. If you find sun-dried tomatoes are too dry, steep them in enough boiling water to cover and allow to sit for a few minutes. Discard the water or add to a soup in progress.

Pizza

PREPARING. On Making Good Dough. Don't dawdle when making pizza. The dough gets sticky very quickly. The longer you wait, the more trouble you'll have getting the pizza off the peel. The water used to make pizza dough should be lukewarm—110° F. is ideal. Water that is too hot will kill the yeast; water that is too cold will not allow the yeast to dissolve. If you have any doubts about the temperature, use a meat thermometer. **Forming.** Don't worry about forming a pizza into a perfect circle, and don't use more dough than the recommended amount. It's almost impossible to get a perfect circle, and odd-shaped pizzas are more interesting anyway. Until you're an expert, don't even think of making a large pizza: the smaller the amount of dough, the easier it will be to work with. Start out by rolling the dough on a surface coated with cornmeal or flour and then let the heel of your hand take over. **Frozen dough.** If you are using frozen dough that has not been formed, simply defrost it and proceed with forming the dough. If you are using frozen dough that has been formed, defrost it and proceed by arranging the topping on the pizza. **Grilling.** Transfer the rolled-out, formed dough (the side you intend to put toppings on) to the grill and cook until it is lightly browned, about 2–4 minutes. Remove the pizza to a pan or a pizza peel and place the topping on the cooked side. Transfer the pizza back to the grill and cook for about 10 minutes, or until the topping is done.

Cheese

COOKING TIPS

1. Always use low heat when melting cheese. Try to mix the cheese into the recipe toward the end of the cooking process to avoid getting stringy pieces.

2. Cheese sauce can easily get overheated and grainy. Try cooking the sauce in the top of a double boiler over simmering water, but make sure that the top pan does not touch the water.

3. If cheese gets overcooked, you can rescue it. Cut it into medium-sized pieces and blend it in a food processor until smooth. If it's part of a sauce, blend the cheese and some of the sauce together. Then add the cheese mixture to the sauce and stir constantly over low heat.

4. Low-fat processed cheese does not melt well, so avoid trying to use it for melting. However, processed cheese melts more easily than natural cheese because it contains emulsifiers.

COMING TO TERMS WITH CHEESE

SAY CHEESE. To smile, especially broadly. First recorded in 1918.

CHEESED OFF. Angry or fed up. First recorded in 1914 and attributed to the troops of Liverpool. It may have been inspired by the phrase, "browned off," which referred to the brown rind of cheese.

CHEESE DOWN. To coil rope so neatly that it resembles a wheel of cheese. First recorded in the 1920s.

CHEESECAKE. A display, especially pictorial, of the charms of the female body; early porn. In the 1940s it was attributed to the photographer's instruction, "say cheese," but the term can be traced to the British Isles. In 1662, it was synonymous with "tart." [Male equivalent: Beefcake.]

Salads

MORE GREENS

CHERVIL: licorice-y. **WATERCRESS:** hot and peppery; **DANDELION GREENS:** slightly bitter—good in warm salads. **ESCAROLE:** slightly nutty, best alone. **FRISÉE:** slightly sweet, slightly bitter—good with salads of nuts and cheese. **GREEN CHARD:** spinachlike flavor, good in warm salads. **KALE:** mild cabbage flavor. **MIZUNA:** mustardy Japanese green. **MUSTARD GREENS:** crunchy, slightly cabbage-y. **RED CHARD:** slightly beetlike. **SORREL:** sour, citrus-y taste.

VINEGARS

Although vinegar is an incredibly important flavoring, expensive does not necessarily mean good. In fact, if you are paying a lot of money (except for aged balsamic vinegar), it is probably for fancy packaging. A splash of vinegar can be used to bring out the bean flavor in bean dishes, it can be used to balance a dish that is too salty or too sweet, and it can be used as a flavor enhancer for meat, fish and vegetable dishes: adding a tiny bit of vinegar, especially balsamic vinegar, brings out a richness and depth to the food's flavor. For variety in any recipe, try substituting vinegar with an equal amount of any citrus juice.

BALSAMIC VINEGAR. All balsamic vinegar is produced in Modena, Italy, and is made exclusively from that region's white Trebbiano grapes. While often mistaken for wine vinegar, it is not. The grapes never ferment. Rather, grape pressings are cooked to a desired level of concentration. Although mostly used in vinaigrettes, it can do wonders alone in small amounts on beans, or vegetables for dinner or

strawberries for dessert. **Balsamico Tradizionale.** *Balsamico tradizionale* not only has been produced in Modena, but it is approved by Modena's Balsamic Vinegar Consortium, and is considerably more expensive. While a slow evaporation takes place, balsamic vinegar destined for *balsamico*'s greatness is transferred over many years to ever-smaller casks of specific woods—oak, chestnut, cherry, ash, and mulberry. As the *balsamico* ages, it thickens and becomes increasingly aromatic. By the age of 12, *balsamico* is often used in salads, foie gras or chicken dishes, and frittatas. When it turns 50, it is ready to be drizzled over ice cream and strawberries. By the time *balsamico* has been aged for more than 70 years (100-year-old *balsamicos* are not uncommon), this extravagant liquid has the consistency of heavy syrup and is often served—one drop at a time from special dispensers—as an after-dinner liqueur.

CIDER VINEGAR. This is a fairly fruity, although unexciting, vinegar made from apples. It is used sparingly and infrequently in cooking.

HERB- AND FRUIT-INFUSED VINEGARS. These are available in an endless supply, but are desirable more for their eye appeal than for what they actually add to a dish. If a strong basil flavor is desired, for instance, you would be better off adding fresh basil to your salad than using basil vinegar. If you are growing your own herbs, by all means make herb vinegars. They're pretty to look at and are a great way to use fresh herbs.

WINE VINEGARS. White and Red Wine Vinegars. Made from red and white wines, these are the most popular and versatile vinegars and can be substituted for any vinegar in any dressing. White wine vinegar is less high-pitched than white vinegar, but is sharper than red wine vinegars and often requires plenty of balancing from the sweet side of the flavor spectrum. **Sherry Vinegar.** A type of wine vinegar, it is mild and great mixed with citrus in vinaigrettes or splashed in cream soups to counteract their rich taste.

WHITE VINEGARS. These distilled vinegars are the most intense members of the vinegar family (they do double duty as cleaning products) and are generally reserved for pickling.

OILS

Oils are composed of one or more of several kinds of fats. Monounsaturated and polyunsaturated fats are considered to be the most healthy kinds of fat. Saturated fat, which is easy to identify because it becomes solid at room temperature, is considered to be the least healthy. Cooks prefer vegetable oil over margarine because it's more versatile, lower in saturated fats than butter or lard, and has no hydrogenated molecules—an artificial process that has recently come under suspicion as being potentially unhealthy. Whether an oil made up predominantly of monounsaturated fats (like olive or peanut) is better for you than one high in polyunsaturated fats (like corn or safflower) is still uncertain.

ALMOND OIL. Light and delicate, it is used primarily in salads or for drizzling on vegetables and breads. It is high in monounsaturated fats.

AVOCADO OIL. Although taken directly from the pit and pulp of avocados, it is fairly low in flavor and is best used for salads when you want a dressing that will not overwhelm.

CANOLA OIL (RAPESEED OIL). Relatively new to the market and fairly mild, canola oil is good for baking and frying. High in monounsaturated fats.

CORN OIL. Made from the sweet corn plant, it is used primarily for sautéing and baking, mixed with olive oil for a mellow vinaigrette, or whenever a mild oil is needed. Corn oil is high in polyunsaturated fat.

OLIVE OIL. Extra Virgin. This is oil derived from olives that have been cold-pressed. Traditionally the olives are crushed between two stone wheels that turn them into a pulp, which is then spread on mats and gently pressed down with weights. Because the pressure is low, heat is not built up, allowing the maximum of flavor and—unfortunately for the cost-conscious—the minimum of product. The greener the oil, the closer to the first pressing it is and therefore the more "virginal" (and costly) it is. Don't be fooled into using the most expensive extra virgin for everything: it should be used only when a distinctively olive-like taste is desired—as on salads, pasta, beans, or bread. **Virgin Olive Oil** and **Pure Olive Oil** are best used for sautéing, or when a less pronounced olive taste is desired. Either can be blended with extra virgin olive oil. The largest producers of olive oil are (in order) Italy, Spain, Greece, and France. All olive oils are high in monounsaturated fats.

PEANUT OIL. Made from South American ground nuts, peanut oil has a very faint peanut flavor and is used in cooking, primarily for sautéing and frying. It is high in mono-unsaturated fats.

SAFFLOWER OIL. It contains some saturated fatty acids and is highly unsaturated.

SESAME SEED OIL. There are two kinds. The pale, just slightly nutty oil is a cold pressing; it can be used for sautéing. The rich, amber-colored oil, very prevalent in Chinese cooking, is made from roasted sesame seeds; it is great in salad dressings and sprinkled over stir-fries at the end. Both high in polyunsaturated fat.

SUNFLOWER OIL. Used in margarine and cooking, it is high in polyunsaturated fat.

WALNUT OIL. Extracted from walnut kernels, it is used mainly in salads. Because of its strong flavor, it is best used in combination with either olive or safflower oil. High in polyunsaturated fat.

Nuts

BUYING. The best packaging is vacuum-sealed for freshness in airtight jars or plastic bags.

STORING. Because nuts have a high fat content, they can quickly become rancid. To slow this process, they should be kept in airtight containers in a cool, dry, dark place. Shelled nuts become rancid more quickly than those in the shell. Nuts can be kept for a couple of months in the refrigerator and up to a year in the freezer.

PREPARING. Most nuts are already prepared to eat. If you need to crack their shells, lobster-crackers work well. (See page 181 for toasting pine nuts.)

HEALTH. Nuts seduce with their rich (read: very high in fat) flavor. But in their dietary defense, they also add texture and protein to any dish. Nuts that have been dry-roasted have less oil and are therefore lower in calories.

Herbs, Spices, and Other Flavorings

PRESERVING FRESH HERBS

AIR DRYING. Wash, dry, and tie herbs in small bunches and hang them upside down or right-side up in a dry place, out of direct sunlight, until dry. If the room for drying is very dusty, place an open brown paper bag over the herbs. When dry, store in jars, away from direct light. (Does not work well in humid summer weather.)

MICROWAVE DRYING. Wash, dry, arrange herbs in one layer on paper towels and cover them with more paper towels. Microwave on high repeatedly for 1 minute intervals until dry. This quick method will help herbs retain color better than air-drying, and humidity is not an issue.

OVEN DRYING. Wash, dry, and arrange herbs in one layer on cookie sheet. Place in a 250° F. oven. Check periodically and turn sheet until herbs are dry. In dehydrator, follow manufacturer's instructions for rotating trays and length of time.

FREEZING. Wash, dry, and pack herbs in small, Ziploc bags. They may be stored in the freezer up to 1 year. The tender herbs—basil, fennel, tarragon, chives, dill, and parsley—will benefit from a quick dip in boiling water, then in ice water before packaging for freezing. Most others can go directly into the freezer.

INFUSING IN VINEGAR. To make herb vinegar, slightly bruise (or crush) the herbs to allow them to give off their oils, place them in a bottle, and cover with any kind of warm vinegar. Let sit for 3 weeks; strain and discard herbs. If you would like to add fresh herbs for decoration, consider basil, oregano, cilantro, thyme, and mint, or a combination of these.

INFUSING IN OIL. Herb-infused oils are great for salad dressing and for cooking. To make them, fill one third of a bottle with herbs and then fill it up with olive, sunflower, walnut, or vegetable oil. Let stand about 10 days, then remove the used herbs; if desired, replace them with a fresh sprig. Good herbs for this are oregano, rosemary, sage, and thyme, or a combination of these.

COOKING

SUBSTITUTION OF DRIED FOR FRESH HERBS. Generally, ¼ teaspoon dried, finely powdered herb equals ¾–1 teaspoon fresh; 1 teaspoon loosely crumbled dried herb equals 1 tablespoon chopped fresh herb. **DIETING TIP.** To enhance the flavor of food when you're cutting back on fat, season liberally with herbs.

SALT

TABLE SALT. Fine-textured salt, most commonly used.
KOSHER SALT. An even, coarse texture, not as strong as table salt.
SEA SALT. Coarse texture and fresh flavor. It's often ground in a salt grinder.

PEPPERCORNS

Preground pepper never compares in pungency to pepper ground on the spot. It is worth investing in a pepper grinder that permits grinds of varying coarseness.
BLACK PEPPERCORNS. The brightest, most vivacious taste in pepper.
WHITE PEPPERCORNS. Less flavor than black pepper, but used in light-colored sauces.
GREEN PEPPERCORNS. Found primarily in Madagascar, they are preserved fresh in water or vinegar. Not as sharp as dried pepper. Needed for steak au poivre sauce.

GROUND PEPPER

CHILI POWDER. A blend made primarily from ground Anaheim peppers, with smaller amounts of garlic, cumin, oregano, paprika, and cayenne. There will be some variation among different brands.

CAYENNE PEPPER. Usually made from crushed cayenne peppers, it can also include the pods of other mild-to-hot chiles.
SWEET PAPRIKA. This is made from the pods of dried mild peppers. (Hot paprika includes the seeds and ribs.)
TABASCO. A fiery hot sauce made with red peppers and vinegar, it is often used in Creole, Cajun, and Mexican cooking.

"Routine in cuisine is a crime."

ÉDOUARD NIGNON

DRIED CHILE PEPPERS

ANCHO PEPPERS. Translated from the Spanish means "wide," usually refers to dried poblano peppers. They are wrinkled, a rich brick-brown color, and heart-shaped. They are a mild pepper, and somewhat sweet and fruity.
CASCABEL PEPPERS. So named "jingle bell" in Spanish because when you shake them, their seeds rattle around inside. Smooth, and glove-shaped, they are medium hot, and have a flavor reminiscent of tomatoes.
CHIPOTLE PEPPERS. These are jalapeños that have been dried and smoked. Hot, smoky in flavor, they are invaluable in long-cooking dishes, such as soups and chilis.
DE ARBOL PEPPERS. Bright red and transparent, usually about 3 inches long and tapered at the end. Although sweet, they are extremely hot and somewhat like cayenne peppers.
PASILLA PEPPERS. Also known as *negros*, they are so named for their dark purple, almost black color. They are intense and smoky.

Fruits and Berries
FRESH FRUITS

BUYING. Color. Beware of green coloration on the skins of peaches, strawberries, raspberries, or any other fruit whose skin is edible (excluding Granny Smith apples)—it's an indication that the fruit was picked too early to ever reach sweet maturity. The more jewel-toned the fruit or berry, the richer the flavor. Any wrinkling, browning, or molding on the fruit's skin means it's past its prime. **Smell.** Smelling fruit can help determine ripeness; fruit should have a pleasant but not overpowering fragrance. A sickly sweet or foul smell indicates that the fruit has begun to rot. Conversely, no smell at all is an indication that the fruit is not yet ripe. **Listen.** When buying melons, thump the side with a flick of the finger—it should have a satisfying resonance. **Touch.** Check for firmness. With the exception of apples, distrust anything that is rock-hard. Fruit should give slightly when gently squeezed. Make sure the fruit has good weight for its size. If a piece of fruit seems too light, it's probably lost a lot of its water weight and is spoiled. **Taste.** Discreetly popping a grape or berry in your mouth is the best on-site freshness test.
STORING. To ripen fruit, place it in a well-ventilated, room-temperature space—direct sunlight accelerates the ripening process. Refrigerate fruit only if you want to prevent any further ripening.
HEALTH. Fruits and berries contain little sodium and no cholesterol and, in addition, they pack in fiber, vitamins, minerals, and certain types can actually reduce cholesterol. **Potassium.** Bananas, pears, oranges. **Iron.** Berries, dried fruits. **Vitamin C.** Citrus fruits (lemons are highest), berries, melons, kiwis, papayas. **Beta Carotene.** Apricots, cantaloupes, peaches, nectarines, mangoes.

Most fruits can be found in specialty stores year-round, thanks to importing and hothouse growing. Here are the fruits for all seasons. Of course, these seasonal guidelines may vary according to where you live.

APPLES. (See pages 242–43 for lexicon.) Year-round; they're at their peak in late summer and fall—when cider is finest.

BLUEBERRIES. Spring and fall. They can be frozen.

CRANBERRIES. September through January. Cranberries can be difficult to purchase off-season. If you like them throughout the year, be sure to keep a few bags in your freezer. They usually can be found between Thanksgiving and Christmas.

MANGOES. April through September.

MELONS. Cantaloupes from May through September; casabas, July to November; Crenshaws, August and September; honeydews, July through October; watermelons, June through August.

ORANGES. Available year-round, but the fruit is more expensive and of poorer quality during summer months.

PEACHES. Late spring and fall. Never substitute canned peaches for fresh ones. Do not store peaches in the refrigerator until they are fully ripe.

PEARS. Varieties like Bartlett are available in August and fall; others like Anjou, Bosc, and Comice are around through the winter.

RASPBERRIES. Height of season is June and July.

RHUBARB. Although a vegetable, rhubarb is eaten as a fruit. It is available from January through June. Do not use the poisonous leaves.

STRAWBERRIES. Year-round; they peak in May and June.

FROZEN. As long as it hasn't been cooked in the freezing process, frozen fruit has the same nutritional value as fresh fruit, yet may have less flavor.

CANNED. Syrup-packed. Watch out—it could be a caloric nightmare. **Water-packed.** Use the water and fruit juice the fruit is canned with, and you will retain many of the nutrients lost in the canning process.

DRIED. Pound for pound, dried fruits have a more concentrated amount of vitamins and minerals than fresh fruit. **A Note for the Allergy-prone.** Be wary of light-colored dried fruits such as apples, peaches, pears, apricots, and golden raisins. Undesirable sulfites often lend the fruit an artificial color.

Eggs

BUYING. Freshness is by far the most important aspect of eggs, because they dry and age quickly depending on time and temperature. The eggshell color depends on the breed of the hen and does not affect the nutritional value or quality of the egg. For eggs to be properly certified organic, they must be produced by chickens fed organic feed on an organic farm (basically, without the aid of artificial pesticides and chemicals). Though organic farming is environmentally sound, organic eggs taste better primarily because they tend to be fresher.

STORING. Raw eggs can be refrigerated for up to 2 weeks but should not be frozen. Don't use the egg storage unit located on the door of your refrigerator because the door is the warmest part of the fridge and therefore the worst place to store eggs. Store eggs in their original cartons, which will keep the yolk centered in the white and away from the air trapped in the large end of the egg. **Taste.** Since eggshells are porous, they are best kept away from strong-smelling foods. Storing eggs in the carton also prevents other flavors from penetrating the shells.

PREPARING. (See egg recipes, page 123.) **Before Cooking.** Room-temperature eggs will become a larger volume when beaten; when added to baking batter, they will not cause already creamed butter and sugar to coagulate. A jiffy (and salmonella-safe) method is to take eggs directly from the refrigerator and place in a bowl of warm water for a few minutes. **Separating.** Holding an egg lengthwise in one hand, crack it quickly against the sharp edge of a bowl or counter across the middle. The trick is to do it hard enough to crack the shell, but not so hard that the yolk inside is broken. Over a bowl, break the shell apart into two halves, allowing the white to fall into the bowl and cupping the yolk in one of the shells. Transfer the yolk from one shell to the other, mad-scientist-with-test-tube style, one or two times, until all the remaining white is gone; then empty the yolk into another bowl. **To Remove Unwanted Eggshell Fragments.** If you go after small pieces of eggshell with a finger or spoon, you're doomed to frustration. When fragments of eggshell accidentally drift into a mixture, they can be easily scooped out with an eggshell half. The shells will almost seem magnetically attracted to each other. **Soft- and Hard-boiled.** Place eggs in a saucepan and cover with cold water. Turn heat to high. Once the water comes to a boil, immediately reduce heat (to prevent shells from cracking) so that the water gently boils around the eggs—7 minutes for soft-boiled, 15 minutes for hard-boiled. Drain hot water and put eggs immediately into a bowl of cold water until the eggs themselves are cool to the touch (this helps the meat separate from the shell, which makes peeling easier). Peel soon afterwards under cold water.

HEALTH. Gone are the days of eating an egg and side of bacon every morning. Eggs may be high in cholesterol but they do have such redeeming qualities as being very high in protein. Plus, if you remove the cholesterol- and fat-packed yolk, you will lose flavor but retain protein. **Kosher Concerns.** If you find that the yolk of an egg has traces of blood, it is not considered kosher to eat.

BIRKENSTOCKS

CAN OPENER

PEPPER MILL

MEASURING
CUP/SPOONS

RECYCLE

DISH CLOTHS

BAKING MITT

WELL STOCKED

There are a hundred sentimental things one could say about the kitchen. It's the heart of the home, the comfort zone, and the most popular room at any given party. But when the clock strikes supper o'clock, that kitchen is your personal workshop. So be an artisan about it. Surround yourself with the best tools and the best ingredients you can get your hands on, and keep them accessible, clean, and sharp. Your final culinary masterpiece will be better for it, and so will your nerves (and feet!).

Tools

What does it take to make a kitchen work? A professional chef may insist that he or she needs only a good knife, a sauté pan, and a spoon to turn out a fabulous meal. Though such thinking may be a bit minimalist, too many kitchen gadgets can be overwhelming. Before you're seduced by the strawberry hullers, the butter curlers, or the 20-piece skillet set, get basic. For instance, if you rarely bake, don't invest in an army of cake pans, muffin tins, and cookie sheets. But if you're a whiz with soups and stews, spend some real money on heavy-bottomed pots that will distribute heat evenly and stand up to years of simmering and scrubbing. The following list includes the bare basics. Adapt the list according to your own needs, but no matter what you end up buying, be sure to have a fire extinguisher handy.

KNIVES

Knives are one of the most important tools in the kitchen. Invest in good ones and keep them clean and sharp. Remember: A sharp knife is safer than a dull one.

BASIC NECESSITIES

- Paring knives, 4-inch
- Chef's knife, 8-inch
- Bread knife, serrated 8-inch
- Sharpening steel

BEYOND NECESSITIES

- Cook's knife, 6-inch
- Carving knife, 10-inch
- Boning knife, 5-inch

UTENSILS AND MORE

Everyone has his or her favorite kitchen tools. These are the ones we find most useful.

BASIC NECESSITIES

- Bowls, assorted stainless steel
- Can/bottle opener
- Colander, stainless steel
- Corkscrew
- Cutting board, of thick, hard wood or acrylic
- Grater, 4-sided stainless steel
- Ladle, 8-ounce
- Measuring cups, 1-cup & 2-cup, Pyrex glass
- Pepper grinder allowing for different grades
- Pot holders; preferably mitts above the wrist
- Potato masher/ricer
- Salad spinner
- Scissors, utility
- Spatula, rubber
- Spatula, stainless steel, ideally with a heat insulated handle
- Spoons, wooden mixing and stainless steel
- Spoons, measuring, heavy gauge, stainless steel
- Spoon, slotted
- Strainer, 8-inch
- Vegetable peeler
- Vegetable steamer, collapsible
- Wire whisk

BEYOND NECESSITIES

- Brush, mushroom
- Brush, pastry
- Bulb baster
- Citrus juicer
- Fish spatula
- Fork, carving
- Garlic press
- Kitchen timer
- Meat pounder/tenderizer
- Pizza cutter
- Pizza peel
- Pizza stone
- Skewers, stainless steel
- Thermometer, for meat, instant
- Thermometer, oven
- Tongs, heavy-duty, long-handled
- Zester

POTS AND FRYING PANS

Don't buy cheap pots and pans; good ones, if properly cared for, can last a lifetime. Pots should be made of stainless steel, highly conductive, heavy-gauge aluminum with a nonoxidizing surface, or enamel-coated cast iron. Skillets should be aluminum (a nonstick surface makes for easier cleanups and requires less oil when sautéing) or cast iron.

BASIC NECESSITIES

- Roasting pan, shallow, 15 x 10 x 2 inches
- Roasting rack
- Saucepan, 2-quart
- Skillet or sauté pan, non-stick, 8-inch
- Skillet or sauté pan, nonstick, 13-inch
- Stockpot, 8-quart

BEYOND NECESSITIES

- Double boiler
- Fish poacher, stainless steel, 15-inch
- Skillet, cast-iron, 9-inch

How to care for a cast-iron pan: When you first purchase a cast-iron pan (or an old one has rusted), scrub it clean with hot water and scouring powder, then rinse and dry completely. Lightly coat it with vegetable oil and place it in a preheated oven at 300° F. for 30 minutes. Rub clean with paper towels. If any evidence of rust appears on the towels, alternate rubbing pan with salt and towels until the towels come away clean. Rub in a final layer of oil. If possible, after subsequent use, do not wash it with soap and water; instead, wipe it with a paper towel lightly moistened with water and then with one that has been lightly moistened with vegetable oil.

BAKING

Metal, glass, or ceramic are all fine materials for bakeware. Make sure that pans are heavy gauge and well balanced for even baking.

BASIC NECESSITIES

- Baking sheets, 18 x 12 x 1 inch
- Bundt pan
- Loaf pan, 8-inch
- Rectangular pan, 9 x 12-inch
- Square pan, 8-inch

BEYOND NECESSITIES

- Electric beater
- Measuring cups, stainless steel
- Muffin tins
- Pie plate, 9-inch
- Rolling pin
- Springform pan
- Wire racks

MACHINES

Sometimes technology really does make things easier.

BASIC NECESSITIES

- Blender or food processor (a food processor is more flexible)
- Oven with stove range

BEYOND NECESSITIES

- Chimney flue (for outdoor grilling)
- Microwave oven, with convection feature preferred
- Toaster oven

MUST HAVES

- Fire extinguisher
- Leftover packaging: aluminum foil, freezer bags, plastic storage containers, plastic wrap

Pantry

Want to make cooking effortless? Then stock your pantry, refrigerator, and freezer with staples. The advantages to maintaining a working pantry are almost endless. For one thing, a good pantry is so adaptable that you can serve up a delicious, filling meal with what's on hand—and nary a trip to the market. (Keep a running shopping list on the fridge to make shopping a breeze.) With plenty of fixin's in the cupboard, even the simplest scrambled egg becomes special— just add snipped chives or sweet basil. The following may seem to be a long list of kitchen staples, but if you're starting from scratch, it's a worthwhile investment. With these items at your fingertips, all you'll need to make dinner are a few fresh ingredients and some inspiration.

DRIED HERBS AND SPICES

Make sure you store these in a cool, dark place. A good tip is to date each container. Since dried herbs and spices lose their kick over time, it's best to replace them after a year.

BASIC NECESSITIES

- Basil
- Bay leaves
- Caraway seeds
- Cardamom
- Cayenne powder
- Chili powder
- Cinnamon
- Cumin, ground
- Curry powder
- Dill
- Fennel seeds
- Ginger, ground
- Marjoram
- Nutmeg, ground
- Oregano
- Paprika
- Pepper—crushed red pepper flakes, whole black and white peppercorns
- Rosemary
- Sage
- Salt—table and kosher
- Sesame seeds
- Tarragon
- Thyme

CUPBOARD

Keep in mind that even items with a long shelf life can lose their flavor (or even worse, go bad) with time. So try to use first what you've had the longest. Also note storage information carefully on the label; many foods can remain on the shelf for a long time, but must be refrigerated after opening.

BASIC NECESSITIES

- Alcohols: bourbon, red wine, white wine, vermouth
- Beans, either canned or dried—black, red kidney, cannellini
- Cornmeal
- Dried fruits (apples, apricots, currants, figs, raisins)
- Flour, unbleached all-purpose
- Honey
- Ketchup
- Mushrooms—assorted dried, shiitake
- Mustard (Dijon, whole-grain, flavored)
- Oils—olive, vegetable
- Pasta, dried—assorted shapes and sizes
- Rice—white, brown, wild, arborio
- Soy sauce
- Stock (bouillon cubes, powdered, canned broth)
- Sugar—white and brown
- Tabasco sauce
- Tea
- Sun-dried tomatoes
- Tomato paste
- Tomatoes, canned—whole, crushed
- Tuna, packed in water
- Vinegar—balsamic, white
- Worcestershire sauce

BEYOND NECESSITIES

- Anchovies—fillets and paste
- Artichokes, hearts of, in marinade
- Bottled water and sodas
- Capers
- Crackers
- Chutney, assorted kinds
- Granola bars/fruit bars
- Hearts of palm, canned
- Olivada
- Olives
- Peanut butter
- Popcorn/popcorn cakes
- Preserves
- Pretzels

BAKING

- Baking powder
- Baking soda
- Chocolate— unsweetened, semi-sweet
- Chocolate chips, semi-sweet
- Flour—unbleached all-purpose, whole wheat
- Oats, rolled
- Sugar—confectioners', superfine
- Vanilla extract

VEGETABLE BIN

These staples should be kept loose or in open paper bags in a cool, dry, well-ventilated place.

BASIC NECESSITIES

- Garlic
- Onions, Spanish
- Potatoes

BEYOND NECESSITIES

- Avocados
- Onions, Red
- Mangoes
- Shallots
- Yams

REFRIGERATOR

These are all items that should be included in any civilized person's fridge. But remember—any of these can turn into a biology experiment if used when past their prime.

BASIC NECESSITIES

- Bell peppers
- Broccoli
- Butter, unsalted
- Carrots
- Celery
- Cheeses—Cheddar, cream cheese, mozzarella, Parmesan
- Eggs, large
- Lemons
- Limes
- Mayonnaise
- Milk
- Salad greens

BEYOND NECESSITIES

- Sour cream

FREEZER

Just because it's in the freezer doesn't mean it'll last forever.

BASIC NECESSITIES

- Beef—ground lean, chops
- Bread
- Coffee beans
- Chicken, cut-up
- Chicken stock
- Fruits (blueberries, cranberries, raspberries, strawberries)
- Gingerroot
- Herbs, bagged in the summer
- Vegetables (beans, peas, chopped spinach, snap peas)

BEYOND NECESSITIES

- Nuts—pecans, pine nuts, walnuts
- Sunflower seeds

G L O S S A R Y

How the Raw Becomes the Cooked

BASTING. Usually associated with meats and poultry, basting involves brushing on or pouring liquid over foods while they are cooking, to keep them moist and flavorful. When basting meat, the basting liquid is usually a combination of pan drippings and fat. Seasonings or other ingredients may be added to enhance taste. The best basting brushes are made of natural boar bristles. Make sure the bristles are securely attached to the handle.

BLANCH. To cook foods—most often vegetables—briefly in boiling water and then set briefly in cold water until completely cool. Food is blanched for one or more of the following reasons: to loosen and remove skin (almonds, peaches, tomatoes); to enhance color and reduce bitterness (raw vegetables for hors d'oeuvres); to extend storage life (raw vegetables to be frozen); to draw out excess salt from meats, such as bacon and salt pork.

BRAISING. To sauté food in either fat (traditionally), beer, wine, broth, juice, or water, then simmer at low heat, in a covered saucepan.

BROILING AND GRILLING. Both cooking methods are quick processes of cooking food close to a very hot heat source. When grilling, you're usually outside (unless you have a stove-top grill), using your barbecue to cook food over glowing charcoals. When broiling, you're indoors, using your oven to cook food under a heat source (a gas oven is better for this than electric coils). Grilling should make meat crisp on the outside and moist inside. The oven or barbecue should be hot before cooking food.

When using either method, cook meat and vegetables 4 inches from heat; chicken or turkey 6–8 inches from heat. Always remove charred areas from food before eating.

MICROWAVING. For the impatient, microwave ovens are a godsend. And because they cook food so quickly, there's less time for nutrients to escape. Microwaves are also wonderful for thawing and reheating. (If you store leftovers in the refrigerator in microwave-save serving dishes that you then reheat the food in, you cut down on the load of dishes to wash.) **Warning.** Never microwave food that is touching plastic wrap; the microwaving process releases chemicals directly from the wrap onto your food. Microwaving food in a bowl covered with plastic pulled tautly across is safe as long as it's an inch or so above the food below. An environmentally superior option is to cover your bowl with a microwave-safe plate.

DREDGE. To lightly coat moist ingredients with a dusting of powderlike substance (e.g., herbs, spices, flour, cornmeal). Always shake loose any excess coating, as it will cook faster and burn easily.

FRYING VS. SAUTÉING. Frying is a way of cooking food (usually predipped in flour or batter) by submersion in hot oil. Sauté, from the French *sauter* (to jump), means to rapidly cook small pieces of food over high heat in oil or fat. The Chinese version is called stir-frying; it usually involves less oil and a wok.

GREASE. To coat the interior of a pan with fat to prevent food from sticking.

PREHEATING. Turn on oven to the desired temperature at least 20 minutes before baking, roasting, or grilling to insure that the oven has reached the desired temperature.

SEAR. To brown food quickly by sautéing in a pan, under a broiler, or on a grill to seal in a food's juices while making the food's exterior pleasantly crisp.

SIMMER. To cook liquid, and anything in it, over a low heat just shy of the boiling point. Small bubbles may rise to the surface. If left uncovered, the liquid will become concentrated.

STEEP. To allow dry ingredients (tea, dried fruits, sun-dried tomatoes) to sit in warm liquid. In the case of tea, the steeping liquid is the desired product. In the case of dried fruits and tomatoes, more often than not the liquid is discarded, as its only purpose is to plump things that have become overly desiccated.

How to Cut It

CHIFFONADE. To cut leaves of easily bruised fresh herbs, like basil, by rolling the leaves and then slicing them across into very fine strips.

CHOPPING. To cut food into small, but not necessarily even, pieces. To chop: Hold the blade firmly and bring a large knife up and down all over the material to be chopped.

DICING. To cut into even, tiny cubes. Dicing results in smaller pieces than does chopping but larger than does mincing. Remove a small slice from the bottom of whatever you want to dice, so that it lies flat on the board. Cut the vegetable into sticks, then cut the sticks into cubes. The size of the sticks and how thick you slice them determine the size of the dice.

FILLET. To debone a cut of meat or fish. (A fillet as a noun refers to the meat once its bones have been removed.)

JULIENNE. To cut into fine, even-sized sticks, which are also called matchsticks. These strips are used to garnish soups, stews, and salads, or they can be steamed and served as a side dish.

MINCE. Mince means to chop food very finely. Parsley and garlic are typically minced.

How to Handle Your Liquids

CURDLE. Certain foods will separate, or curdle, when heated too rapidly (dairy products are especially susceptible); flour acts as a binding agent to prevent this from happening. If a dish curdles on you, all is not lost; you can often incorporate the ruined batch into the new.

DEGLAZE. To pour liquid—water, stock, wine, or liquor—into a pan in which food has been roasted or sautéed in order to absorb the glaze and the browned, crusty bits formed on the bottom of the pan. These concentrated, coagulated meat essences add wonderful flavor to a dish or sauce.

DEGREASE. To skim fat from the surface of a soup or sauce. This can be done with a spoon and additional fat can be absorbed with paper towels. A less labor-intensive solution is to ladle the liquid into a special degreasing pitcher with a trap door at the bottom. Then you can allow the non-fatty meat juices to escape from below, stopping the flow when only the fat remains. If there is time enough to allow the liquid to thoroughly chill, then the fat rises to the top in a semisolid layer that is easily removed.

GLAZING. Applying any thick liquid that lends luster to food.

REDUCE. To heat a liquid to a boil, and leave uncovered and simmering so that liquid will condense in volume and flavor.

RENDER. To extract an animal fat from its connective tissue by melting. Two rendered fats used in cooking are chicken fat and lard, which is pork fat. Rendering is a slow process, done in a heavy-bottomed pan over low heat. It continues until all the fat has liquefied, the tissue has turned brown and crispy, and any impurities have sunk to the bottom of the pan. The remaining clear fat is strained carefully through filter paper. The practice of rendering is losing favor among health-conscious cooks.

SCALD. To scald milk is to heat it just shy of boiling. To scald solid food is to briefly immerse it into already boiling water.

"Let him kiss me with the kisses of his mouth: for thy love is better than wine."

SONG OF SOLOMON 1:2

Wine Glossary

ACIDITY. This refers to the quality of tartness and freshness. The acid also protects the wine from bacteria, which make it "turn," or go bad. As a rule, white wine is less acidic than red.

AERATING/BREATHING. When wine is exposed to air, it loses any unpleasant odors and exudes its own inherent aroma, or bouquet.

AGING. Wine must age to undergo the process of fermentation. During this time, wine is stored in oak barrels, stainless steel tanks, or glass.

AROMA. The wine's fragrance depends on how advanced the fermentation process is. Wines with strong aromas are those that still have some of the original grape sugar.

BALANCE. A fine wine should have an equilibrium of flavors—no one quality (acidity, fruit, sugar, etc.) should dominate.

BODY. The degree of the wine's richness and flavor as affected by its alcohol and tannin levels.

BOUQUET. Wine should smell clean, like grapes, not moldy. The scent that endures is the aroma.

BREATHING. See **AERATING**.

BRUT. When a champagne is very dry, all the grapes' sugar has fermented into alcohol. Brut is the superlative of "extra dry."

COMPLEX. If a wine has many identifiable attributes (acids, alcohol, fruit, and tannin) it is usually an older, more expensive wine.

CRISP. A light wine that is acidic and tastes clean and fresh.

DECANT. As a wine (usually red) is poured from the bottle to another container (often a carafe or a decanter), the wine breathes, releases its bouquet, and leaves behind its sediment in the bottle. As you are pouring out the wine, stop once you notice dark, cloudy wine rise to the neck—you may lose 1–6 ounces, but the rest of the bottle will taste so much better, it's worth the sacrifice.

DRY/SEC. Once all the sugar in the grape has completely fermented, the sugar disappears and only alcohol is left.

FAT. Wine that is rich and intense.

FINISH. Once the wine is swallowed, this term refers to its aftertaste.

FLAT. A wine that's low in acidity will have an unappealing lack of body, character, and flavor.

FRUITY. A term referring to wines that have a refreshing fragrance or taste reminiscent of grapes and other fruits.

HEAVY. Wine that is full-bodied but otherwise lackluster.

LEGS. The transparent liquid that trickles down the inside of a wine glass after it has been swirled.

LIGHT. Wine low in alcohol content and tannin; can be a pleasant quality.

SEC. See **DRY**.

SWEET. Wine that still retains much of the grape sugar.

TANNIN. Organic compounds (phenols) in the skins, stems, and seeds that give wine its bitter, acidic taste. More prevalent in reds than whites.

THIN. See **FLAT**.

General Notes. American wines are named for the grape and European wines for their region.

Some White Categories. Chardonnay, Gewürztraminer, Muscat, Nebbiolo, Riesling, Sauvignon Blanc, Sémillon, Viognier

Some Red Categories. Cabernet Sauvignon, Gamay, Grenache, Merlot, Pinot Noir, Sangiovese, Shiraz, Syrah, Zinfandel

where.
Preparing and presenting your food is as essential to the meal as the cooking process itself. Nothing is more frustrating than a garlic press that won't press. Refer to our list of Resources (see page 277) and our list of Tools (see page 270) for help on better serving it up.

FREEDOM OF CHOICE

MANUFACTURERS

ALL-CLAD
800/ALL-CLAD
(Cookware)

AMANA
800/843-0304
(Kitchen appliances)

BRAUN
800/272-8610
(Cooking appliances)

CALPHALON
419/666-8700
(Cookware)

CHANTAL COOKWARE
800/365-4354
(Cookware)

CORNINGWARE/REVERE
800/999-3436
(Cookware)

CUISINART CORP.
800/726-0190
(Food processors)

FARBERWARE
800/562-4226
(Cookware)

GENERAL ELECTRIC
800/626-2000
(Kitchen appliances)

KENWOOD
800/536-9663
(Kitchen appliances)

KITCHENAID
800/422-1230
(Restaurant-quality blenders and mixers)

KRUPS
800/526-5377
(Kitchen appliances)

LE CREUSET OF AMERICA
800/729-0908
(Enameled cast-iron kitchenware, wine accessories)

REPLACEMENTS, LTD.
800/562-4462
(Stainless flatware, crystal)

TUPPERWARE
800/858-7221
(Kitchen storage)

NATIONAL RETAILERS/MAIL ORDER CATALOGS

BED, BATH & BEYOND
212/255-3550
(Kitchen storage items)

BERGDORF GOODMAN
800/967-3788 for catalog
(Tableware)

BLOOMINGDALE'S
800/777-4999 For store catalog
800/777-0000 For Bloomingdale's by Mail Ltd.
(Upscale department store; kitchen- and tableware)

BRENTHAM SAUSAGE COMPANY
800/460-5030
(Air-dried German and Tex-Mex sausages)

BRIDGE KITCHENWARE
800/274-3435 Outside of NYC only
212/688-4220
(Kitchenware)

CHEF'S CATALOG
800/338-3232
(Professional kitchenware)

CIVELLO'S RAVIOLISMO
800/80PASTA
(Stuffed pasta)

CORRALITOS CHEESE COMPANY
408/722-1821
(Wide selection of goat cheeses)

CRATE & BARREL
800/323-5461 for catalog information
(Kitchen utensils)

DAYTON HUDSON MARSHALL FIELD
800/292-2450
(Department store; kitchenware)

DEAN & DELUCA
800/221-7714 for catalog
212/431-1691 for store
(Gourmet foods and spices, cooking supplies)

DILLARD'S PARK PLAZA
501/661-0053
(Kitchenware, cookware, tableware)

HOME DEPOT
404/433-8211. Call for locations.
(Kitchenware)

GARLIC SURVIVAL COMPANY
800/3Garlic
(Wide selection of garlic condiments)

GOURMET AMERICA
800/352-1352
(Importers of exotic foods and spices; call them for store referrals in your area for Inner Beauty Real Hot Sauce)

IKEA
908/352-1550
(Cookware)

JOHNSON BROTHERS BY WEDGWOOD
800/677-7860
(Cookware)

LECHTER'S
800/605-4824
(Kitchenware and utensils)

R. H. MACY & CO., INC.
(BULLOCK'S, AÉROPOSTALE)
800/45-MACYS
212/695-4400 for East Coast listings,
415/393-3457 for West Coast listings
(Department store)

NORDSTROM'S
800/285-5800
(Kitchenware, cookware)

POTTERY BARN
800/922-9934 for catalog
(Housewares)

SILETZ TRIBAL SMOKEHOUSE
800/828-4269
(A variety of smoked Pacific salmon)

SPECIALTY SAUCES
800/SAUCES1
(Barbeque sauces from around the country)

TARGET
612/370-6073 for location nearest you
(Cookware, tableware, kitchen utensils)

TIFFANY'S
800/526-0649 for catalog
(Tableware)

WILLIAMS-SONOMA
800/541-2233
(Kitchenware, kitchen storage items)

UNITED STATES

ARIZONA

SHAR'S BOSCH KITCHEN
CENTER
6204 North 43rd Street
Glendale, AZ 85301
602/ 937-3974
(Kitchenware)

CALIFORNIA

CAPRICORN GOURMET
COOKWARE
100 Throckmorton Avenue
Mill Valley, CA 94941
415/388-1720
(Gourmet cookware)

COOKING
339 Divisadero Street
San Francisco, CA 94117
415/861-1854
(Nostalgic and professional cooking equipment)

HERB PRODUCTS
11012 Magnolia Boulevard
North Hollywood, CA 91691
818/984-3141
(A variety of domestic and imported herbs)

HOMECHEF
329 Corte Madera Town Center
Corte Madera, CA 94921
415/927-3191
(Kitchenware and cooking school)

HOMECHEF
3525 California Street
San Francisco, CA 94115
415/668-3191
(Kitchenware and cooking school)

KITCHEN ART
142 South Robertson Boulevard
Los Angeles, CA 90048
310/271-9499
(Kitchenware)

SWISS KITCHEN
228 Bon Aire Center
Green Brae, CA 94904
415/461-1011
(Kitchenware,cookware)

CONNECTICUT

CHEESE & STUFF
550 Farmington Avenue
Hartford, CT 06105
203/233-8281
(Cookware, selection of imported cheeses)

FOOD FOR THOUGHT
221 Post Road West
Westport,CT 06880
203/226-5233
(Cookware)

THE PANTRY
Titus Road
Washington Depot, CT 06794
203/868-0258
(Cookware, tableware)

THE SILO
44 Upland Road
New Milford, CT 06776
203/355-0300
(Cookware, kitchen appliances, cooking school)

ILLINOIS

ELKAY MANUFACTURING
COMPANY
2222 Camden Court
Oak Brook, IL 60521
708/574-8484
(Cookware)

ST. CHARLES MANUFACTURING
COMPANY
1611 East Main Street
St. Charles, IL
708/584-3800
(Cookware)

OHIO

KITCHEN COLLECTION
71 East Water Street
Chillicothe, OH 45601
614/773-9150
(Kitchenware, appliances)

NEW MEXICO

CHILI SHOP
109 East Water Street
Santa Fe, NM 87501
505/983-6080
(Mail order chilis)

NEW YORK

ABC CARPET & HOME
888 Broadway
New York, NY 10003
212/473-3000
(Kitchenware, tableware)

AD HOC SOFTWARES
410 West Broadway
New York, NY 10012
212/925-2652
(Kitchenware, tableware)

BROADWAY PANHANDLER
520 Broadway
New York, NY 10012
212/966-3434
(Cookware, kitchenware)

E.A.T.
1064 Madison Avenue
New York, NY 10028
212/772-0022
(Gourmet foods, kitchenware)

FELISSIMO
10 West 56th Street
New York, NY 10019
212/956-4438
800/708-7690 for catalog
(Serving pieces)

FISHS EDDY
889 Broadway
New York, NY 10003
212/420-9020
(Tableware)

GOURMET GARAGE
453 Broome Street
New York, NY 10013
212/941-5850
(Gourmet foods)

THE RYE COUNTRY STORE
50 Purchase Street
Rye, NY 10580
914/967-3450
(Gourmet foods and serving pieces)

TAKASHIMAYA
693 Fifth Avenue
New York, NY 10022
212/350-0100
(Serving pieces)

TARZAN HOUSEWARES
194 Seventh Avenue
Brooklyn, NY 11215
718/788-4213
(Cookware)

WOLFMAN-GOLD & GOOD
116 Greene Street
New York, NY 10012
212/431-1888
(Serving pieces)

"Couples who cook together, stay together. (Maybe because they can't decide who'll get the Cuisinart.)"

ERICA JONG

ZABAR'S
2245 Broadway
New York, NY 10024
212/787-2000
(Gourmet foods)

ZONA
97 Greene Street
New York, NY 10012
212/925-6750
(Dishware)

MICHIGAN

THE KITCHEN PORT
415 North Fifth Avenue
Ann Arbor, MI 48105
313/665-9188
(Cookware, kitchenware)

WASHINGTON

SUR LA TABLE
84 Pine Street
Seattle, WA 98101
206/448-2244
(Kitchenware, tableware)

WASHINGTON, D.C.

SUTTON PLACE GOURMET
3201 New Mexico Avenue, NW
Washington, DC 20016
202/363-5800
(Gourmet foods)

INTERNATIONAL LISTINGS

CANADA

**GINGER'S
AT ELTE CARPETS & HOME**
80 Ronald Avenue
Toronto, M6E 5A2
416/785-4774
(Everything for the hobby chef, including the kitchen sink)

FRANCE

AU BAIN MARIE
12, rue Boissy d'Anglais
Paris 8e
142/266-5974
(Selection of tableware items)

CULINARION
99, rue de Rennes
Paris 6e
45/48-94-76
(Practical kitchen equipment)

GREAT BRITAIN

ALGERIAN COFFEE STORES
52 Old Compton Street
London W1V 6PB
71/437-2480
(Herbal and fruity teas, coffees, and gourmet grocery items)

BERWICK STREET MARKET
Berwick Street
London W1
(Fruit and vegetable market and inexpensive household goods)

BRIXTON MARKET
Electric Avenue
London SW9
(Afro-Caribbean food, such as goat's meat, pigs' tails, salted fish, breadfruit, and exotic fish)

THE CONRAN SHOP
Michelin House
181 Fulham Road
London SW3
71/589-7401
(Kitchenware, tableware)

DAVID MELLOR
4 Sloane Square
London SW1W 8EE
71/730-4259
(Kitchen equipment and tableware)

FORTNUM AND MASON
188 Piccadilly
London W1A 1ER
71/734-8040
(Founded from the eighteenth-century court of Queen Anne, makes high art of selling fine tableware, groceries, jams, preserves, teas, and crocks of Stilton cheese)

HABITAT UK LTD
206 King's Road
London SW3 5XP
71/351-1211 Call for branch listing
(kitchen and tableware)

HARRODS FOOD HALL
Knightsbridge
London SW1X 7QX
71/730-1234

HEAL'S
196 Tottenham Court Road
London W1P 9LD
171/636-1666
(Accessories for the home)

HOLLAND AND BARRETT
19 Goodge Street
London W1P 1FD
71/580-2886
(Health-food retailer, vitamins)

JERRY'S HOME STORE
163-167 Fulham Road
London SW3 6SN
71/581-0909
(Kitchenware)

JUSTIN DE BLANK
123 Sloane Street
London SW1X 9BL
71/730-3721
(Specialty foods)

LEADENHALL MARKET
Whittington Avenue
London EC3
(Market of food shops selling gourmet foods, seafood and game available in season)

MUJI
26 Great Marlborough Street
London W1V 1HB
71/494-1197. Call for branch listing.
(Special Japanese foods; selection of cookware and tableware)

PAXTON AND WHITFIELD
93 Jermyn Street
London SW1Y 6JE
71/930-0250
(Dating from 1830; over 300 cheeses including baby Stiltons and Cheshire cheeses, along with pork pies, elegant biscuits, oils, and preserves)

THE TEA HOUSE
15 Neal Street
London WC2H 9PU
71/240-7539
(Interesting selection of teas, including fruit-flavored, and teapots)

ITALY

C.U.C.I.N.A
Via del Babuino 118A
Rome 00168
396/684-08-19
(Kitchenware)

THE NETHERLANDS

BALKJE
Kerkstraat 46-48
1017 GM
Amsterdam
20/622-0566
(Gourmet foods)

RESOURCES

(Uncredited items are from the collection of Edward Kemper Design)

SOUP

20–21 **LADLE**—Broadway Panhandler

23 **ENAMEL STOCKPOT**—Broadway Panhandler

25 **BOWL**—Macy's

30 **PAN**—Calphalon Cookware

32 **TABLE**—Takashimaya

POULTRY

43 **ENAMEL ROASTING PAN** and **PLAID LINEN** —Broadway Panhandler

45 **PLATE**—Bergdorf Goodman

47 **PLATE**—Bergdorf Goodman

54 **SMALL** and **LARGE PLATES**—Fishs Eddy; **NAPKIN**—Bergdorf Goodman

61 **PLATE**—Wolfman-Gold & Good; **FORK**— Tiffany & Co.

62 **TONGS**—courtesy of Chris Schlesinger

65 **BRUSH**—Broadway Panhandler

MEAT

70 **PLATE**—Bergdorf Goodman

73 **MIXING BOWLS**—(clockwise from upper left) Broadway Panhandler; Lechter's Housewares; Macy's

75 **PLATE**—Fishs Eddy; **SPATULA**—Broadway Panhandler

76 **NAPKIN**—ABC Carpet & Home

78 **NAPKIN**—Felissimo

81 **SHALLOW ROASTING PAN**—Broadway Panhandler

83 **PLATE**—Johnson Brothers; **LINEN**—antique

92 **PLATE**—Mikasa; **GLASS**—Elsa Peretti, from Tiffany & Co.

95 **BOWL**—Bergdorf Goodman

96 **FISH SPATULA**—Williams-Sonoma

VEGETABLES

117 **BOWL**—Ikea

118 **PLATE**—Pottery Barn

106 **BAKING PAN**—Broadway Panhandler

107 **PLATE**—Felissimo

POTATOES, GRAINS, AND RICE

132–33 **WHITE GARDEN TRELLIS BOWL**—Williams-Sonoma

135 **MEASURING CUP**—Broadway Panhandler

141 **POLENTA DISH**—Barneys

145 **CAST-IRON FRYING PAN**—Broadway Panhandler

147 **BLUE-RIMMED CHARGER**—Bergdorf Goodman

148–49 **CUTTING BOARD**—Williams-Sonoma

151 **DISH**—antique

BEANS

157 **BEAN JAR**—Lechter's Housewares

164–65 **ANTIQUE STEW POTS**—(left) Tortoise Orchard Antiques

167 **ANTIQUE HAND-PAINTED PLATE**— collection of Robert Valentine; **LINEN NAPKIN**—Barneys

PASTA

178 **COLANDER**—Williams-Sonoma

179 **SAUTÉ PAN**—Calphalon cookware

184 **LINEN**—Takashimaya; **PLATE**—Felissimo

189 **BOWL**—Bergdorf Goodman; **GLASS**— Tiffany & Co.; **ANTIQUE TABLE**— Takashimaya

196 **LINEN NAPKIN**—Takashimaya

202 **PIZZA PEELS**—(top) antique; (bottom) Williams-Sonoma

205 **PLATE**—Fishs Eddy; **BAKERS TOWEL**— Williams-Sonoma; **TABLE**—Tortoise Orchard Antiques

214 **PIZZA CUTTER**—Williams-Sonoma

SALADS

222–23 **SINK**—courtesy of Schnoodle Studios; **COLANDER**—Broadway Panhandler

225 **SOUP BOWL** and **PLATE**—Fishs Eddy

227 **SMALL PITCHER**—Williams-Sonoma

231 **STAR PLATE**—Bergdorf Goodman

DESSERTS

240 **SILVER SPOON**—collection of Robert Valentine

244 **BUNDT PAN**—Broadway Panhandler

245 **CAKE STAND**—Wolfman-Gold & Good

251 **ANTIQUE SILVER SPOONS**—Tortoise Orchard Antiques

254 **SIFTER**—Broadway Panhandler

255 **PLATE**—Barneys; **GLASS**—Tiffany & Co.

QUOTES

Unless otherwise noted, all VOICES quotes are from original interviews. For publishing information on VOICES cookbooks, see page 279.

2 Jim Harrison, "Midrange Road Kill" from *Just Before Dark: Collected Nonfiction* (Clark City Press, 1991)

6 Australian aboriginal saying

14 R. Fitzhenry, ed., *The Harper Book of Quotations* (HarperCollins, 1993)

18 Lewis Carroll, *Alice's Adventures in Wonderland* (1865)

22 Maria Polushkin Robbins, ed., *The Cook's Quotation Book: A Literary Feast* (Penguin Books, 1984)

26 R. Fitzhenry, *The Harper Book of Quotations* (HarperCollins, 1993)

36 Jeanette Winterson, *The Passion* (Atlantic Monthly Press, 1988)

38 Michael Cader and Debby Roth, eds., *Eat These Words: A Delicious Collection of Fat-free Food for Thought* (Cader Books/ HarperCollins, Publishers, 1991)

42 John Goode, ed., *The Cultured Glutton: A Collection of Culinary Quotes* (Headline Book Publishing, 1987)

46 Anne Tyler, *The Accidental Tourist* (Knopf, 1985)

50-51 Julia Child, *The Way to Cook:* "I would much..." page xi; On Stock, page 137; On Fish, page 80; On Pasta Salad, page 367

53 S. Herbst, ed., *A Food Lover's Companion* (Harper & Row, 1979)

63 Chris Schlesinger, *The Tab* of Newton, Mass., June 16, 1992: "Part of the fun..."; *The Thrill of the Grill*: On Salt, page 370

64 John Wayne, *The Man Who Shot Liberty Valance,* 1961

68 Deuteronomy XII:20, *The Bible*, King James Version

71 Merrit Malloy and Marsha Rose, eds., *The Comedian's Quote Book: Quick Takes from the Great Comics* (Sterling Publishing Company, Inc., 1993)

79 Jim Harrison, "Piggies Come to Market" from *Just Before Dark: Collected Nonfiction* (Clark City Press, 1980)

82 James Leeds, *Children of a Lesser God*, 1986

85 Marion Cunningham, *The Supper Book*: "Supper is more..." page xiii; On Enhancing Flavors, page 57; *The Fannie Farmer Cookbook*: On Presentation, page 3

88 Ernest Hemingway, *The Sun Also Rises* (1926)

94 Peter Mayle, *A Year in Provence* (Vintage Books, 1991)

96 Maria Polushkin Robbins, ed., *The Cook's Quotation Book: A Literary Feast* (Penguin Books, 1984)

98 Pierre Franey, *A Chef's Tale*: "It is literally...", page 4

99 Pierre Franey, *A Chef's Tale*: On Ingredients, page 128; *Pierre Franey's Low-Calorie Gourmet*: On Equipment, page 6; On Sauces, page 5

102 Jim Harrison, "Hunger, Real and Unreal," *Just Before Dark: Collected Nonfiction* (Clark City Press, 1991)

104 Dr. Hannibal Lecter, *The Silence of the Lambs*, 1991

108 Robert Andrews, ed., *The Columbia Dictionary of Quotations* (Columbia University Press, 1993)

110 R. Fitzhenry, ed., *The Harper Book of Quotations* (HarperCollins, 1993)

114-15 Paula Wolfert, *The Cooking of the Eastern Mediterranean*: On Oil and On Nuts, page 402; *The Cooking of South-West France*: Inspiration in Situ: p. 1; "For me, one...", page 26

116 Maria Polushkin Robbins, ed., *The Cook's Quotation Book: A Literary Feast* (Penguin Books, 1984)

126 Nora Ephron, *Heartburn* (Knopf, 1983)

134 Italian proverb, *The New Basics Cookbook* by Julee Rosso and Sheila Lukins (Workman Publishing, 1989)

136-37 Annie Somerville, *Fields of Greens*: "Stocking your pantry...", page xix; On Tools, page 2; On Beans, page 3; On Fruit, page xx; On Salads, page 4; On Vegetables, page 4

138 Robert Byrne, ed., *1,911 Best Things Anybody Ever Said* (Ballantine Books, 1988)

148-49 Maria Polushkin Robbins, ed., *The Cook's Quotation Book: A Literary Feast* (Penguin Books, 1984)

154 Louis Armstrong

166 R. Fitzhenry, ed., *The Harper Book of Quotations* (HarperCollins, 1993)

174 Ortensio Landi, secretary to Lucrezia Gonzaga, sixteenth century.

177 Robert Byrne, ed., *1,911 Best Things Anyone Ever Said* (Ballantine Books, 1988)

178 Ragú TV commercial from the late 1970s

190-91 Pino Luongo, *A Tuscan in the Kitchen*: "For me, cooking...", and "Keep the meal...", page 9; On Olive Oil, page 30; On Garlic, page 31

200 Calvin Trillin, *Travels with Alice* (Ticknor & Fields, 1989)

203 Maria Polushkin Robbins, ed., *A Cook's Alphabet of Quotations* (Dutton, 1991)

208 Maria Polushkin Robbins, ed., *The Cook's Quotation Book: A Literary Feast* (Penguin Books, 1984)

212 Michael Cader and Debby Roth, eds., *Eat These Words: A Delicious Collection of Fat-free Food for Thought* (Cader Books/HarperCollins Publishers, 1991)

213 Shakespeare, *Butter in the Bard* by Robert D. Bernoskie (Original Traveling Chef, 1992)

214-15 Wolfgang Puck, *Adventures in the Kitchen*: "It took me...", and "Think of cooking...", page xv; All tips, page 108

218 Justin Kaplan, ed., *Bartlett's Familiar Quotations* (Little, Brown & Company, 1992)

224 John Goode, ed., *The Cultured Glutton: A Collection of Culinary Quotes* (Headline Book Publishing, 1987)

228 Robert Byrne, ed., *The Fifth and Far Finer Than the First Four 637 Best Things Anybody Ever Said* (Ballantine Books, 1993)

230 Allen Ginsberg, "A Supermarket in California," 1955

232-33 Alice Waters, *Chez Panisse Menu Cookbook*: "I opened a restaurant..." page xi; On Quality Not Quantity, page 10

236 Colette, *The Claudine Novels* (Penguin, 1995)

244 Shirley Maclaine, *The New York Times*, March 17, 1994

254 Mr. Tyrrell, *Blade Runner*, 1982

258 Alka-Seltzer ad slogan

259 Colin Jarman, ed., *The Guinness Book of Poisonous Quotes* (Contemporary Books, 1993)

263 John Goode, ed., *The Cultured Glutton: A Collection of Culinary Quotes* (Headline Book Publishing, 1987)

264 Fred Metcalf, ed., *The Penguin Dictionary of Modern Humorous Quotations* (Penguin, 1988)

267 Maria Polushkin Robbins, ed., *A Cook's Alphabet of Quotations* (Dutton, 1991)

273 Song of Solomon I:2, *The Bible*, King James Version

276 Fred Metcalf, ed., *The Penguin Dictionary of Modern Humorous Quotations* (Penguin, 1988)

288 Clifford Cook Furnas and Sparkle Moore Furnas, *Man, Bread & Destiny* (Reynal & Hitchcock, 1937)

VOICES RECIPES

51 CHICKEN SIMMERED IN WHITE WINE from Julia Child's *The Way to Cook*, page 144

63 GRILLED WEST INDIES SPICE-RUBBED CHICKEN BREAST WITH GRILLED BANANA from Chris Schlesinger's *The Thrill of the Grill*, page 165

85 QUICK THEATER STEAK from Marion Cunningham's *The Fannie Farmer Cookbook*, page 161

99 BROILED FLOUNDER À LA MOUTARDE from *Pierre Franey's Low-Calorie Gourmet*, page 54; ZUCCHINI BORDELAISE also from *Pierre Franey's Low-Calorie Gourmet*, page 233

115 SHRIMP IN TOMATO SAUCE WITH ALMONDS AND PINE NUTS from Paula Wolfert's *The Cooking of the Eastern Mediterranean*, page 255; STEWED POTATOES WITH TOMATOES AND FETA also from *The Cooking of the Eastern Mediterranean*, page 201

137 CORN AND BULGUR SALAD WITH CILANTRO AND LIME from Annie Somerville's *Fields of Greens*, page 36; COUSCOUS SALAD WITH APRICOTS, PINE NUTS, AND GINGER also from *Fields of Greens*, page 34

191 PASTA WITH TOMATOES, MOZZARELLA, AND BASIL from Pino Luongo's *A Tuscan in the Kitchen*, page 101; BAKED PEACHES STUFFED WITH WALNUTS AND CHOCOLATE also from *A Tuscan in the Kitchen*, page 224

211 SPICY CHICKEN PIZZA from Wolfgang Puck's *Adventures in the Kitchen*, page 180

233 WARM GREEN BEAN SALAD WITH ROCKET AND GARDEN LETTUCES from Alice Waters' *Chez Panisse Menu Cookbook*, page 214

VOICES

BIBLIOGRAPHY AND RESTAURANTS

JULIA CHILD

- *The French Chef Cookbook* (Knopf, 1968)
- *From Julia Child's Kitchen* (Knopf, 1975)
- *Julia Child & Company* (Knopf, 1978)
- *Julia Child at Home with the Master Chefs* (Knopf, 1993)
- *Julia Child's Menu Cookbook* (Wings Books, 1978)
- *Julia Child & More Company* (Knopf, 1979)
- *Mastering the Art of French Cooking,* with Simone Beck and Louisette Bertholle (Knopf, 1961)
- *Mastering the Art of French Cooking, Volume Two,* with Simone Beck (Knopf, 1970)
- *The Way to Cook* (Knopf, 1989)

MARION CUNNINGHAM

- *The Breakfast Book* (Knopf, 1987)
- *The Fannie Farmer Baking Book* (Knopf, 1984)
- *The Fannie Farmer Cookbook* (Knopf, 1990)
- *The Supper Book* (Knopf, 1992)

PIERRE FRANEY

- *A Chef's Tale: A Memoir of Food, France & America,* with Richard Flaste and Bryan Miller (Knopf, 1994)
- *Cooking with Craig Claiborne and Pierre Franey,* with Craig Claiborne (Columbine, 1985)
- *Craig Claiborne's Gourmet Diet,* with Craig Claiborne (Times Books, 1980)
- *Craig Claiborne's New New York Times Cookbook,* with Craig Claiborne (Times Books, 1979)
- *Cuisine Rapide,* with Bryan Miller (Times Books, 1989)
- *The New York Times: Sixty-Minute Gourmet* (Times Books, 1979)
- *The New York Times: More Sixty-Minute Gourmet* (Columbine, 1985)
- *The Seafood Cookbook* with Bryan Miller (Times Books, 1986)
- *Pierre Franey's Cooking in America,* with Richard Flaste (Knopf, 1992)

- *Pierre Franey's Cooking in France,* with Richard Flaste (Knopf, 1994)
- *Pierre Franey's Low-Calorie Dessert: The New York Times 60-Minute Gourmet's Lighter Approach to Classic Cuisine,* with Richard Flaste (Times Books, 1995)
- *Pierre Franey's Low-Calorie Gourmet,* with Richard Flaste (Times Books, 1989)

PINO LUONGO

- *Fish Talk: Recipes from Le Madri, Coco Pazzo & Sapore di Mare,* with Barbara Raives (Clarkson N. Potter, 1994)
- *A Tuscan in the Kitchen: Recipes and Tales from My Home* (Clarkson N. Potter, 1988)

RESTAURANTS

(Does not cook but oversees menus and chefs)

AMARCORD
7 East 59th Street
New York, NY 10022
212/935-3535

COCO PAZZO
23 East 74th Street
New York, NY 10021
212/794-0205

COCO PAZZO
300 West Hubbard
Chicago, IL 60610
312/836-0900

LE MADRI
168 West 18th Street
New York, NY 10022
212/727-8022

MAD. 61
10 East 61st Street
New York, NY 10021
212/833-2200

PICCOLA CUCINA
South Coast Plaza, Space 3001
3333 Bristol Street
Costa Mesa, CA 92626
714/556-5844

PICCOLA CUCINA
Galleria One
5015 Westheimer
Houston, TX 77056
713/622-4544

PICCOLA CUCINA
1030 NorthPark Center
Dallas, TX 75225
214/691-0488

SAPORE DI MARE
Montauk Highway
Wainscott, NY 11975
516/537-2764

WOLFGANG PUCK

- *Adventures in the Kitchen* (Random House, 1991)
- *The Wolfgang Puck Cookbook* (Random House, 1986)
- *Wolfgang Puck's Modern French Cooking* (Houghton Mifflin, 1986)

RESTAURANTS

CHINOIS ON MAIN
2709 Main Street
Santa Monica, CA 90405
310/392-9025

GRANITA
23725 West Malibu Road
Malibu, CA 90265
310/456-0488

POSTRIO
545 Post Street
San Francisco, CA 90265
415/776-7825

SPAGO, LOS ANGELES
1114 Horn Avenue
West Hollywood, CA 90069
310/652-4025

SPAGO, MEXICO CITY
Avenida Presidente Masaryk 214
Col. Polanco
D.F. 11580
Mexico City, Mexico
011-525-280-7800

SPAGO, VEGAS
c/o The Forum at Caesars
3500 South Las Vegas Boulevard
Las Vegas, NV 89109
702/369-6300

CHRIS SCHLESINGER

(with John Willoughby)

- *Big Flavors of the Hot Sun: Techniques and Recipes from the Spice Zone* (Morrow, 1994)
- *Salsas, Sambals, Chutneys & Chowchows* (Morrow, 1993)
- *The Thrill of the Grill: Techniques, Recipes & Down Home Barbecue* (Morrow, 1990)

RESTAURANTS

BLUE ROOM
1 Kendall Square, Bldg. 200
Cambridge, MA 02141
617/494-1376

EAST COAST GRILL
1271 Cambridge Street
Cambridge, MA 02139
617/491-6568

JAKE & EARL'S
1273 Cambridge Street
Cambridge, MA 02139
617/491-RIBS

ANNIE SOMERVILLE

- *Fields of Greens: New Vegetarian Recipes from the Celebrated Greens Restaurant* (Bantam, 1993)

RESTAURANTS

GREENS
Building A, Fort Mason
San Francisco, CA 94123
415/771-3472

ALICE WATERS

- *Chez Panisse Menu Cookbook* (Random House, 1982)
- *Fanny at Chez Panisse: A Child's Restaurant Adventure with Forty-two Recipes* (HarperCollins, 1992)
- *Chez Panisse Cooking,* with Paul Bertolli (Random House, 1988)
- *Chez Panisse Pasta, Pizza & Calzone,* with Patricia Curtan and Martine Labro (Random House, 1984)

RESTAURANTS

CHEZ PANISSE
1517 Shattuck Avenue
Berkeley, CA 94709
510/548-5525

CAFE FANNY
Cedar and San Pablo Avenues
Berkeley, CA 94709
510/524-5447

PAULA WOLFERT

- *The Cooking of South-West France: A Collection of Traditional and New Recipes from France's Magnificent Rustic Cuisine* (HarperCollins, 1988)
- *Couscous and Other Good Foods from Morocco* (HarperCollins, 1988)
- *Mediterranean Cooking* (HarperCollins, revised, 1994)
- *Paula Wolfert's World of Food* (HarperCollins, 1994)
- *Paula Wolfert's World of Food 2* (HarperCollins, 1995)

I N D E X

ACKNOWLEDGMENTS

You've probably had the experience of tasting something delectable at a friend's home. You timidly ask if he or she would mind sharing the recipe. "Of course," declares your magnanimous host as he or she scribbles down the recipe while letting you know how easy it is to make. Days later you try to re-create the dish and find that while not quite a disaster, it lacks the distinction you remember. Is it just that everything served at someone else's home tastes better, especially when there's plenty of wine, music, and laughter, or did your host neglect to include that small but necessary detail needed to transform the ordinary into something memorable? That is why we have invited a variety of real people—people who aren't professional cooks, yet enjoy cooking and eating—to try the recipes included in this book and give us their opinions. We are extremely grateful for their candid and creative feedback. We also thank Georgia Downard for her professional advice.

RECIPE TESTERS Liz Abbott, Susan Johnson Banta, Lucy Bartley, Georgia Downard, Teri and Nick Galluccio, Lise Gescheidt, Barbara Gnaedig, Betty Hudson, Boyd Matson, Lorca Peress, Victoria C. Rowan, Raquel M. Scott, Carleen Simone
Special thanks to Glenna, Carolyn, and David Gross for being my tasters in residence (**K.J.G.**)

ADDITIONAL RECIPE INSPIRATION Many recipes were contributed or inspired by friends. We thank the following for allowing us to share these dishes with you: Joan Didion, Nora Ephron, Laurel Gross, Toby Gross, Robert Hughes, Todd Lyon, Jacqueline de la Chaume, Jeffrey Miller, Victoria C. Rowan, Russ Solito

QUOTE RESEARCH Lilly Golden, Kate Doyle Hooper, and Lige Rushing

MANUFACTURER AND RETAIL RESEARCH Susan Claire Maloney

ADDITIONAL COOKING RESEARCH Mary Ann Daly, M. Scott Cookson, Deborah Freeman, Babs Lefrak, Victoria C. Rowan, Sally Sampson, Heather Starr

WINE CONSULTANT Richard J. Shiekman, Parliament Import Co., importers and marketers of fine wines from France, Italy, Germany, Australia, and the United States

AND SPECIAL THANKS TO Suzi Arensberg, Claire Bradley, Amy Capen, Lauren Clarke Caldwell, Cara Chaiet, Tony Chirico, Jin Chung, Jill Cohen, Lauri Del Commune, the experts at Dean & Deluca, Michael Drazen, Jane Friedman, Hayward Hill Gatling, Carla Glasser, Janice Goldklang, Dr. Jeffrey Gross, Margaret Gross, Patrick Higgins, Susan Horowitz, Katherine Hourigan, Andy Hughes, Marilyn Knowlton, Carol Janeway, Judith Jones, Barbara Jones-Diggs, Nicholas Latimer, Carl Lennertz, William Loverd, M. Kathryn Lyon, Anne McCormick, Dwyer McIntosh, Sonny Mehta, Anne Messitte, Colleen Mohyde, Lan Nguyen, Cathy O'Brien, Nancy Olin, Alicia Rusch, Anne-Lise Spitzer, Cynthia Stuart, Shelley Wanger, Kate Westerbeck, Amy Zenn.

CHIC SIMPLE STAFF

PARTNERS Kim & Jeff
ART DIRECTOR Wayne Wolf
OFFICE MANAGER Jo-Anne Harrison
MARKETING/PR Deborah Freeman
ASSOCIATE EDITOR Victoria C. Rowan
DESIGN/PRODUCTION Alicia Chang, Aileen Tse
COPY EDITOR Borden Elniff
INTERNS Ji Byol Lee, Heather Starr

COMMUNICATIONS

The world has gotten smaller and faster but we still can only be in one place at a time, which is why we are anxious to hear from you. We would like your input on stores and products that have impressed you. We are always happy to answer any questions you have about items in the book, and of course we are interested in feedback about Chic Simple.
Our address is:
84 WOOSTER STREET, NEW YORK, NY 10012
Fax: **(212) 343-9678**
Compuserve number: **72704,2346**
email address: **info@chicsimple.com**
Stay in touch because . . .
"The more you know, the less you need."

KIM JOHNSON GROSS & JEFF STONE

A NOTE ON THE TYPE

The text of this book was set in two typefaces: New Baskerville and Futura. The ITC version of **NEW BASKERVILLE** is called Baskerville, which itself is a facsimile reproduction of types cast from molds made by John Baskerville (1706–1775) from his designs. Baskerville's original face was one of the forerunners of the type style known to printers as the "modern face"—a "modern" of the period A.D. 1800. **FUTURA** was produced in 1928 by Paul Renner (1878–1956), former director of the Munich School of Design, for the Bauer Type Foundry. Futura is simple in design and wonderfully restful to read. It has been widely used in advertising because of its even, modern appearance in mass and its harmony with a great variety of other modern types.

SEPARATION AND FILM PREPARATION BY
ULTRAGRAPHICS
Dublin, Ireland

PRINTED AND BOUND BY
R. R. DONNELLEY & SONS
Willard, Ohio

HARDWARE

Apple Macintosh Power PC 8100, Quadra 800 personal computers; APS Technologies Syquest Drives; MicroNet DAT Drive; SuperMac 21" Color Monitor; Radius PrecisionColor Display/20; Radius 24X series Video Board; Hewlett-Packard LaserJet 4, Supra Fax Modem

SOFTWARE

QuarkXPress 3.3, Adobe Photoshop 2.5.1, Microsoft Word 5.1, FileMaker Pro 2.0, Adobe Illustrator 5.0.1

MUSICWARE

Chet Baker (*Chet Baker Sings*), John Barry (*Goldfinger: Motion Picture Soundtrack*), Greg Brown (*The Poet Game*), Chopin (*Nocturnes*), Clerks (*Motion Picture Soundtrack*), Diva (*Motion Picture Soundtrack*), generica (*Glass Eye*), Hole (*Live Through This*), Billie Holiday (*As Time Goes By*), House of Groove (*Arista's Most Fierce Tracks*), Brenda Kahn (*Epiphany in Brooklyn*), Madonna (*Bedtime Stories*), Sarah McLachlan (*Fumbling Towards Ecstasy*), Liz Phair (*Whip-Smart*), Opus III (*Guru Mother*), Pearl Jam (*Vitalogy*), Portishead (*Dummy*), Pulp Fiction (*Motion Picture Soundtrack*), Jimmy Scott (*All the Way*), Andrés Segovia (*The Segovia Collection, Vol. 9: The Romantic Guitar*), Frank Sinatra (*Live in Paris*), Tribute to Curtis Mayfield, True Romance (*Motion Picture Soundtrack*), Welcome to the Future[2], Shannon Worrell (*Three Wishes*), The Youngbloods (*Elephant Mountain*)

"Books which suggest simplicity in the kitchen never sell well."

CLIFFORD COOK FURNAS AND SPARKLE MOORE FURNAS

Man, Bread & Destiny
(1937)

Standard U.S. (Imperial) Volume/Weight Equivalents

NOTE: American (Imperial) pint = 16 ounces; British pint = 20 ounces

3 teaspoons = 1 tablespoon = ½ ounce
4 tablespoons = ¼ cup = 2 ounces
5⅓ tablespoons = ⅓ cup
8 tablespoons = ½ cup = 4 ounces
1 cup = 8 ounces = ½ pound
16 ounces = 2 cups = 1 pint = 1 pound
16 cups = 8 pints = 4 quarts = 1 gallon

Common Conversion Formulas

NOTE: All measurements are approximate to the closest round number

CONVERTING OUNCES (OZ.) TO GRAMS (G):

To convert ounces to grams: multiply number of ounces by 28.35
To convert grams to ounces: multiply number of grams by .0353

NOTE: 1 ounce is approximately 30 grams.

1 ounce = 30 grams
4 ounces = 115 grams
8 ounces = 225 grams
12 ounces = 340 grams

CONVERTING POUNDS (LB.) TO GRAMS (G) OR KILOGRAMS (KG):

To convert pounds to grams: multiply number of pounds by 453.6
To convert pounds to kilograms: multiply number of kilograms by 0.45

NOTE: 1 pound is approximately half a kilogram.

½ pound = 225 grams
1 pound = 450 grams
1½ pounds = 675 grams
2 pounds = 900 grams
2.21 pounds = 1 kilogram

CONVERTING QUARTS (QTS.) TO LITERS (L):

To convert quarts to liters: multiply number of quarts by 0.95

NOTE: One liter is approximately equivalent to one quart.

1 quart = .95 liter
1½ quarts = 1.4 liters
2 quarts = 1.9 liters
3 quarts = 2.85 liters

TEMPERATURE CONVERSIONS AND SETTINGS

To convert Fahrenheit to Celsius, subtract 32 from the Fahrenheit figure; multiply the resulting number by 5, then divide by 9.
To convert Celsius to Fahrenheit, multiply the Centigrade figure by 9; divide the resulting number by 5, then add 32.

NOTE: British Gas Mark/Regulo Settings are included in last three entries

−10° F = −23.3° C = freezer storage
32° F = 0° C = water freezes
68° F = 20° C = room temperature
212° F = 100° C = water boils
350° F = 177° C = 4 = baking
400° F = 204° C = 6 = hot oven
500° F = 260° C = 9 = broiling